ANGLISTIK UND ENGLISCHUNTERRICHT

Herausgegeben von
Gabriele Linke
Holger Rossow
Merle Tönnies

Band 75

MERLE TÖNNIES
HEIKE BUSCHMANN (Eds.)

Spatial Representations of British Identities

Universitätsverlag
WINTER
Heidelberg

Bibliografische Information Der Deutschen Nationalbibliothek

Die Deutsche Nationalbibliothek verzeichnet diese Publikation
in der Deutschen Nationalbibliografie;
detaillierte bibliografische Daten sind im Internet
über *http://dnb.d-nb.de* abrufbar.

Herausgeber:

Prof. Dr. Gabriele Linke
PD Dr. Holger Rossow
Prof. Dr. Merle Tönnies

ISBN 978-3-8253-5960-7
ISSN 0344-8266

Imprimé en Allemagne · Printed in Germany
Druck: Memminger MedienCentrum, 87700 Memmingen

Gedruckt auf umweltfreundlichem, chlorfrei gebleichtem
und alterungsbeständigem Papier

Den Verlag erreichen Sie im Internet unter:
www.winter-verlag.de

Contents

Merle Tönnies & Heike Buschmann (Paderborn)

Introduction: Space in and beyond Literature

In the second decade of the twenty-first century, the spatial turn is clearly no longer an exciting novelty. The key tenets which in the 1990s came to dominate studies of space as an abstract entity and of concrete spaces and their uses are now more or less self-understood: spaces not only have a 'real', material side but are endowed with a whole range of cultural meanings closely connected with social and personal constructions of identity. Famously, Michel de Certeau differentiated between tangible geographical 'place' and its constructed counterpart, the 'space' perceived and used by different people in different ways.[1] The constructed character of space obviously foregrounds the issue of representation. In how far do different representations of a particular space influence its cultural meanings and, vice versa, how can spaces be instrumentalised within cultural representations to project particular desired meanings and identities? While Henri Lefebvre already distinguished between 'spatial practice', 'spatial representation' and (most subjectively from the user's point of view) 'representational space',[2] these questions have been addressed in more recent studies as well. Indeed, with its attention to the ways in which space is constructed and read, the more specific 'topographical turn' (propagated particularly by Sigrid Weigel) directly shifts the focus to the mutual interaction between 'real' places and their representations as well as the identities that are bound up with them.[3]

As Gerhard Hard has argued,[4] the main focus of the discussion has nevertheless remained on the material side of space so far. He therefore calls for an understanding of the spatial turn as a 'rhetoric turn' and for putting the role of space(s) in communicative processes centre-stage. With such an agenda, literary representations of space acquire an important role. As Elizabeth Jones has documented, the realisation of so-called New Cultural

Geography that spaces can become an active force in society and can carry (and be made to carry) ideological and political meaning, gradually led geographers to abandon their traditional wariness about literature.[5] As maps, too, came to be seen as just one possibility of constructing space, literature was no longer the opposite of the 'reality' that geographers wanted to study but was increasingly credited with a constitutive as well as a mimetic force with regard to space.[6] More or less at the same time, literary studies started to go beyond the traditional descriptive approach of treating the 'setting' as a passive back-drop to or 'container' of the action, moving towards a more dynamic conception of space and allowing it an active role in the process of literary meaning-making.[7] This includes transcending a mimetic understanding of the relationship between literary spaces and their real-life equivalents. As Wolfgang Hallet (who considers this development in literary studies to be by no means finished yet) has analysed in detail, the highly complex and constructed literary text 'translates' experiences and constructions of space into another medium. To some extent it then functions as a second-order semiotic system that builds on existing (already constructed) perceptions and readings of the space concerned and then forms a new spatial reality itself.[8]

Since space and identity formation are closely linked, spaces in literary texts provide an insight into the characters' identity, while the characters in turn allow the reader to share their experience of space directly. The characters' movement in space creates relations between different spaces and can thus generate whole spatial networks in the text, just as in real life it is movement that allows us a direct experience of space.[9] Forms of transition between different kinds of spaces and the way in which spaces are categorised in relation to each other become very important, so that spatial boundaries and their readings in terms of self and other often form a central topic in research. This is by no means restricted to studies with a postcolonial focus, as can for instance be seen in Hartmut Böhme's edited volume *Topographien der Literatur*.[10] In the introduction, Böhme examines in detail how topographies function as spatial structuring devices which create semiotically organised space.[11] If one focuses on the reception process, this means that literary spaces always convey a picture of the world in an ideological sense as well, 'hailing' the recipient and offering a subject position to him or her along the lines of Louis Althusser's concept of ideology.[12] The spaces, their interrelations and the identities connected with them draw readers into a complex web of meanings which – even beyond explicitly political literature – invite them to share a particular vista on events by identifying with the characters.

In general, space is a powerful category as far as the naturalisation of meanings and identities is concerned. Its apparently unmediated material reality seems to offer a secure grounding that deflects attention from the inherent constructedness of ideological positions and concepts of self. Gerhard Hard as well as Moritz Csásky and Christoph Leitgeb have stressed this aspect by using the terms 'Verräumlichung' and 'Verortung' respectively.[13] This also gives additional strength to Doreen Massey's classic point that space is inherently bound up with power relations in society, which it not only reflects but to which it also contributes.[14] It is an active force in the ongoing struggle for social dominance not only as far as the claiming and reclaiming of places is concerned, but also on the level of representation and of the power to determine acceptable meanings. What makes literature interesting from a cultural studies point of view here is its general tendency to defamiliarise.[15] Its affinity with playful construction means that the ideological potential of literary spaces will only relatively rarely end up supporting a dominant ideology unequivocally. Rather, there is an anti-hegemonial potential in literary spaces that can work against the social use of space for naturalising power positions. Wolfgang Hallet has coined the category of 'fictions of space' to designate literary texts which exploit this potential to the full by foregrounding spatial defamiliarisation and deconstruction.[16] Such works draw explicit attention to the constructedness of space and to the factors involved in its conceptualisation and use. Although Althusser would of course stress that there is no outside of ideology, they can thus literally create space for non-conformist meanings and identities and negotiate between them in spatial terms.

It becomes obvious here that a comprehensive perspective on literary spaces can only be reached when the aims and methods of literary studies are combined with those of cultural studies and their interest in social power structures and (especially in the tradition of British cultural studies) ways of undermining them. With such an interdisciplinary approach and the overall tendency of cultural studies to analyse a very wide range of different cultural products, the question of intermediality automatically becomes important. In how far do the representational strategies and the resulting spatially constructed identities differ in other, particularly visual media and in how far can they, too, realise a certain anti-hegemonial potential? As is obvious from the annotations in this introduction, the role of space in literature has been addressed by a number of analysts so far, both from a theoretical perspective and with regard to concrete analyses especially of novels.[17] Indeed, space in literature seems to be a preoccupation at present especially in the German academic context, with seminal theoretically oriented collections like Böhme's (2005a), Döring and Thielmann's (2008) and Hallet and Neumann's (2009a) appearing in close succession. None of these volumes, however, includes a comparison with artistic representations of space outside literature itself. This is even slightly surprising with Böhme, who starts out with a definition of topographies on a very general semiotic level,[18] which would have allowed comparisons with other kinds of 'texts' and their functioning as spatial representations. In his definition of 'fictions of space', Hallet explicitly stresses the unique quality of literature as a second-order semiotic system which distinguishes it from other cultural phenomena.[19] Due to the abstract nature of his analysis at this point, it is not quite clear of which other kinds of representations he is thinking here, but it needs to be noted that from a semiotic perspective, artistic efforts in non-literary media can definitely achieve a comparable degree of complexity in their constructions of space. If one leaves aside the traditional wariness of literary studies towards popular culture and its perceived excessive visuality, it is clear that the concrete medium used is not as important as the deliberate attempt to represent space and thereby potentially reflect on its current social constructions and their implications for identity. In this way, visual representations, too, can become potential sites of alternative meaning-making and 're-location'. Indeed, if one wants to go as far as John Fiske, one can even observe a potential for resistant readings in the most commercial products of popular culture, should the recipient choose to respond to the gaps and contradictions contained in them.[20]

On this basis, the 2009 Annual General Conference of the German Association for the Study of British Cultures held at Paderborn had as one of its aims to compare the strategies of spatial representation and self-representation in literature and in other media. While the Paderborn volume of the *Journal for the Study of British Cultures* entitled *Reading British Spaces* (17:2, 2010) collects some of the conference papers dealing with space in non-literary 'texts', this volume of 'anglistik & englischunterricht' focuses on the conference's comparative aspect from the point of view of representation and identity. The contributions focus on the period from the nineteenth to the twenty-first century and are grouped in such a way that the representation of space and its implications for identity concepts can be compared both from the perspective of different aspects of identity and with regard to the similarities and differences between literature, artistically oriented visual 'texts' (photographs and films) and non-artistic material representing spaces. It becomes clear that similar degrees of complexity can be achieved in the spatial representations irrespective of the medium used, while the materiality of the medium at the same time remains a central focus in the articles themselves, which study selected examples. Proceeding from such case studies, it can then become possible to compare the mediality of literature and other forms of topography, as Hallet and Neumann sketch with regard to maps in a relatively brief passage of their introduction.[21] The present volume thus considers itself one step in the direction of analysing the media-specific representational strategies that can be used in making space signify in identity construction, especially as far as anti-hegemonial agendas are concerned.

The wide range of available representational strategies opens up a space of opportunities for artists, writers or filmmakers and scholars alike. Novelist Patricia Duncker and photographer Mark Hall combine the writer's/artist's point of view with the perception by readers and scholars to illustrate how this diversity of possibilities can be translated into concrete representations and readings. They thereby map this space of opportunities and lay the groundwork for the case studies, which focus on single phenomena. Duncker offers an insight into the inner workings of fiction writing, disentangling parts of the intertextual and spatial web that formed the basis for her novel *Hallucinating Foucault* (1996). She addresses two different yet overlapping spaces which contribute to the creation of a literary text: On the one hand, these are spaces of reading and writing in which meaning is created through productive encounters between readers or writers and texts. On the other hand, these encounters depend on the (fictional) worlds and spaces formed in the writing process itself. Mark Hall focuses on one particular aspect and investigates the potential of light and darkness in constructing identities and spaces in different media formats, ranging from photography to fiction. He uses the issue of visibility as well as hegemonic and physical boundaries created by light and darkness to highlight various media-specific effects that illumination can create.

The case studies in this volume all deal with texts which exploit some of the abundant choices and techniques revealed by Duncker and Hall. The first set of contributions focuses on national, regional and local identities as expressed and formed in a variety of spaces.

Wolfgang Funk and Florian Kläger explore the constructions of different versions of national identity in and through space. Funk discusses contemporary novelistic attempts to construct new versions of English national identity as the traditional one is perceived as irreparably damaged. He monitors the success of the selected novels in arriving at such new spaces of identity through a discussion of the interplay between personal and national identities in the arena of memory and spatial representation. Kläger concentrates on a space that has commonly been used to signify Englishness and looks into the state of the contemporary condition-of-England novel through the pub window. The novels he concentrates on all face the challenge of trying to represent an England which is becoming increasingly evasive – a process that does not stop short even of key icons, so that the core question is whether national emblems like the pub can persist under such conditions.

Sandra Heinen takes up the connection between temporal and spatial aspects in processes of identity formation, studying the River Thames as portrayed in Peter Ackroyd's eponymous 'biography' (2007). Both the Thames and the public house have a double function as national icons or links between members of the English nation as an 'imagined community' and as a focal point of personal understandings of 'self' on a local level. Heinen's article investigates the point where these two functions converge to form overlapping personal and national identities as an intersection between the temporal development and progression through space, which the Thames experiences in Ackroyd's representation.

The next two case studies in this section focus on local contexts and investigate the identities of/in London and Liverpool. Although Sonja Frenzel and Elke Schuch both focus on cities, their methods vary beyond the differences inherent in their subjects. Frenzel examines London identities though readings of late-nineteenth-century poetry and opens up new interpretational space by suggesting an approach through London as a body. She thus creates opportunities for gendered readings not only of Londoners but of the city itself. Schuch traces the development of Liverpool identity through various phases from its rise as a port city via periods of decline to its recovery in the late twentieth century. This sense of historical development along with changes in the physical appearance and social composition of the city results in a decidedly local identity, clearly set off against the North as a regional frame for identity construction and other local identities in that region.

Ingrid von Rosenberg completes the picture with her study of Northern regional identities. She examines the correlation between constructions of place identities in the North East of England and its changing land- and cityscapes. Tracing the formation of new 'patchwork place identities' alongside transformations of the context in which they take shape allows insights into the ways in which identity formation processes respond to spatial developments which are relevant to all case studies in the first part of this collection.

The second set of contributions further explores the relations between space, individual identities and mobility which were hinted at in some of the approaches outlined so far. Gabriele Linke uses contemporary Scottish autobiographies by Glaswegian authors to study individual identity constructions in the context of a specific city. While the point of (spatial) reference – Glasgow – is the same for all biographers here, they position themselves differently in relation to it. Linke uncovers the resulting multiplicity of stories, highlighting connections between space, its use and specific identity constructions in the fields of class, religion, education and social mobility. Christiane Bimberg establishes a similar link between the construction of individual identities and the urban environment. Her approach, however, focuses on fictional spaces and examines how Virginia Woolf uses interactions between London and the people in the city to create and communicate identities. This process involves the function of the city as a frame for constructions of self but goes far beyond this to the point where the boundaries between movements through the physical place of the city and the characters' thought processes become blurred and tangible landscapes blend with mental ones.

While mobility has so far been considered in relation to upward social movement (Linke) and states of mind (Bimberg), Timo Lothmann and Antje Schumacher take movement literally. They study nineteenth-century railway poetry and its strategies of coming to terms with the enlarged radius and pace of mobility that resulted from the invention of the steam train. In a sense, Yousef Awad then takes up the contemporary effects of increased mobility by focusing on new constellations of identity construction in the multicultural spaces created by migration. His study of Fadia Faqir's novel *My Name is Salma* (2007) traces how the experiences of a disadvantaged female Arab immigrant to Britain are represented in literature and reveals conflicts over space and belonging.

The final articles in this volume examine literary and filmic representations in which two contested spaces of belonging and representation melt into one. Elahe Haschemi Yekani and Simon Dickel open up various perspectives on interethnic gay desire. Haschemi Yekani focuses on gay melancholy as an aesthetic strategy in Hollinghurst's *The Line of Beauty* (2004). Conflicts over inclusion and exclusion, as well as a spatially grounded sense of belonging and owning a place as a representational anchor for one's identity, are confronted with the ephemerality of shifting reference points. In his exploration of queer and ethnic spaces in film Dickel approaches the interspace between a 'politics of resistance' as a struggle over the ownership and right to contested spaces and a 'politics of representation', as mono-cultural venues and representational strategies begin to be absorbed for cultural practices that stem from many different backgrounds.

Through the diverse media, representational strategies and identity concepts investigated by the contributions, this volume provides an outline map of different approaches towards representing space across media formats and modes of identity construction. This map equips its readers with an overview of a rewarding field of research and includes close-up views of key landmarks, as for example the question of shifting realities as well as contested or (anti-)hegemonial spaces. Readers are invited to use the paths introduced here and explore further territory that remains uncharted.

Finally, we would like to thank all those who helped to create this volume and give it its shape: the contributors for providing such a variety of topics and approaches and for being so patient, all those who offered feedback at the Paderborn conference and during the preparation for publication and last but certainly not least Nele Reichert, who gave invaluable support in the formatting and proofreading process.

Notes

1 De Certeau (1984: 117). It should be noted that the two terms have also been applied with different meanings by other cultural theorists.
2 Lefebvre (1991: 38-46).
3 Weigel (2002), see also Günzel (2008: 220-230) and Günzel (2010: 114).
4 Hard (2008: 304-305).
5 Jones (1991: 222-229).
6 *Ibid.* 227.
7 Cf. Nünning (2009).
8 Hallet (2009: 84, 92, 108-109). Cf. also Frank (2009: 64) and Neumann (2009: 116).
9 Hallet/Neumann (2009b: 17, 90); Böhme (2005b: xv).
10 Cf. especially Böhme (2005a: 597-599). See also Moretti (1999 [1997]: 65-67).
11 Böhme (2005b: xix-xx). Cf. also Frank (2009: 64).
12 Cf. Althusser (2001 [1969]: 1502-1505).
13 Hard (2008: 305); Csásky/Leitgeb (2009: 7).
14 Massey (1994: 4-5).
15 Cf. e.g. Hallet/Neumann (2009b: 23).
16 Hallet (2009: 108-109).
17 As far as the latter point of view is concerned, James's (2008) overview of space in contemporary British fiction is particularly prominent among recent works. It is of limited value for this introduction, however, as it only briefly touches upon more theoretical issues.
18 Böhme (2005a: xix-xx).
19 Hallet (2009: 109), cf. also Neumann (2009: 117).
20 Fiske (2006 [1989]: 103-106).
21 Hallet & Neumann (2009b: 26).

Althusser, Louis, "From *On Ideology*". – In Vincent B. Leitch (Ed.): *The Norton Anthology of Theory and Criticsm*, New York, 2001, pp. 1496-1508 [original 1969].

Böhme, Hartmut (Ed.): *Topographien der Literatur. Deutsche Literatur im transnationalen Kontext*, Stuttgart & Weimar, 2005a.

---: "Einleitung: Raum – Bewegung – Topographie". – In H.B. (Ed.): *Topographien der Literatur. Deutsche Literatur im transnationalen Kontext*, Stuttgart & Weimar, 2005b, pp. ix-xxiii.

Csásky, Moritz & Christoph Leitgeb: "Kommunikation – Gedächtnis – Raum. Orientierungen im *Spatial Turn* der Kulturwissenschaften". – In M.C. & C. L. (Eds.): *Kommunikation – Gedächtnis – Raum. Kulturwissenschaften nach dem "Spatial Turn"*, Bielefeld, 2009, pp. 7-10.

De Certeau, Michel: *The Practice of Everyday Life*, Berkeley, 1984 [1980].

Döring, Jörg & Tristan Thielmann (Eds.): *Spatial Turn*, Bielefeld, 2008.

Fiske, John: *Understanding Popular Culture*, London & New York, 2006 [1989].

Frank, Michael C.: "Die Literaturwissenschaften und der *Spatial Turn*. Ansätze bei Jurij Lotman und Michail Bachtin". – In Wolfgang Hallet & Birgit Neumann (Eds.): *Raum und Bewegung in der Literatur. Die Literaturwissenschaften und der Spatial Turn*, Bielefeld, 2009, pp. 53-80.

Günzel, Stephan: "*Spatial Turn – Topographical Turn – Topological Turn*. Über die Unterschiede zwischen Raumparadigmen". – In Jörn Döring & Tristan Thielmann (Eds.): *Spatial Turn*, Bielefeld, 2008, pp. 219-235.

---: "On Reading Space". – In Merle Tönnies & Ina Grimm (Eds.): *Reading British Spaces* [= *Journal for the Study of British Cultures* 17:2], Tübingen, 2010, pp. 107-115.

Hallet, Wolfgang: "*Fictions of Space*. Zeitgenössische Romane als fiktionale Modelle semiotischer Raumkonstitution". – In W.H. & Birgit Neumann (Eds.): *Raum und Bewegung in der Literatur. Die Literaturwissenschaften und der Spatial Turn*, Bielefeld, 2009, pp. 81-113.

Hallet, Wolfgang & Birgit Neumann (Eds.): *Raum und Bewegung in der Literatur. Die Literaturwissenschaften und der Spatial Turn*, Bielefeld, 2009a.

---: "Raum und Bewegung in der Literatur: Zur Einführung". – In W.H. & B.N. (Eds.): *Raum und Bewegung in der Literatur. Die Literaturwissenschaften und der Spatial Turn*, Bielefeld, 2009b, pp. 11-32.

Hard, Gerhard: "Der Spatial Turn. Von der Geographie her betrachtet". – In Jörg Döring & Tristan Thielmann (Eds.): *Spatial Turn*, Bielefeld, 2008, pp. 263-316.

James, David: *Contemporary British Fiction and the Artistry of Space. Style, Landscape, Perception*, London, 2008.

Jones, Elizabeth: "Literature and the New Cultural Geography", *Anglia* 126, 2008, 221-240.

Lefevbre, Henri: *The Production of Space*, Oxford, 1991.

Massey, Doreen: *Space, Place and Gender*, Cambridge, 1994.

Moretti, Franco: *Atlas des europäischen Romans. Wo die Literatur spielt*. Köln, 1999 [1997].

Neumann, Birgit: "Imaginative Geographien in kolonialer und postkolonialer Literatur. Raumkonzepte der (Post-) Kolonialismusforschung". – In Wolfgang Hallet & B.N. (Eds.): *Raum und Bewegung in der Literatur. Die Literaturwissenschaften und der Spatial Turn*, Bielefeld, 2009, pp. 115-138.

Nünning, Ansgar: "Formen und Funktionen literarischer Raumdarstellung. Grundlagen, Ansätze, narratologische Kategorien und neue Perspektiven". – In Wolfgang Hallet & Birgit Neumann (Eds.): *Raum und Bewegung in der Literatur. Die Literaturwissenschaften und der Spatial Turn*, Bielefeld, 2009, pp. 33-52.

Tönnies, Merle & Ina Grimm (Eds.): *Reading British Spaces* [= *Journal for the Study of British Cultures* 17:2], Tübingen, 2010.

Weigel, Sigrid: "Zum 'topographical turn'. Kartographie, Topographie und Raumkonzepte in den Kulturwissenschaften", *KulturPoetik* 2:2, 2002, 151-165.

Patricia Duncker (Manchester)

The Lunatic, the Lover and the Poet. On Writing *Hallucinating Foucault*

Let me begin with Shakespeare. *A Midsummer Night's Dream* recounts a night of sexual mayhem in the woods, a league from Athens. The fairies are locked in battle for the possession of a little Indian boy, and the human lovers are 'quick bright things', tangled in amorous confusion. Lysander loves Hermia, but so does Demetrius, who used to love Helena until he set eyes on Hermia, and alas, poor Helena, she still adores Demetrius, who now does not love her anymore. Desire falls victim to the fairies' interference. Titania, the fairy queen, is duped and drugged by her lord Oberon, so that she falls in love with Bottom the weaver, disguised as an ass. The players, hidden in the woods to rehearse in private, are also overtaken by magical disaster. Ridicule, humiliation, love potions and mistaken identities transform the lives of both mortals and immortals in the night woods. Act V supposedly sees order restored. The lovers are married off to the correct partners, and the audience is treated to royal wedding celebrations and entertainments. The mechanicals deliver their play in a hectic, if slightly over-explanatory performance, and are generously applauded by the nobles.

And it is right at the beginning of Act V that Theseus sounds off about the relationship between the lunatic, the lover and the poet. His new wife, the conquered Amazon Hippolyta, ventures to comment "Tis strange my Theseus, that these lovers speak of." (V.i.1)[1] Theseus, in reply, manages to be both pompous and dismissive. Here is his great speech on the imagination:

> More strange than true. I never may believe
> These antique fables, nor these fairy toys.
> Lovers and madmen have such seething brains,
> Such shaping fantasies, that apprehend
> More than cool reason ever comprehends.

The lunatic, the lover and the poet,
Are of imagination all compact:
One sees more devils than vast hell can hold;
That is, the madman: the lover, all as frantic,
Sees Helen's beauty in a brow of Egypt:
The poet's eye, in a fine frenzy rolling,
Doth glance from heaven to earth, from earth to heaven;
And as imagination bodies forth
The forms of things unknown, the poet's pen
Turns them to shapes, and gives to airy nothing
A local habitation and a name.
Such tricks hath strong imagination,
That, if it would but apprehend some joy,
It comprehends some bringer of that joy:
Or in the night, imagining some fear,
How easy is a bush supposed a bear! (V.i.2-22)[2]

Theseus dismisses lunatics, lovers and poets in one breath, even as he draws them all together. Creative inspiration, sexual passion and madness all create unnecessary worlds and turn bushes into bears. Theseus ignores Hippolyta's objection:

But all the story of the night told over,
And all their minds transfigur'd so together,
More witnesseth than fancy's images,
And grows to something of great constancy;
But howsoever, strange and admirable. (V.i.23-27)[3]

This is, in fact, the voice of cool reason, which has listened to 'the story of the night', and reached somewhat different conclusions. Men, in Shakespeare's plays, usually ignore women at their peril.

Hallucinating Foucault (1996) begins and ends with dreams.[4] The action of the text vindicates the content of both dreams. The dreams are therefore both strange and true. Many of the characters are unnamed: the narrator, the Germanist, The Bank of England. When a character is unnamed, or given a generic name, the reader's attention shifts from identity to role, as it does in fairy tales. Characters have pre-established parts. Here is the King, the Orgre, the Miller's youngest son, the Princess, the Fairy Godmother, the ugly Witch. Who the characters are proves to be far less important than what they represent, or indeed what they actually do. When a character is named, like Rumpelstiltskin, the name itself becomes significant as does the name of Paul Michel, in *Hallucinating*

Foucault.[5] I wanted my readers to be aware of the fact that this tale is not entirely realist fiction, but a symbolic narrative, which refers, quite self-consciously, to earlier texts and other meanings. And, as in Renaissance drama or in eighteenth-century fiction, my plot is crucial, and will give the reader meanings. I wanted the text of *Hallucinating Foucault*, however extraordinary the tale, to grow to 'something of great constancy'. My character, Paul Michel, actually refers to Theseus' speech, more than once. The clearest reference comes towards the end of the novel, when the unnamed student refuses to acknowledge that the summer will end and that he must be parted from the writer he now loves. Paul Michel describes the projected end of their relationship and the student objects:

> "So ... you will take me back to the loving care of Pascale Vaury and her cohorts of sadists. You will then proceed to England, marching with military precision, and take up your studies again. You will write to me whenever your schedule allows, usually with academic queries on my texts. Is that clear?"
>
> I lost my temper.
>
> "No. It's not clear. There's no way that I'm letting you get locked up again in that inferno. We'll get you past the medical commission and then we'll go back to Paris. We'll find somewhere to live. I'll get a job or something. You have to start writing again."
>
> He let out a wild cackle of laughter and dropped my hands.
>
> "Ah ... well, in that case ..." He lit a cigarette. "My God, petit, you ought to be riding a white horse and bearing an ensign. You take your role of saviour much too seriously."
>
> I got up and left him there in the café. I didn't want him to see that I was crying, with anger, frustration and pain. He left me alone on the beach for an hour or so. Then he came down and rubbed wet sand onto my back. I hadn't heard him approaching.
>
> "Listen, petit," he said gently, "you are twenty-two and very much in love. I am forty-six and a certified lunatic. You are much more likely to be insane than I am."
>
> I couldn't help it. I laughed. (151)

Here, Paul Michel acknowledges the gift of love, but hides his answer behind Shakespeare's ironies. What links the lunatic, the lover and the poet in Theseus' argument, and in Paul Michel's comments, is that they are all deluded people. They misunderstand and misinterpret reality, not only because they lack cool reason, but also because they suffer from seething brains. They all possess imagination, which, through a process of transformation, not only enables them to create fictive worlds, but also to believe that these worlds are real and true. Lunatics, lovers and poets do also sometimes have the power to persuade other people that their worlds are real. Notice that Hippolyta uses still more powerful, resonant language than Theseus does: 'transfigured' and 'witnesseth' are both religious words. The student both imagines and believes that there is a future for himself and the man with whom he has fallen in love. But for the mad writer and the student who came to find him there is no future beyond the one that continues through the imaginary texts that exist when the novel ends: Paul Michel's writing and the doctoral thesis on his work.

For behind every book stands not just another book, but a dense web of texts. *A Midsummer Night's Dream* is not the only play lurking behind *Hallucinating Foucault*. There is also *King Lear*, where madness becomes a metaphor, not for passion and creative inspiration, but for the disintegration of the state. Here is Paul Michel describing the significance of madness.

> "Have you read what Foucault wrote about Bedlam? Madness is theatre, a spectacle. We have very few words to designate what we mean by madness in French. You, the English, you have a galaxy of words for the demented: crazy, foolish, simple, idiotic, rabid, distracted, manic, absurd, insane. It is important to traverse all those meanings. Look at you, petit, only a madman would have come all the way to Clermont to find someone who had been incarcerated for nearly ten years, with so little hope of ever finding me. Without knowing whom you would find."
>
> He looked at me carefully.
>
> "Madness and passion have always been interchangeable. Throughout the entire western literary tradition. Madness is an abundance of existence. Madness is a way of asking difficult questions. What did he mean, the powerless tyrant king? O Fool, I shall go mad." (125-126)

Paul Michel's riff on the possible significance of madness traverses the different languages and registers, which have always been florid and abundant and are still used to describe seething brains. States of madness are sometimes accepted in the social world, and sometimes excluded from all company. The clinical definitions are both fluid and dangerous. What are the origins of madness? That question is crucial, because, depending on the answer we choose, we decide whether it is to be tolerated within civil society and domestic space, and accepted within the social world, or excluded, locked up, treated and cured – that is, extinguished and destroyed. What indeed did he mean, the powerless tyrant king? 'O Fool, I shall go mad.' For what is at stake here is the *value* of madness. It is a commonplace in Shakespeare criticism to note that this is the world turned upside down: just as Gloucester cannot see until he is blind, so Lear cannot grasp the truth until he is mad; thus, for Lear, madness is revelatory, a visionary state. But I would insist that madness, as a metaphor, cannot be separated from the work within which it is represented. The metaphoric meanings and sources are as fluid and unstable as the clinical terminology used to describe the mental conditions commonly described as mad.

So Shakespeare sits at my elbow, by my left hand. His poetry remains a touchstone in my writing, just as it does for Michel Foucault in his early work *Folie et déraison* (1961), strangely re-titled in English, *Madness and Civilisation*. In an interview with *Le Monde* in 1961, Foucault said this about his study of madness:

> Madness only exists in society … It does not exist outside of the forms of sensibility that isolate it, and the forms of repulsion that expel it or capture it. Thus one can say that from the Middle Ages up to the Renaissance, madness was present within the social horizon as an aesthetic and mundane fact; then in the seventeenth century – starting with the confinement (of the mad) madness underwent a period of silence, of exclusion. It lost the function of manifestation, of revelation, that it had had in the age of Shakespeare and Cervantes, (for example, Lady Macbeth begins to speak the truth when she becomes mad) it becomes laughable, delusory. Finally the twentieth century collars madness, reduces it to a natural phenomenon, linked to the truth of the world. From this positivist expropriation derive both the misguided philanthropy that all psychiatry exhibits towards the mad, and the lyrical protest that one finds in poetry from Nerval to Artaud, and which is an effort to restore to the experience of madness the profundity and power of revelation that was extinguished by confinement.[6]

'Profundity' – 'power of revelation' – those are strong words to describe madness. And it is perhaps the point where I would separate myself and my views from those of Foucault. The 'power of revelation' begs many questions. What is revealed? And to whom? The writing that is art is about judgement and selection. When Paul Michel goes mad he ceases to write. He no longer creates the self-conscious writing that is art. True, he does scrawl messages across the walls of the asylum and, later, on other people's houses. These graffiti are not without meaning; they are messages. But the writing on the wall is not art, it is a warning.[7]

The most abstract spaces in the construction of fiction are the most dangerous. There are two spaces of which I am constantly aware, two spaces that require constant, careful negotiation. The first is the space between texts. This space is filled by reading, the creative act of reading; I make my work out of gaps, the gaps within and between other books. My reading is easily the most important thing that I will do every day, and so, that deadly space between texts, the space of influence and anxiety, is the first and most crucial terrain upon which I work. But the space between texts is the space where every writer can take risks and be supported doing so. It is not empty space. The space between texts has signposts and landmarks, emotional textual markers, maps and directions. It is a space that has precise parameters, is both known and strange, and it is a space that can be reclaimed by re-reading.

The second space, however, is the most dangerous space of all, because it is the space where meaning is created, and that is the space between the writer and the reader. That shared space is the page. Meaning is constructed out of a relationship that has to be imagined, before it can be negotiated. The writing will imagine and create its own reader. As a writer your contract with the reader must be at the forefront of your mind, even if that reader is only yourself. You write for yourself not as a writer, but as a reader. It is a contract that must be continually re-negotiated, but never broken. And this is the central subject of *Hallucinating Foucault*; the precarious link between the writer and the reader.

Paul Michel is in fact the *Doppelgänger* of Michel Foucault. Paul Michel was Foucault's real name: Paul Michel Foucault. The book is about a ghostly haunting. The two men haunt one another. Here is Paul Michel, describing his imagined relationship between the writer and the reader, that is the connection between himself and Foucault.

> "It's rare to find another man whose mind works through the same codes, whose work is as anonymous, yet as personal and lucid as your own. Especially a contemporary. It's more usual to find the echo of your own voice in the past. You are always listening, I think, when you write, for the voice that answers. However oblique the reply may be. Foucault never attempted to contact me. He did something more frightening,

> provocative, profound. He wrote back, in his published work. Many people have observed that our themes are disturbingly similar, our styles of writing utterly different. We read one another with the passion of lovers. Then we began to write to one another, text for text. I went to all his public lectures at the Collège de France. He saw me there. He gave no sign. He was teaching in California when I was in America for the publication of Midi. I went to his seminars. There were over 170 people there. Once I was slightly late. He was standing silent at the lectern, looking at his notes when I joined the crowd standing at the back of the hall. He looked up and we stared at one another. Then he began to speak. He never acknowledged me. He always knew when I was there." (154-155)

This passage is in fact about the illusory nature of the relationship between the writer and the reader. It is indeed a complex hallucination. Paul Michel, as the handsome outlaw writer, who openly lived that life of abandonment and excess, which Foucault lived only in secret, insists that he is 'the wish made flesh', Foucault's own desires, unleashed into the world. Both men are writers, but they are also each other's reader. Is the pact real? Did Foucault know about the pact? Is this likely? Or are we simply inside that kind of book, where writers and readers concoct hidden pacts with one another? Or is this another way of reading, a writing back that is both argument and interpretation? My novel, which is filled with many different kinds of readers, raises, but never answers these questions.

All the locations in *Hallucinating Foucault* are spaces that have been theorised, discussed and reconfigured both by Foucault himself and other French historians and political theorists: the library, the archive, the asylum. And for those of us who can still remember Louis Althusser and the Ideological State Apparatuses, they are all ISAs. The Library and the Archive are not necessarily museums of knowledge, but instruments for the social control of knowledge, and the restriction of its use. Both the Library and the Archive are spaces of enchantment and entrapment. They are the magic castles of fairy tale, but they are also spaces where the forces which control and govern them, are largely invisible. Here is the student attempting to gain access to Paul Michel's private letters to Foucault. This passage describes his stand-off with the Archivist.

"These letters are on reserve," she said. "I don't think you can see them."

"On reserve?"

"Yes. There's another scholar working on them. These letters are not available for consultation."

"Is he – or she – working on them now?"

"They are on reserve for publication," she hissed.

I suddenly turned obstinate.

"But I only want to read them."

"I'll have to check."

She disappeared again. I sat down in a rage. I had come all the way to Paris to read these letters. I glared at the innocent executive American, who had no obvious designs on either Foucault or Paul Michel. Eventually the Secretary returned. She chanted a formula.

"The letters in question have been purchased for publication by Harvard University Press. All rights reserved. You may read the manuscripts, but photography, photocopying or reproduction of any passage therefrom is forbidden. You will be required to sign an undertaking to that effect. In addition you must make a detailed declaration concerning your reasons for wishing to read these manuscripts and the use you intend to make of the information contained therein. All publication, including précis, abstract or detailed commentary in any form whatsoever is forbidden. This declaration will be forwarded along with your name, status and institutional address to the holders of the copyright. This declaration will have legal force."

I nodded, astounded.

"Go into the reading room and choose a seat."

I sharpened my pencils very, very, carefully while she stood over me, taking all the time in the world. Then I bowed with obnoxious politeness. I had turned love-fifteen into fifteen-all. (58-59)

The student's encounter with bureaucracy at the Archive reveals two things: the actual, material body of the writing is owned. It has become a commercial literary product. But what cannot be owned or controlled is the creation and interpretation of meaning. Reading is anarchic, unfettered and subversive. The student inserts a version of reading as measurement between himself and the archive authorities. He claims to be counting how many times Paul Michel uses the conditional; but he is in fact reading with the heart. This is the most dangerous kind of reading anyone can undertake, because it is the reading that is closest to hallucination. He believes that the letters reveal themselves to him: "I believed that I was capable of reading them differently to anyone else" (75). The student has become trapped in the deadly space between the reader and the text.

His gesture – setting out to find Paul Michel – is the moment of error and entrapment. The most dangerous method of reading is informed by desire, the reading that thereby unleashes both the imagination and the heart.

Just as the reader cannot be kept within boundaries, neither can the imagination. The first scene I wrote, on 26 July 1993, when I began the book, was the encounter between the mad writer and the reader who set out to find him. This remains in many ways the key moment in the narrative, the scene when they meet for the first time, because Paul Michel makes clear that he is entirely aware of his metaphoric identity.

> "And they told me in Paris that you keep getting out. Though I can't see how."
>
> He smiled again. The same wonderful, transforming smile.
>
> "Voilà," he said, "it's a professional secret. You can imprison the imagination. You can drug it into oblivion. You can even drive it mad. But you cannot keep it locked up." (99)

Paul Michel, like Shakespeare's fairies, represents the ambiguous hallucinatory force of the imagination, the double-sided gift that brings light and joy, but also the dangerous, violent, destructive forces, both of which are unleashed in Shakespeare's play. The Library, the Archive and the Asylum are all closed spaces. They are all indoors. There is a peculiar and arresting tension throughout British literature between indoors and outdoors. We have inherited a strongly class-marked language, and I notice in my reading that indoors, inside all the houses, courts, castles and places, we are, as readers, usually forced to occupy strongly class-marked, socially policed spaces, whereas outdoors, the usual hierarchies break down. Gendered spaces collapse into one another; the fine lady chats to the peasant and the courtiers change places with the gardeners. Open space is free space; the wilderness sets its own rules, and quite different structures of power suddenly assume ascendancy over the characters in any drama, poem or fiction.

Let me return to Shakespeare. The woods outside Athens in *A Midsummer Night's Dream* are a dangerous, but liberated space. The fairies become the unseen agents of power and transformation, the lovers change places. These woods represent not only the unconscious night world of dreams and desires, but also the imagination. Theseus is gazing at the bears and seeing only bushes.

The forest of Arden in *As You Like It* translates the court into an unwilling band of merry men in the greenwood. Pastoral romantic comedy always does create a world where class and gender are subverted and disrupted by desire. E.M. Forster and Lawrence knew this and exploited the possibilities offered by the woods, fields and forests of England. Their working-class lovers are masters in open space; the prize they offer to the trapped heroine in *Lady Chatterley's Lover* and the hero in *Maurice* is the same: sexual liberty in the green world. E.M. Forster actually names that space as the 'greenwood' in the utopian moment of escape. Thus the homo-social community of Robin Hood's merry band is subverted and invoked. But the reference to outlaws escaping from tyranny is appropriate; this world turned upside down also offers the possibility of a virgin space in which to imagine a commonwealth that is both more honest and more just.

Nevertheless, 'outdoors' is also dangerous space. The classic nineteenth-century theatre for the marriage proposal is the conservatory; that mid-point between the drawing room and uncontrolled vegetation. Of course, not all proposals in the conservatory are honourable, but the wild 'outdoors' sometimes becomes the menacing sexual space of woman's undoing. In Jane Austen's *Mansfield Park* (1814) the walk in the wilderness leads out towards a landscape into which Maria Bertram and Henry Crawford actually do disappear. Maria's fiancé, Mr Rushworth, takes too long fetching the key. Their exit is accompanied by a quite explicit tempter's speech from Henry Crawford, who says,

> 'And for the world you would not get out without the key and without Mr Rushworth's authority and protection, or I think you might with little difficulty pass round the edge of the gate here, with my assistance; I think it might be done, if you really wished to be more at large, and could allow yourself to think it not prohibited.'[8]

Their affair effectively begins here, when they leave the park – un-chaperoned. And the consequences of passing round the edge of the gate, into uncontrolled outdoor space, lead to Maria's ruin.

Outdoors, for women who really wish 'to be more at large', can even prove fatal. Thomas Hardy's Tess of the D'Urbervilles is seduced and betrayed in the ancient Chase. The outdoor space of the coliseum in Henry James's *Daisy Miller* proves fatal both to the heroine's reputation and her life. My point is simply this: open space, wild space, in my tradition of writing, is never neutral, and always possesses the power to subvert and transform the relationships that have been established indoors. Outdoors, the forest, the heath, the wilderness and woods can become a politically free space, a *tabula rasa* on which to rebuild the state. More often, the uncharted wilderness becomes a sexually open space; a forest of desire in which the subject loses herself.

The student frees Paul Michel from the enclosed spaces of the asylum – and the library, where they first encountered one another – and lets him loose in open space. The reader sets the imagination free. Paul Michel is mad, not only because he has lost his chosen reader and his Muse; the sign of his madness is his delusion that there is only *one* chosen reader. There is no one single reader, or one single reading. The reader is created by the text; he has thousands of readers. Hence the moment of his capitulation to the disease which claims him, is the moment where he begins to write upon himself, and becomes the body of his own text. The text is then entrapped within the mind of the writer. The imagination is shut down, introverted, doomed. All writers need the dream of the reader, to create, to exist.

My novel is about kinds of reading. What kinds of reading can liberate the imagination? The answer is legion. At the end of the novel the mass of pilgrims climbing to the graveyard where Paul Michel is to be buried, represent the readers, the mass of readers who are faithful and unknown. As the Germanist argues in her last letter to Paul Michel, "I was your reader too. He was not your only reader. You had no right to abandon me." (173) And here I agree with the Germanist; there is no limit that can ever be imposed upon the reader, and no end to the creation of meaning.

I began with Shakespeare and I'm going to end with the last scenes of *A Midsummer Night's Dream*. The sleeping Theseus never knows how thoroughly he has been confounded; as the nobles retire to bed, the fairies invade the palace. They are real, powerful, present, and the nobles are lucky that they come not to curse, but to bless. The dark chambers of the court are abandoned, the play within the play is over, the human theatre of the imagination is extinguished, but the fairies return, bringing with them recognition of the dark places that have been evoked throughout the play, but are now finally discarded. Here in Puck's final speech the violent, predatory world of destruction, the lion, the wolf, the open graves yielding up their ghosts, is acknowledged, before it is set aside and swept away. The powers of the woods, that is, the fairies, representing the anarchy of outdoors, the freedom of unlocked spaces, now rush in, bringing light and dancing. I placed this moment too in *Hallucinating Foucault*. Paul Michel, freed from the asylum, leads the dance in the light spray from the motorway showers. The imagination, once more unleashed in the hot light of the south, explodes with joy. Shakespeare gives his audience a carefully tempered happy ending.

> Now the hungry lion roars,
> And the wolf behowls the moon;
> Whilst the heavy ploughman snores,
> All with weary task fordone.
> Now the wasted brands do glow,
> Whilst the screech owl, screeching loud,
> Puts the wretch that lies in woe
> In remembrance of a shroud.
> Now it is the time of night
> Then the graves, all gaping wide,
> Every one lets forth his sprite,
> In the church-way paths to glide.
> And we fairies, that do run
> By the triple Hecate's team
> From the presence of the sun,
> Following darkness like a dream,
> Now are frolic; not a mouse
> Shall disturb this hallow'd house.
> I am sent with broom before
> To sweep the dust behind the door. (V.i, 357-376)[9]

The screech owl, both in Shakespeare's play and in *Hallucinating Foucault*, represents the messenger of death. He is part of the symbolic structure of the novel, a reminder of the encroaching darkness, and a measure of what is at stake. The imagination, so foolishly scorned by Theseus, is not only the source of wisdom and liberty, but also the place where we recognise the oncoming presence of our own deaths. I chose a darker end to my story than the one offered by Shakespeare in *A Midsummer Night's Dream.* I returned to the unconscious world of dream. The student sees Paul Michel, free at last, outdoors, with a shadowy figure behind him.

> The detail of my dream has a hallucinatory intensity, which I cannot shake off. […] The shape of a man, a long way off, behind Paul Michel, glimmers through the smoke of the stubble fires. I cannot make him out. I do not know who he is. The scene freezes before me, like a painting I can never enter, a scene whose meaning remains unreachable, obscure. (179,180.)

This is the last encounter between the writer and the reader in *Hallucinating Foucault.* And its significance remains unreadable and opaque. There is a warning here to readers in search of easy answers and to writers who assume that they always know what they are doing, or what they have unleashed. Not all writing is transparent, accessible, facile. Some meanings will always elude us. Not every text yields up its meanings, all its meanings, to every reader.

Notes

1 Arden ed., 103.
2 *Ibid.* 103-104.
3 *Ibid.* 104-105.
4 Duncker (2006 [1996]), references to this edition will be included in the text.
5 I have written at length elsewhere about the fairy tales. See Chapter v of my collection of essays, "Re-imagining the Fairy Tales. Angela Carter's Bloody Chambers" in *Writing on the Wall. Selected Essays* (2002: 67-83). I first delivered this essay as a paper to the Modern Fiction Society in Oxford, back in 1982, where my argument generated a fight. I am happy to report that it has been often reprinted, and gone on generating fights ever since.
6 Cited in Miller (1993: 98).
7 See the title essay "Writing on the Wall" in *Writing on the Wall. Selected Essays* (2002: 187-201). In this essay I discuss the significance of the metaphor, writing on the wall, and the passages in *Hallucinating Foucault* which describe the graffiti.
8 Austen (1990: 89).
9 Arden ed., 124-125.

Bibliography

Austen, Jane: *Mansfield Park*, Oxford, 1990.

Duncker, Patricia: *Hallucinating Foucault*. London, 2006 [1996].

---: "Re-imagining the Fairy Tales. Angela Carter's Bloody Chambers". – P.D.: *Writing on the Wall. Selected Essays*, London, 2002, pp. 67-83.

Miller, James: *The Passion of Michel Foucault*, London, 1993.

Shakespeare, William: *A Midsummer Night's Dream*. Ed. Harold F. Brooks, London, 2007 [Arden edition].

Mark Hall (*Derby*)

Longing for the Light. Darkness, Dislocation and Spaces of Exile

There have been many studies of light and this paper acknowledges all of the scholarship that goes before. However, this is not a study of light but a study of how light defines perceived identity and how our relationship to it in turn defines our own sense of self. I shall be examining work from different areas of the arts, literature, photography and film to develop my argument, showing how writers and artists have located both the subject and the reader/viewer to exploit this dynamic.

Light, as Foucault reminds us, became the most visible symbol of those who, during the Enlightenment, sought to banish darkened spaces and create a visible society. This eventually led to Bentham's design for the Panopticon which became a model of "'power through transparency', [and] subjection through 'illumination'".[1] As Foucault points out, it could serve as a template for other areas of society where visibility was a necessary adjunct to other forms of more physical control (the police or the army). Light itself defines space, sets its visible limits, reveals, creates and, as I shall show, establishes identities. Where one positions oneself in relation to the light, depends on a number of factors and determines the limits of inclusion into what we may term 'civilised society'. This paper sets out to look at instances where both spatial and individual identity is established through the position in which the subject is placed in relation to the light and its source.

Ever since the Enlightenment, western culture has had a strange relationship to the dark, alternating between ignorance, fear and suspicion that all things not visible could potentially do us harm or a belief that darkness was the only precondition of the sublime. What followed was an institutional struggle to control light and the nocturnal visibility it afforded, and a private, perhaps more spiritual desire for darkness. Habermas refers to the control exerted upon communal areas as the "public sphere of authority",[2] and in the seventeenth century this 'authority' became increasingly interested in the activities of dissident groups. Attempts were made to flood darkened spaces with light in an effort to control and police nocturnal space, thus mapping the territory of authority and identifying those in that territory as subject to that control. This, though, did not extend to domestic space, which was largely autonomous until the control of power such as gas, and later, electricity became centralised.

The hegemonic use of light in the street, advocated by Robespierre to banish darkened spaces and produce a visible, transparent and regulated society, attracted some resistance at its inception in Paris during the French Revolution. This resulted in lantern smashing, thereby "symbolically unseating the authority they [the lights] represented: the darkness that prevailed after the lanterns had gone out stood for disorder and freedom".[3] It is worth noting too that the brackets on which the lanterns hung were also used as makeshift gallows: "[B]y day, 1,500 uniformed police were on the streets. By night, 3,500 Lanterns (*réverbères*)[4] achieved the same result."[5]

Fig. 1: Hall, Mark (2006) *Untitled #2*

Bachelard refers to the power and solitude of the single light. It becomes a haven existing subconsciously at the centre of the house, with its power emanating from our desire to be at this centre. As the light travels outward it becomes the axis of vigilance, "a symbol of prolonged waiting".[6] "And the narrower the ray of light, the more penetrating its vigilance".[7] In its vigilance it becomes the watcher, sequestering those who see its light; "its light becomes for me, before me, a house that is looking out".[8] There exists then a spatial ambiguity if, as Bachelard suggests, we imagine ourselves in the warmth of the circle of light that metaphorically exists at the heart of the house, but are watched and sequestered by the light it emits and ultimately remain outside.

Foucault examines the spatial properties of light and control in his analysis of Bentham's Panopticon, which he sees as a paradigm for institutional control. He maps it to other institutional uses and 'scopic regimes'[9] concluding that "Visibility is a trap".[10] One can, however, observe a correlation between the 'trap' of visibility that Foucault identifies and that of performative spaces. The invisibility that darkness affords, identifies the audience. The Panopticon provided a space that served a dual purpose: its architecture was set out with a central tower where a guard would watch inmates arranged in individual cells around the periphery. The surveillance by the guard represented the institutional control, which was intended to modify the inmates' behaviour. However, the spaces arranged in this manner and lit from behind by windows in the exterior wall were also theatrical making a performer of each inmate. The light reveals each cell and identifies each occupant as a prisoner. Each space can be identified by the intensity and direction of the light that illuminates it, and that light can be instrumentalised by institutional control.

The house was different, normally considered a place of refuge and spatial autonomy, though this too had its areas of insecurity (as C.J. Jung suggests):[11] the polarised spaces of the attic and basement, the two places where the servants would primarily live and work in an English stately home. There are also domestic spaces for both employers and employees in which they intersect at different points, occupying the same space but for different reasons, one to serve and the other to be served. Both groups would therefore treat the space quite differently; the employers (let us say the upper classes) occupy space often oblivious to the presence of the other, whereas the servants are always aware of their own visibility. This becomes even more apparent at night when light begins to separate spaces, lit from un-lit, creating areas where identity becomes associated with the levels of visibility the light and darkness affords.

In *The Remains of the Day*, for instance, the butler Stevens describes the anxiety of visibility. In a large room he is waiting on two diners in a space that the light has made difficult for him to negotiate.

> On that occasion, much of the room was in darkness, and the two gentlemen were sitting side by side midway down the table – it being much too broad to allow them to sit facing one another – within the pool of light cast by the candles on the table and the crackling hearth opposite. I decided to minimize my presence by standing in the shadows much further away than I might usually have done.[12]

He clearly feels easier in the anonymity created by the shadows, feeling 'trapped' in the light of the candles, his presence made explicit, entering into a spatial relationship with the two diners. He then has difficulty with the transition from one state to another, from the darkness into the light, which is surely a metaphor for the book as a whole.

The arc of Stevens's story traces his situation from a mute observer of 'Negative Capability', which Keats describes as "when a man is capable of being in uncertainties, mysteries, doubts, without any irritable reaching after fact and reason"[13] to the realisation that his marginal life in the service of others has left him unable to act on his own behalf. He revisits this situation at different points in the book, mapping his journey from darkness to the enlightenment of self-knowledge, epitomised in the final scene by his reaction to the switching on of the lights on Weymouth pier.

Stevens' exile, though, is self-imposed. He exists on the edge of things, subjugating his sense of self almost completely into the role he has created, that of an automaton. As we can see in the scene in the dining room described above, he stands on the edge of the light, a voyeur whose particular fetish is the repression of emotion.[14]

Berberich suggests that the only indication of his true feeling occurs when he again enters the room after hearing of his father's death,[15] seeing "a forest of black dinner jackets, grey hair and cigar smoke".[16] Again he stands on the edge of darkness, this time though with the determination of an explorer: "he wended his way past the gentlemen, searching for glasses to replenish",[17] concerned only with his sense of purpose and inanimate objects.

Darkness can be a refuge as it was for Stevens; however, as Burke suggests darkness can also be capable of generating feelings of the sublime and light itself is so commonplace as to make little impression on the mind. Light, he goes on to say, if too intense, can overwhelm the mind and the sharp transition from one state to another (light to dark and dark to light) can be startling.[18] Darkness, when complete, also closes spatial phenomenology and as such inverts the locus of perception to a partial sensory deprivation. A state in which images cease to bombard the mind, "where the brain is [...]" as Deleuze suggests, "[...] an interval, a gap between action and reaction. [...] It constitutes a centre of indetermination in an acentred universe of images."[19] This interval may have been the moment Burke was describing, a moment of inner stasis, a 'sublime moment' between different conscious states, between 'action and reaction'. Roger Caillois uses the term *"legendary psychasthenia"*[20] to express the dissolution of spatial boundaries between self and environment and finds Eugene Minkowski's analysis of schizophrenia useful to describe the 'assimilation into space' a schizophrenic may experience. He adds that darkness has a

> positive quality [... it] is 'thick'; it directly touches a person, enfolds, penetrates, and even passes through him. Thus the 'self is *permeable* to the dark but not to light'; [... therefore] the role played by the inner/outer distinction and thus by the sensory organs as well [... becomes] minimal.[21]

Rather than the dislocating effect that light might have he here sees the subject become at one with the environment.

The transitions between different perceptive phenomenological states was what concerned Walter Benjamin. When writing about a trip to Naples in 1924 he identifies a concept Asja Lacis described as 'porosity' where in the city at night there are no discernable boundaries between inside and out, a kind of spatial anarchy. As Gilloch suggests, this "directs attention to a number of motifs. With respect to the physical structure of the city, it highlights the notions of dislocation and disorientation within an urban environment."[22] The disorientation that Gilloch identifies in Benjamin's analysis is one of identification. One finds a different situation from Caillois in that the ceaseless movement between spaces creates a dizzying array of possible spaces with which to identify: inside/outside, public/private, state/church.

Victor Burgin [discussing Benjamin] states,

> In this space it is not simply that the boundaries are 'porous', but that the space itself is soluble. This space is the source of bliss and terror, of the 'oceanic' feeling, and of the feeling of coming apart; just as it is in the origins of the feelings being invaded, overwhelmed, suffocated.[23]

'Bliss and terror' might easily describe the sensation of being in total darkness where physical boundaries dissolve into the surrounding space, creating, as Burgin suggests, a dichotomy between the 'oceanic' feeling of limitless dark, inspiring terror, and the intimacy and suffocation inspiring bliss.

The porous nature of both public and private space at night also poses a problem for the photographic image, where the slippage between light and dark is brought about not by any philosophical construct but by the limitations of technology. Consequently, this leads to selection and control of the limits of what is visible (in the image), and therefore what is ultimately recorded becomes its hegemonic subject even in instances where this subject is a fraction of the frame. However, new technologies have allowed a much simpler way to overcome this by layering different exposures to compensate for the extremes of contrast found at night. This, though, adds elements of temporal and spatial compression, which is not within the scope of this paper.

Notions of interpenetration suggest boundaries, territories with some investment of the individual in each. Some of the photographic work I have done recently explores this concept, specifically the transition between public and private spaces and the interpenetration of one into another, blurring these perceived boundaries. It is a symptom of anxieties that exist in some quarters about the reaches of visibility and its effect on notions of the private (hidden) self.

Fig. 2: Hall, Mark (2006) *Untitled #1*[24]

In *Untitled #1* the porous nature of the street at night to which Benjamin refers is evident: light emanates from the window, inverting the situation of daylight. One feels drawn to the light, to its inclusion; however, each area – the street and the interior – is separate. They are separated by their very nature and their hegemony. The brightness of the interior has primacy over the gloom of the street, its utilitarian function; life, quite literally, is inside. As a consequence, viewers find themselves, perhaps unwillingly, in the position of a voyeur since this is the selection the camera and its technologies have made (quite apart from those of the photographer).

The intimacy of dark space is what is at the heart of *Western Deep* (2002) by British-born artist and filmmaker Steve McQueen.[25] The work was commissioned to document conditions in South Africa's deepest mine Western Deep to undertake the "representation of nearness as the dominant mode of understanding the present condition of globalization".[26] It is not surprising that what emerges in the opening minutes of the film is the spatial disorientation of darkness. The viewer is also assailed by the screech and grind of heavy machinery which, in the darkness of the auditorium, echoes the situation of the miners as they travel below ground in the cage lift. The miners themselves are also in close proximity to each other in the darkness, sharing a spatial sense of community, their silence punctuated only by the shriek of the winding mechanism and the random flashes of their helmet lamps making small details specific. These details become monumental in scale, as they are the only pieces of information by which the miners can locate each other in the dark. This sense of dislocation and spatial separation from the light locates us as viewers (and the miners) in the suffocating and claustrophobic darkness. The isolation and fracture of peering into the small patches of light is at odds with the 'communion' of the dark and erases any racial, or social divisions, which only become apparent in the light. However, in this dark place, light still stands in for the power of the mine owners, who literally own the power. Kate Kellaway commented in *The Observer* in 2002,[27] "This is the darkest film I have ever seen. A lift descends blindly, goes miles underground, carrying its workers – and us with them – like damned men. We long for the light […]." Accompanied by the screeching mechanical sounds and occasional flashes of light the screen and the auditorium are closed in claustrophobic darkness – gone is the spatial harmony that Caillios referred to.

The camera becomes a co-conspirator in the anxiety choosing to film the darkness. It inverts the representation of Plato's cave and the normal situations of the cinematic experience. If what we see is darkness where there should be light, the implication is that this darkness represents reality. It certainly does for the miners, who are expected to descend into this damp darkness every day.

In *Rings of Saturn*, W.G. Sebald also sees the darkness at a distance – "[a]s darkness closed in from the horizon like a noose being tightened",[28] placing himself in the light as the noose tightens around him. Here the protagonist is on an island of light but is surrounded by a darkness that will inevitably overwhelm him. Another example of Sebald's use of light is the description of Somerleyton house at night "when the incomparable glasshouses, borne on cast iron pillars and braces and seemingly weightless in their filigree grace, shed their gleaming radiance on the dark [… –] an oriental palace in a fairy tale",[29] a beacon, though this time of fantasy, of the imagination that the reality of economics eventually snuffed out.

Sebald's darkness in *Rings of Saturn* is linked with that of Joseph Conrad (another exile), with whom Sebald had an affinity. There are examples of a more explicit pairing of their situations: "In the evenings, when the darkness settled upon the sea, he will have strolled along the esplanade, a twenty-one-year-old foreigner alone amongst the English."[30] The implicit identification here is with the otherness of darkness as an indistinct state that exists within and has a visible expression at dusk, a time when we are reminded of our own fears and capacity for evil, throughout the book Sebald to the 'heart of the dark continent' as distant, advancing over the sea towards him on the land, though for Conrad it was only too close: "A dark figure obscured the lighted doorway of the manager's hut, vanished, then, a second or so after, the doorway itself vanished too."[31] The moral decay in society links both books as the edges between fantasy and reality, between commerce and humanity are blurred. Both are solitary travellers and exiles in their own way, always on the edge of things, in the light but not of it, commenting on others who find themselves in the same position.

Chateaubriand's father, Sebald writes,

> paced up and down the enormous dining hall until it was time for bed […] Once he was at a certain distance from the centre of the hall, which was lit only by the flickering fire in the hearth and a solitary candle, he would begin to disappear into the shadows, and, when he was completely immersed in the darkness, all one would hear was his footfall until he came back like a ghost in his peculiar attire.[32]

It is in the darkness that meaning itself becomes porous, indicated by the envelopment in darkness of Chateaubriand's father, who is isolated and alone in a cavernous house: "Those who walked beneath its vaults felt much as one might when entering a Carthusian monastery."[33] He would have been aware of the collapsing of space, feeling less isolated and alone in the darkness.

Light and its captor, the photograph, have an unusual relationship in that both are often invisible. One looks at artificial light and what it reveals but seldom notices the quality or direction and indeed who has placed the light and for what purpose. This, though, is a key element in the establishment of perceived identity in contrast to how one might identify oneself. As I have shown, how one negotiates this spatial relationship can determine one's identification with such things as suspicion (search lights), sexual availability (red light district), commerce (shop windows and neon signs), fear and security (outdoor domestic PIR lights) etc. Artificial light also has associations with theatrical space and therefore attracts mute observation such as photography or surveillance cameras. Some artists have exploited this implicit understanding and have subverted surveillance footage (The Surveillance Camera Players) or have coerced the camera into recording everyday occurrences, lifting them out of the ordinary temporal flow and remarking on their specificity. The space of the photograph has also often collapsed, becoming for some 'a window on the world'. Although this relationship has been more exhaustively examined, the light that is at its heart has been generally regarded solely for its technical contribution rather than its hegemony. However, control of light has been a fundamental aspect of photography since its inception. Its relationship with truth is also bound up with much of what we believe (or used to believe) about news or documentary photography – a relationship that is at best uneasy and at worst corrupt.

Artificial light itself is too often placed in such a way as to represent what is already believed about something. One may, for instance, consider the difference in lighting between police 'mug shots' and children's school photographs – both taken in a similar manner but with very different outcomes (The photographs of Jamie Bulger's killers are just one example.)[34] Although the differences are often subtle, photographers have known since the beginning how to light to flatter or to critique and how to choose the quality of light to the best advantage. Over the years, light and its source have been enslaved to underpin theological and ideological philosophies for different purposes; more recently, photography has become a silent partner.

Things that fall outside of this circle of light are often marginalised, as fear of the unknown grips even the most robust cultures. The desire though to know and to see or witness, drives much cultural output, and the anxiety of not knowing or being able to control through vision drives politics. Darkness then, one supposes, will become the refuge, the spiritual home of the private, the unseen and un-surveilled as the backlash against total visibility begins.

Notes

1 Foucault (1980: 154).
2 Habermas (1989: 30).
3 Schivelbusch (1988: 98).
4 The exact number is 3,528.
5 Schivelbusch (1989: 97-98), emphasis in the original.
6 Bachelard (1994: 34).
7 *Ibid.*
8 *Ibid.*
9 The term 'scopic regime' appears in an essay by Martin Jay entitled "Scopic Regimes of Modernity" (in Foster [1988]).
10 Foucault (1977: 200).
In this book Foucault specifically discusses the advances made in penal reform from the dungeon to more open types of confinement, where (as in Bentham's Panopticon) prisoners are subjected to the constant and invasive regard by the prison guard situated in a central tower and isolated from the prisoners.
11 Quoted in Bachelard (1994: 18-19).
12 Ishiguro (1989: 72).
13 Expressed in a letter to his brother dated 28 December 1817.
14 Repression (noun):
"1. Being kept down by force […] 2. Psychological protective mechanism: in Freudian psychology, a mechanism by which people protect themselves from threatening thoughts by blocking them out of the conscious mind […]." (Encarta Dictionary).
15 Berberich (2007: 145).
16 Ishiguro (1989: 106).
17 *Ibid.* 106-107.
18 Burke (1998: 121).
19 Deleuze (1986: 62-63).
20 Minkowski, "Le Problème du temps en psychopathologie" (1932-33), quoted in Caillois (2003: 100), emphasis in the original.
21 *Ibid.* 100-101, emphasis in the original.
22 Gilloch (1996: 25).
23 Burgin (1996: 155).
24 Hall, M (2006) *Untitled #1*, (Original in colour).
25 Commissioned by Okwui Enwezor for Documenta XI Exhibition, 2002.
26 Okwui Enwezor, "The Black Box", quoted in Demos (2005: 63).
27 Kellaway (2002).
28 Sebald (2002: 229).
29 *Ibid.* 34-35.
30 *Ibid.* 113.
31 Conrad (1989: 60).
32 Sebald (2002: 258).
33 *Ibid.* 258.

34 http://www.inewscatcher.com/timages/2beed13e73fe683a3ca14c16053 b4bc4.jpg, 10 December 2009 and http://img.dailymail.co.uk/i/pix/2008/03_01/killersL0203_468x396.jpg, 10 December 2009.

Bibliography

Bachelard, Gaston: *The Poetics of Space*, Boston, MA, 1994.

Berberich, Christine: *The Image of the English Gentleman in Twentieth-Century Literature. Englishness & Nostalgia*, Aldershot, 2007.

Burgin, Victor: *In/Different Spaces. Place and Memory in Visual Culture,* Berkeley, CA, 1996.

Burke, Edmund: *A Philosophical Enquiry into the Sublime and Beautiful*, London, 1998.

Caillois, Roger: *The Edge of Surrealism. A Roger Caillois Reader*. Ed. Claudine Frank, London, 2003.

Conrad, Joseph: *Heart of Darkness*, London, 1989.

Deleuze, Gilles: *Cinema 1. The Movement Image*, London, 1986.

Demos, T.J.: "The Art of Darkness. On Steve McQueen", *OCTOBER* 114, 2005, 61-89.

http://www.encarta.msn.com/dictionary_1861700605/repression.html, 15 January 2010.

Foucault, Michel: *Discipline and Punish. The Birth of the Prison*. Trans. Alan Sheridan, London *et al*., 1977.

---: "The Eye of Power". – In: Colin Gordon (Ed.): *Power/Knowledge. Selected Interviews and Other Writings, 1972-1977*, New York, 1980, pp. 146-165.

Gilloch, Graeme: *Myth and Metropolis. Walter Benjamin and the City*, Cambridge, 1996.

Habermas, Jürgen: *The Structural Transformation of the Public Sphere. An Inquiry into a Category of Bourgeois Society*, Cambridge, Mass., 1989 [German original 1962].

Ishiguro, Kazuo: *The Remains of the Day*, London, 1989.

Jay, Martin: "Scopic Regimes of Modernity". – In Hal Foster (Ed.): *Vision and Visuality*, Seattle, 1988, pp. 3-23.

Kellaway, Kate: "From Grenada to Jo'burg, Everyone's in Deep Trouble", *The Observer*, 6 October 2002.

Schivelbusch, Wolfgang: *Disenchanted Night. The Industrialization of Light in the Nineteenth Century*. Trans. Angela Davies, Oxford, 1988.
Sebald, W. G. *The Rings of Saturn*, Trans. Michael Hulse, London, 2002.

Wolfgang Funk (Hannover)

Puzzling Memories, Displacing Ideologies. Utopias of National Identity

1. States of the Mind – On the Memory and Utopia of National Identity

Memory – or rather attempts at reconstructing memory – play a significant role in all three novels I want to discuss in this essay. Of the three protagonists, it is only Thomas Parry in *Divided Kingdom* who claims a definite moment for the first thing he remembers. This memory is of the night he was taken away from his parents and given a new identity in a move, which not only obliterated every potential memory Thomas might have had before but also completely redefined the space that constitutes England.

The protagonists in the other two novels, in contrast, concede that it is impossible to really remember their first memory. While Brian Marley in *Speak for England* is busy speculating about the

> shattered relics, the small evidence of the era of his […] little Life On Earth, which would be dug out by anthropologists or archaeologists from dusty library vaults, mounds of radioactive waste or ice-cap-flooded cities three hundred years from now.[1]

When pressed for exact details about this evidence, his memory remains somewhat blurred: "I remember lying in bed and thinking about atom bombs when I was very little. But actually, one of the first things I really remember at all is Winston Churchill's funeral." (179) Martha Cochrane in *England, England* approaches the question from a distinctly more philosophical angle and treats the reader to a concise treatise on the constructedness of every kind of memory before the end of the first page of the novel. Practising what she preaches, she presents as "her first memory, her first artfully, innocently arranged lie" the assembling of a counties-of-

England jigsaw puzzle.[2] What all these memories have in common is that they link the construction of a personal to that of a national identity, both of which are constituted by similar processes of remembering and forgetting.

The national memory, which Benedict Anderson sees as constitutive for any 'imagined community', is structurally oriented towards the past, which acts both as a projection screen and a repository for fragments from which a supposedly stable national identity is assembled. A clear definition of the space in which this collective identification occurs is essential for its success. The boundaries of the nation state figure as both the precondition for and the result of the establishment of 'cultural memory' in Jan Assmann's sense.[3] I would argue, now, that the novels under investigation in this essay redirect the momentum of this cultural memory insofar as they sketch utopias of national identity. They do this by rearranging the spaces within which the processes of national identification are negotiated.

Julian Barnes's 1998 novel *England, England* unmasks the fundamental futility and hollowness of the concept of 'national identity' in an unbounded world of global enterprise and entertainment. At the same time it muses about possible re-definitions of this concept, which might lead back towards a 'better place'. In *Speak for England*, James Hawes creates such a ‘good place’ by re-awakening the ghosts of the past in the shape of the survivors of a plane crash, who have been cut off from civilization (and more to the point English civilization) since 1958 and come back with a vengeance against the evils of today. Rupert Thomson, in *Divided Kingdom*, quite literally redraws the map of England along the lines of the ancient theory of the four bodily humours. What all three novels (and possibly all utopian texts) share is the conviction that contemporary society has in many ways reached an impasse and I would argue that this impasse is above all due to the failure or obsoleteness of traditional mechanisms of national identity formation such as its spatial demarcation with boundaries.

2. *Condensed Landscapes – The Destruction and Reassembling of National Identity in Julian Barnes's* England, England

The counties-of-England jigsaw puzzle which Martha constructs as her first memory illustrates in more than one way the spatial dimension of the interplay of national and personal identities. The jigsaw, for Martha, is more than just a toy, as it comes to represent the most dramatic episode of her childhood. When her father leaves his wife and his daughter, the significance of this event manifests itself in Martha's understanding mainly because her father's departure coincides with the loss of the county of Nottinghamshire from the jigsaw. In a puerile misinterpretation of cause and effect, Martha feels guilty about her father's leaving – "Daddy had gone off to find Nottinghamshire" (14) – and disposes of the jigsaw puzzle by stuffing the counties one by one into the seats of her school bus.

Benedict Anderson identifies the desire "to create a community out of signs" as the driving force behind nation building.[4] This community is not real, but always already a construction; or rather an effect of imagination, as it lacks the concrete interpersonal ties that bind together family or friends. These are replaced with an abstract notion of spiritual affinity, which can manifest itself in various forms, both sensual and cerebral. A glimpse of the White Cliffs of Dover or the smell of Fish and Chips (or nowadays probably rather Chicken Tikka Masala) can equally serve as symptoms of a feeling of belonging, which is then couched in the boundaries of a nation state.

The main part of Barnes's novel describes the birth of a rather different sort of nation. 'England, England' is a theme park located on the Isle of Wight and starts out as a pure business venture the aim of which is to present the most prominent markers of English identity, the "legends and landscapes" as Stephen Daniels calls them,[5] in a condensed (but easily manageable and navigable) version. In order to guarantee the 'authenticity' of this endeavour, a survey is carried out, which results in a list of 50 English 'quintessences' (83-85), including abstract notions like 'Snobbery' (no. 12 on the list) or the 'Stiff Upper Lip' (no. 21), landscape or architectural features like the White Cliffs of Dover (a surprising no. 9) or Wembley Stadium (no. 47) or historical/mythological characters like Shakespeare, Churchill, Robin Hood or Alice in

Wonderland. These assembled signifiers of Englishness are without further ado relocated to or recreated on the Isle of Wight.

Even though the project's originator, Sir Jack Pitman, is at pains to portray himself as a true-blue English patriot (e.g. by wearing MCC braces), there can be no doubt that it is net revenue rather than national sentiment that really powers the enterprise. The project thus serves as a sign of the time in more than one regard. First and foremost, it uncovers the tenuous state of the idea of 'national community' in general. The quintessential identity markers of (Old) England are simply transferred across the Solvent to serve as attractions for the theme-park and therefore primarily as means for making money, without too much patriotic resistance on the mainland.[6]

The fact that this shift in material (if not in symbolic) function meets with little to no impediments, makes obvious the irreparable rift that has opened up between the markers of national identity and any form of communal identity, however feeble, they are intended to call forth. The signs that once were part of a heterogeneous image of Englishness have lost their referential value and location in time and space. The past, as a space accessible via the interpretation and serialisation of symbols, has comprehensively been abolished and in its place a continuous present reigns supreme, which all the same pretends to be all about the past. The symbols have been freed from any referential obligation in order to facilitate their role as generators of profits.

The entire planning stage of the theme-park can be understood as an applied lesson in the contingency of historical narrative in the sense of Hayden White, who defines traditional historiography as "a narrative prose discourse that purports to be a model, or icon, of past structures and processes in the interest of *explaining what they were by representing* them".[7] The reasons for the streamlining of representations of the historical and geographical raw material in 'England, England' differ in purpose rather than in scale. In order to assure the historical unassailability of his project and to guarantee that his theme-park is in keeping with the latest philosophical and epistemological tendencies, Sir Jack invites a French intellectual to expound on the present-day fatigue with reality and the fact that we "prefer the replica to the original" (53). This is, of course, a thinly veiled send-up of Jean Baudrillard and his ideas on simulation. Set up in opposition to representation, which is still bound by "the principle of the equivalence of the sign and the real",[8] simulation consists in "substituting the signs of the real for the real itself",[9] thereby both freeing the signifiers of any conventional link to a referent outside itself and once and for all rendering the representation of reality with the help of images impossible. Sir Jack himself presents us with an apt illustration of this unreliability of the things we see. At one point he relates how he came to admire a scenic view of seemingly unscathed landscape replete with hill, fields, copse, river and even a pheasant, only to find out later that the

> hill was an Iron Age burial mound, the undulating field a vestige of Saxon agriculture, the copse was a copse only because a thousand other trees had been cut down, the river was a canal and the pheasant had been hand-reared by the gamekeeper (60).

This is to say that human in(ter)vention rather than real 'nature' was responsible for the idyllic scenario in the first place. Is it not possible, he asks, and the question is trickier than we might think, that all the things we take for granted, including landscape, are always already preconfigured either through actual human intercession (as in the example above) or by the way we are conditioned to look at them.[10] Why are the White Cliffs of Dover so fraught with national significance? Certainly not due to some intrinsic connection to whatever we think England stands for, but rather because they represent the first bit of English soil many a traveller crossing the Channel used to see. This has nowadays become an anachronism, of course, but the connotation of homecoming and belonging still sticks, while the runway at Stansted Airport (most likely the first English soil that today's traveller touches upon) has yet to inspire an equal measure of mythical fascination.

In 'England, England' the integrative force of the nation state has been displaced not only literally but also ideologically by the convenience culture (if you want to call it thus) of the "pure market state" (183).[11] But this is only one side of the coin. The novel's final part permits us a short glimpse at an alternative version of communal life. The country formerly known as England has been rechristened 'Anglia' and undergone a fundamental change in terms of communal identification.[12] Due to a self-imposed confinement (travelling to and in Anglia is well neigh impossible; there are no mass media to speak of and therefore little interpersonal communication), space has once again become a concrete rather than an abstract concept. The village is the reference point for integration, with the symbols of identification being local rather than global. The community described here, and we must assume that there are many of the same kind all across 'Anglia', is, of course, no more 'natural' than the one across the Solvent. Most of the inhabitants are acting the roles of village dwellers in just the same way as the employees of Pitco enact the cast of 'England, England'. The myths created to endow the village society with a common ground for identification – such as the Village Fete or the stories invented by retired American legal expert Jack Oshinsky, now known as Jez Harris – are approximations of traditional folklore at best and structurally resemble the streamlined and consumer-friendly version of English culture Sir Jack provides (and the analogy concerning names is certainly no coincidence). So, is there any difference between the two varieties of utopian England at all? Both are certainly not real in the sense of being original, as they are pure simulations, inhabited and brought to life by people acting their parts. On the other hand, both are real in the sense of not being imagined, as the integrative exchanges happen between the individuals themselves rather than on an abstract symbolic level.

Landscape features, however, can serve as a potent symbol of a general discrepancy in approach. The White Cliffs of Dover, for example, are relocated to 'England, England' by superimposing the traditional name and associated mythological connotations onto a totally different cliff, thereby perpetuating the myth while rewriting the location. In 'Anglia', on the other hand, new mythologies are foisted onto existing landscape features like Halley's copse, thus mapping out the given topography with new stories, a process that can be seen as an early step in the formation of any common experience.

3. *Every Citizen in his Humour – National Identity as a Matter of Character in Rupert Thomson's* Divided Kingdom

Having experienced both worlds, Martha opts for the nostalgic simulation of pre-modern 'Anglia' over the capitalist simulation of postmodern 'England, England', while still acknowledging and bewailing the loss of authentic experience in general. No such freedom of choice is on hand for the citizens in Rupert Thomson's divided kingdom. In his eponymous novel, the political topography of the UK is radically redrawn in the course of a single night. The country is split up into four separate and independent quarters, marked by the four colours red, blue, green and yellow. The inhabitants are allocated to the respective quarters according to the ancient model of the four bodily humours. The reasoning behind the 'Rearrangement', as this transformation is euphemistically called, is fairly deep-rooted in Western political philosophy. It is assumed that the state functions similarly to the human body and consequently is in its best shape if the balance of the four humours is safeguarded. In order to bring about this balance, the instigators of the 'Rearrangement', who are actually never explicitly revealed in the novel, break up families and friendships and relocate all citizens to their respective quarter, thus forcefully fabricating a new, divided topography of the formerly united Kingdom. Wales and the South West are turned into the Blue, phlegmatic country, the East Coast and the whole of Scotland are rechristened the Green (i.e. melancholic) quarter, the East Midlands up to Cumbria become the Yellow (hence choleric) quarter, while the South East and a triangle roughly between London, Bristol and Liverpool is designated as the habitat for the sanguine people. London is itself divided up into four capital cities.

Just like Martha Cochrane, Thomas Parry, the sanguine protagonist of *Divided Kingdom*, amalgamates personal and national identity configurations from the very beginning of his existence. His memory sets in when he is forcefully taken away from his family and put into a re-education facility called Thorpe Hill, where young boys are spoon-fed the new state philosophy before being reinstated in their new, matchingly-humoured families. Thomas's initiation into the new state of the nation and his subsequent career as a relocation officer for the government of the Red Quarter comes at the price of a thorough annihilation of all memories prior to the 'Rearrangement'. In stark contrast to *England, England*, where both utopian states are very much constituted on the principle of collective memory (however distorted), this divided kingdom has the abolition of all form of memory written into its fabric. In its place, the spatial limits of each quarter, in the form of heavily guarded boundaries, become the defining feature for collective identity. Small wonder, then, that the indulgence in memory eventually leads Thomas astray. On an official visit to the Blue Quarter he is tempted to visit a shifty entertainment facility called the 'Bathysphere', where he is confronted with the memory of his former life. This experience uproots him, literally cuts him loose from his sanguine existence. What follows is a tour-de-force through all quarters of the divided kingdom, resulting in the understanding that "perhaps, in the end, the four countries didn't vary as much as was commonly believed. Perhaps our famous differences were no more than convenient fictions."[13] The intrusion of personal memory, which in *England, England* functions as a projection screen for the collective memory, eventually leads to the destabilization of the ideological and purely spatial construct of the divided kingdom. This is aptly symbolised by Thomas joining the White People, a scattered group of pariahs, who resisted the initial division into the four quarters and as a consequence are now at home nowhere and constantly on the move. They have lost their ability to use language and are to all intents and purposes *vogelfrei*, which means that they are constantly exposed to violence, rape and even mob killings. The White People represent the abject other of the divided kingdom. They have retained the freedom of movement and character but only in exchange for the complete loss of all means of representation. Thomas reflects on the possibility that "if I'd seen so little of the White People recently it was because they had mapped out an alternative geography. Their existence lay parallel to everybody else's" (240). He thereby implicitly acknowledges the contingency of the geo-political construction he has hitherto taken to be all but self-evident.

It is interesting to note that the initial necessity for the 'Rearrangement' is – in good utopian tradition – explained with the deficiency of the previous, i.e. our contemporary, society. The Government, or so Thomas is told in Thorpe Hall, was forced to restructure the country as a consequence of

> our country's recent history. It had become a troubled place, she said, obsessed with acquisition and celebrity. A place defined by envy, misery and greed. Crime was rampant: the courts swamped, the prisons overflowing. Divorce followed marriage as quickly and predictably as teenage pregnancies followed puberty. Homeless people slept in every

> doorway, ditch and underpass. Racism was more widespread and more firmly rooted than ever before. Violence lurked round every corner. (7)

The utopian experiment in *Divided Kingdom* and the subsequent re-organisation of national space is thus grounded in a feeling of discontent rather than motivated by monetary incentives as in Barnes. This links it closely to the third novel I want to introduce in this essay, James Hawes's *Speak for England.*

4. *Brave Old World – The Rule of Reaction in James Hawes's* Speak for England

Just like *England, England*, *Speak for England* presents us with different versions of the world to come, and likewise, it is not clear at first sight which is utopian and which dystopian. The England which Brian Marley, the novel's protagonist, leaves behind is a place of moral decay and private destitution. Politicians are a bunch of corrupt and opportunistic scumbags, who happily twist any rule and abandon any principle for the limelight of public exposure time. In their constant craving for public attention, they in effect become slaves to the media, whose representatives are depicted as unscrupulous and superficial drug addicts. Their only objective is the viewing rate, an idol for which they are even willing to sacrifice human lives. This attitude is reflected in the rationale behind the reality TV-show *Brit Pluck, Green Hell, Two Million* as phrased pithily by Grant Brodie, college friend of Brian and executive producer of the show: "We're going to drop six ordinary Brits into the last unexplored jungle on earth, and see who lasts the longest before they go screaming bonkers or die. Or get eaten." (87-88)

Marley, whose life is a mess after a divorce and a rather unspectacular career as an EFL teacher, and who, like Martha Cochrane suffers from the absence of his father, takes the chance to escape from the dystopian jungle of meaninglessness in his contemporary England to the real jungle of the TV-show. He eventually wins the show and a prize-money of two million pounds but after Channel 7's rescue mission to get him back to "an England where at last he could be truly at home" (9) has failed spectacularly, he finds himself cut off from civilisation. Aimlessly wandering through the jungle for a couple of days, he at last climbs a plateau, sends a farewell message to his son and prepares to die. But instead of reawakening in paradise or purgatory, he comes to to the sound of cricket, and soon afterwards is actually hit by a cricket ball. This quintessentially English form of resuscitation marks his introduction to a group of accidental English colonists, the survivors of a plane crash in 1958, school children and (some of) their teachers at that time. They have established a society organised around the virtues and worldviews communicated in boys' magazines like *The Eagle Annual* and run by the patriarchal and authoritarian figure of the Headmaster. Marley immediately feels at home, a fact that is probably not unrelated to the presence of Georgina, who insists on being called George, with whom he enjoys one the most hilarious orgasms in English literature (149-151). After spending a couple of weeks in "this impossible Eden" (163), the memory of the two million pounds prize money returns to Marley. With the help of his batteries, he manages to contact the outside world and the whole colony is rescued. But here, at the meeting point of the two disparate 'English' societies, the clash of values becomes apparent. The Prime Minister and his entourage, flown in to greet the prodigal son of Britain on live television, are accosted by the Headmaster with the legendary words: "Well, I'm the Headmaster of this place. So is it true what Marley here tells me, that you Labour shower have dropped all this unions and nationalisation and disarmament claptrap?" (246). When the PM's 'Best Friend' tries to defuse the situation with the usual petty political soundbites, he is thoroughly caned by the Headmaster. The old ways seem to have more power than New Labour, and once everybody has made their way back to Blighty, the spirit of the moment even leads to a reactionary revolution. In compliance with Brian's assertion that "nothing was ever truly thrown away, no past ever truly got rid of" (285), the Headmaster is elected as the new Prime Minister. He runs England very much in the spirit of the Empire, a regression aided in fact by the socio-cultural conditions left by his predecessors. He confides to Brian:

> I'm amazed no one seems to see how easy this democratic politics is, what with the idiots' lantern and all. Really, you just have to treat them the way we used to treat the locals in the Empire: nothing too complicated, put on a bit of a show, never let them see you blink. (326)

So, eventually, the novel proposes three versions of England, one in the correct place but without the supposedly quintessential English values, one with these values apparently intact but geographically removed and one where values and geography are re-united under the rule of common sense as propagated by the Headmaster. There can hardly be any doubt that all three versions are dystopian in essence. The England Brian leaves is ruled by merciless egotism and withering interpersonal relations, while even the supposed Eden of the colony turns out to be resting on brutal and primeval foundations, like the Headmaster's insistence on the *jus primae noctis* and the fact that the colonists go headhunting for native tribes every once in a while. Small wonder, then, that the new England, instigated by the Headmaster, is a country which though "basking in itself, admiring itself with a touch of incredulity" (299) is a totalitarian system. It relies on forcing its citizens into obedience by way of curfews and strict law and order, thereby throwing out the baby of human rights with the bathwater of free-wheeling consumerism and capitalism. Teaching, for example, is "stripped completely of the hideous sociological guff which the last four decades of trainee teachers had been forced to endure" (294) and handed over to disciplinarians, with even the Headmaster himself regularly descending upon schools to cane discipline into any wayward youngster.

Both *Speak for England* and *Divided Kingdom* present attempts to re-arrange the political landscape as a reaction to the loss of virtues and communality in the face of social decline and unrestrictive individualism. The resulting utopian entities fail, however, to produce 'better places', as they themselves give rise to ideologically motivated societies, governed by abstract notions of membership and exclusion rather than humanity or altruism. These values are still there, but exist outside the reconstructed state systems. For Marley the decision for or against this new state of England is aptly personified in his being torn between George, in many ways (not only in her name) symbolic of both the traditional version of Englishness held up in the colony and of its application in a post-moral context in the new England, and Consuela, an Argentinean and thus decidedly un-English language student. There is no doubt where his heart will lead him.

5. *Conclusion*

When Brian records what he thinks is his final message to his son, he knows exactly what is rotten in the state of the nation:

> It's England that's wrong with me, Tommy. England. […] maybe you'll be fine and England will just be a normal country and everyone will forget all that balls about it mattering how you talk and us being better than everyone else in the world. (317)

English national identity, all three novels seem to suggest, has fallen into permanent disrepair. The utopian spaces and geographies discussed in this essay start out from a presumed assumption of lack and could – in a Lacanian sense – be read as attempts at re-constructing symbolic orders of national identification. However, they all fail to provide a new space around which strategies of collective identification could arise. The protagonists, who start out freely revelling in or pursuing the boons of the new world orders (careers with Martha and Thomas, fame and money in Brian's case), end up as castaways, either exiled from or homeless in their respective national geographies, on a quest for other means of identification.

In all cases, memories trigger a chain of events which eventually leads to an overcoming of artificial boundaries set up by the wilful abuse of collective identity formation. Beware, these novels seem to say, of false prophets of national identification. Neither common space, nor common character, nor common traditions have sufficient rallying potential to provide a place called home in this age of global simulations.

Notes

1 Hawes (2005: 179). Further references to this edition will be included in the text.
2 Barnes (1998: 4). Further references to this edition will be included in the text.
3 Assmann (1995: 126).
4 Anderson (1983: 20).
5 Daniels (1993: 5).

6 This is not to say, however, that national monuments are not used in this very way in (Old) England as well. The heritage industry, i.e. the business of making the past accessible and understandable for the present, is a matter of attracting euros, dollars and yens just like 'England, England', and it is certainly true that the "link between tourism and postmodern existence is made not least through the concept of authenticity", as Barbara Korte claims (2002: 289). I would still argue that there is a fundamental difference between the two concerning the underlying purposes. While today's heritage industry still puts the emphasis in the phrase 'experience England's past' on 'England's past', 'England, England' foregrounds the experience aspect, with the assembled symbols of Englishness serving as a mere and theoretically exchangeable backdrop, not fixed by locus and/or tradition.

7 White (1973: 2), emphasis in the text.

8 Baudrillard (1994: 6).

9 *Ibid.* 2.

10 See also Wendy Joy Darby's study on *Landscape and Identity* and in particular her analysis of the shaping of the Lake District (which strangely enough features neither in the list of 'quintessences' nor on 'England, England') as a national icon for a detailed example of a similar process.

11 For the interesting interrelation of tourism and authenticity, see also Boorstin (1985), Cohen (1988), Handler and Saxton (1988), Hughes (1995), MacCannell (1973) and Wang (1999).

12 The third part of the novel was originally called 'Anglia' and changed to 'Albion' with the 4th edition by the explicit request of Barnes.

13 Thomson (2006: 153). Further references to this edition will be included in the text.

Bibliography

Anderson, Benedict: *Imagined Communities. Reflections on the Origin and Spread of Nationalism*, London & New York, 1983.

Assmann, Jan: "Collective Memory and Cultural Identity", *New German Critique* 65, 1995, 125-133.

Barnes, Julian: *England, England*, London, 1998.

Baudrillard, Jean: *Symbolic Exchange and Death*. Trans. Iain Hamilton Grant, London, 1993 [French Original 1976].

---: *Simulacra and Simulation*. Trans. Sheila Faria Glaser, Ann Arbor, 1994 [French Original 1981].

Bentley, Nick: "Re-Writing Englishness. Imagining the Nation in Julian Barnes's *England, England* and Zadie Smith's *White Teeth*", *Textual Practice* 21, 2007, 483-504.
Boorstin, Daniel: *The Image. A Guide to Pseudo-Events in America*, New York, 1985.
Cohen, Erik: "Authenticity and Commoditization in Tourism", *Annals of Tourism Research* 15:1, 1988, 164-182.
Daniels, Stephan: *Fields of Vision. Landscape Imagery and National Identity in England and the United States*, Princeton, 1993.
Darby, Wendy Joy: *Landscape and Identity. Geographies of Nation and Class in England*, Oxford & London, 2000.
Handler, Richard & William Saxton: "Dyssimulation. Reflexivity, Narrative, and the Quest for Authenticity in 'Living History'", *Cultural Anthropology* 3, 1988, 242-260.
Hawes, James: *Speak for England*, London, 2005.
Head, Dominic: "Julian Barnes and a Case of English Identity". – In Philip Tew & Rod Mengham (Eds.): *British Fiction Today*, London & New York, 2006, pp. 15-27.
Heiler, Lars: "Transformations of the Pastoral. Modernization and Regression in Jim Crace's *Arcadia* and Julian Barnes's *England, England*". – In Stefan Glomb & Stefan Horlacher (Eds.): *Beyond Extremes. Repräsentation von Modernisierungsprozessen im zeitgenössischen britischen Roman*, Tübingen, 2004, pp. 331-349.
Henke, Christoph: "Remembering Selves, Constructing Selves. Memory and Identity in Contemporary British Fiction", *Journal for the Study of British Cultures* 10, 2003, 77-100.
Hobsbawm, Eric & Terence Ranger: *The Invention of Tradition*, Cambridge *et al.*, 1983.
Hughes, George: "Authenticity in Tourism", *Annals of Tourism Research* 22, 1995, 781-803.
Korte, Barbara: "Julian Barnes, *England, England*. Tourism as a Critique of Postmodernism". – In Hartmut Berghoff *et al.*: *The Making of Modern Tourism. The Cultural History of the British Experience, 1600-2000*, Basingstoke, 2002, pp. 285-303.
MacCannell, Dean: "Staged Authenticity. Arrangements of Social Space in Tourist Settings", *American Journal of Sociology* 79:3, 1973, 589-603.

Mergenthal, Silvia: *A Fast-Forward Version of England. Constructions of Englishness in Contemporary Fiction*, Heidelberg, 2003.
Nünning, Vera: "The Invention of Cultural Traditions. The Construction and Destruction of Englishness and Authenticity in Julian Barnes's *England, England*", *Anglia* 119, 2001, 58-76.
Thomson, Rupert: *Divided Kingdom*, New York, 2006.
White, Hayden: *Metahistory. The Historical Imagination in Nineteenth-Century Europe*, Baltimore & London, 1973.

Florian Kläger (Münster)

Reading Iconic Spaces. The Public House in the Contemporary Condition-of-England Novel

"ICONS. A portrait of England," a web-based service commissioned by the UK's Department for Culture, Media and Sport and representing national icons chosen by the public, describes the English public house as "an indispensable part of the national landscape, whether in town, city or countryside", and elaborates that:

> For many people – natives and tourists alike – the pub is the very image of our national social life. There can be no greater contentment than arriving of an evening to a room full of friendly, familiar faces, and settling down with a pint of your favourite brew. The traditional atmosphere of the English pub, with its informality and all-round cosiness, has made it an internationally unique institution.[1]

Note the parameters which allegedly make the pub a national icon: First is its nation-wide presence in town, city, and countryside. Apparently, the pub is so much of an institution that differences between individual places are elided by a nature that is universal to the non-concrete space of 'the' pub, a pub-ness that characterises this half-space/half-place – it is an iconic space constituted by the family resemblances between an immense number of individual places. The same applies for other English spaces between universal iconicity and local particularity that might similarly, and fruitfully, be studied: piers, chippers, and the queue come to mind, as do (with a view to intercultural comparison), the cornershop, the football ground, the village church, the town hall, the bus, the tube, and the phone booth. The supposedly shared nature of these iconic spaces, in being based on abstract family resemblances, is utopian in the literal sense – there is no 'original' pub that would define 'pub-ness', it only manifests itself in particulars. Hence, 'the pub' denotes an abstract space that only emerges by viewing together a large number of concrete places. In that an icon "*somehow* shares the properties of, or resembles, the objects which it denotes,"[2] the pub seems to have something in common with the nation: The relationship between individual pub and iconic pub-ness appears analogous to the relationship between iconic pub and Englishness. Furthermore, this pub-ness is associated closely with English social life. It stands for an atmosphere of friendliness, familiarity, and conviviality, which is thus claimed to be characteristically English. What is more, the pub has allegedly stood for this atmosphere long enough to render it 'traditional'.

In spatial, social, and temporal dimensions, then, 'the pub' is deemed an emblem of Englishness.[3] Like any national icon, it is a fruitful subject for literary and cultural studies in that its representations allow us inferences about English negotiations of traditions, and conceptions of national identity based on these traditions, in the face of a changing world. Obviously, if we look for representations of pubs that tell us something about their iconic state and the way this iconicity is perceived by Englishmen and -women, and that indeed contribute to the discourse of their iconicity in one way or another, fiction presents us with a prime field of such cultural introspection and self-negotiation. The so-called condition-of-England novel is a particularly suitable object of study because here, we can expect representations of pubs in the broader context of the 'state-of-the-nation' question. If the pub is treated, by author and reader, as the iconic site it purportedly is, it offers the opportunity to depict English society in a representative microcosm.[4] In the following, I examine how the problem of representation is, or is not, resolved by four established contemporary authors.[5]

1. *The Condition-of-England Novel, the English Public House, and the Production of Iconic Spaces*

The phrase, 'Condition of England', was coined by Thomas Carlyle in his 1840 pamphlet, *Chartism*,[6] in which he expresses his concerns about the immense division between the working classes and the better-off, and their lack of mutual understanding. These problems were also addressed by many nineteenth-century novels "which sought to articulate and interpret, in the mode of fiction, the changing nature of English society in an era of economic, political, religious, and philosophical revolution" with a view to improving conditions for the working classes.[7] The implicit assumption behind these 'condition-of-England' novels, then, was a faith in the power of fiction to adequately articulate and to alleviate social abuses. David Lodge identifies the particular challenge posed by the nineteenth-century genre as one of a formal nature:

> The major technical problem confronting the Condition of England novelist [was] how to accommodate within an imaginative structure an abundance of material of a kind which is usually treated discursively.[8]

For the twentieth-century successors to these novelists, John Brannigan perceives a different challenge:

> In contemporary 'condition of England' fiction [...], the compulsion to tell the story of the collective is also the compulsion to narrate the dissolution of the collective identity, to unfold the conditions by which England has come to the limits of its own existence.[9]

It is surely significant that the focus of writers', and critics', attention should have shifted from considerations of a formal nature to a question of the subject – whereas the original challenge was *how* to represent the condition of England, the problem now seems to be, *what* to present as 'the' condition of England.[10] As concerns the former question of how, or in what specific setting and through which social spaces, to represent the condition of England, it would appear that the symbolically charged space of the public house as a space oxymoronically located between the public and the private, supremely lends itself to this kind of undertaking: it is a place of work and leisure, of encounters between classes and genders, of conflict and conviviality. In this local place that is supposedly representative of the national space, in this individual site that partakes of a supposedly typically English pub-ness, an immense number of the discourses Lodge mentions intersect, or clash.[11] This is manifest in the history of the English public house: One of its precursors, the eighteenth-century coffee house, was the cradle of what Habermas has called the 'public sphere'.[12] Here, one could read the papers and discuss political matters, which led to the growth of bourgeois political awareness and participation.[13] In the nineteenth century, as the working classes flocked to public houses in the wake of increasing urbanization and the Beer Act of 1830, the same concern prompted anti-Chartist and anti-unionist legislation and the Licensing Act of 1872.[14] Social gatherings in an atmosphere of 'intimacy and all-round cosiness' fuelled by alcohol were not appreciated: For this reason, Saltaire, the Victorian model village built in West Yorkshire in 1853, did not have a pub.[15]

According to the pub novel to end all pub novels, *Ulysses*, space is "what you damn well have to see".[16] But, to adapt Johanna Garvey's pertinent question, "who is this 'you' and what are the spatial arrangements being observed, and further, in what way(s) is the [pub]scape perceived and composed [...]?"[17] The so-called 'topographical turn' in the humanities has, in the past years, pointed out the importance of accounting for the relativity of space Garvey here expresses – there is no such thing as 'space' pure and simple, it only emerges from cultural production and the relations between people, between 'self' and 'other'. This implies a shift of attention, for students of literature and culture, towards the ways in which literature constitutes or effects a transformation of empty space into meaningful place(s).[18] Undoubtedly, it is one of literature's prime functions to give voice to, and contribute to, the cultural interpretation and production of spaces, and to charge these spaces with symbolic meaning. Whether this meaning be old (voicing and examining traditions) or new (ascribing new meaning, or producing it), literature contributes to the ongoing discourse on space and the spatial orders of a given culture. These orders, Urs Urban argues, gesture beyond themselves towards a culture's social and symbolic order, or, in other words, towards its specific 'cultural topography' that defines itself by locating 'self' and 'other'.[19] In the present context, we will thus ask: How do novels that explore the notion of Englishness and the present condition of England employ the iconic space of the pub to comment on their subject?[20] How do they evaluate its cultural role, and do they (attempt to) re-inscribe it? If they do so, this suggests a faith in the power of literature (and perhaps, of the specific genre of the condition-of-England novel) to effect change – a faith maintained by nineteenth-century practitioners of the form. If they do not, it is interesting to explore *why* they should not do so. We also need to ask, with a view to the role of iconic spaces for the fashioning of identities, who is presented, in the pub, as 'subject', 'self' or 'other', and how and for what reasons? These questions point towards "the essential question that informs all 'condition of England' writing: Who will inherit England?"[21] and will yield insights into, if not the 'social and symbolic order of [English] culture', then at least into the role the novel plays in commenting on it.

2. *Reading Pub Spaces in* Nice Work *(1988)*, Last Orders *(1996)*, London Fields *(1989), and* England, England *(1998)*

David Lodge's 1988 *Nice Work* features an ostensibly conventional treatment of the pub space:[22] Protagonists Robyn Penrose and Vic Wilcox stop during a car journey at a pub on the outskirts of Manchester. Robyn is a literary scholar and a feminist, Vic an engineer and to some degree, a traditionalist. Both are characterised by their reactions to the place as soon as they enter. It is

> an undistinguished modern building situated on a roundabout next to a petrol station, but it had a restaurant attached to it done out in mock-Tudor beams and stained imitation oak furniture and enough reproduction antique brassware to stock a gift-shop in Stratford-upon-Avon. […] The clientèle were mostly businessmen in three-piece suits laughing boisterously and blowing cigarette smoke in each other's faces, or talking earnestly and confidentially to well-dressed young women who were more probably their secretaries than their wives. In short, it was the kind of establishment that Robyn would normally have avoided like the plague.
> "Nice place, this," said Wilcox, looking around him with satisfaction. (*NW*, 198-199)

Lodge renders the place simulacral in its outfitting (mock-Tudor beams, imitation furniture, reproduction brassware), though he does not elaborate on this. He uses the setting to characterise his protagonists, and the social space offers the opportunity to enact their different attitudes:

> Robyn observed how the deportment of the secretaries being entertained by their bosses had mutated under the influence of drink from a demure reserve over the starter to giggling irresponsibility by the time the dessert was served. She was less amused by their waiter's evident assumption that she herself was Wilcox's secretary, being set up for seduction. He referred to her throughout the meal as "the young lady",

winked and smirked when Wilcox suggested another glass of wine, and recommended something "sweet and lovely" for dessert. (*NW*, 201)

Wilcox is unaware of the power structures that inform and shape the place. The pub is sketched as a space of male domination both in terms of class and gender. The stereotypes associated with the pub allow for the easy presentation of different reactions to a place that does not need to be created with great effort – this thoroughly unremarkable mid-1980s pub-restaurant belongs with the cultural background. Clear-sighted Robyn critically observes the mechanisms of power at work in this social space, and she explains to Victor about the outrages of late capitalism over dinner. Overall, Lodge renders the place as a stereotype in order to characterise Robyn as critical of her surroundings and elitist in her tastes, and Victor as a man of plain tastes and a business-like, somewhat oblivious nature. It is not made explicit, but the quintessential Englishness of the pub is acknowledged, albeit in a mocking manner – it does serve as a microcosm of English society.

A more extended treatment of pub spaces is to be found, unsurprisingly, in Graham Swift's Booker Prize winning 1996 novel, *Last Orders.*[23] For four friends on their way to Margate pier, where they are to scatter their friend's ashes, pubs mark waypoints on the journey. It begins in the men's symbolically named local, The Coach and Horses, its name reminiscent of an old-fashioned hearse. Ray, the protagonist, opines that this is a "[d]aft name to call a pub [… w]hen it aint ever moved" (*LO*, 7). In a flashback, we are told that Jack, the deceased, once replied to this, "Where d'you think it should be going, Raysy? Where d'you think we've all got to get to that the bleeding coach should be taking us?" (*LO*, 9). On the one hand, this strengthens the connection with the hearse,[24] since it is the dead man's voice that asks this question, and on the other hand, it endows the local pub with symbolic significance that hints at stasis and a sense of futility in the group's social cohesion – key themes explored throughout the novel in various ways. In frequent flashbacks, The Coach and Horses serves as a meeting-place for the friends and a site of male bonding and sociability.[25] If the pub stops on the way to Margate serve as structuring devices that mark their slow geographical progress, The Coach and Horses is the focal point that marks their past immobility. It is the hub of their shared lives, and the scenes set in this space slow down narrative pace.

However, any simplistic notion of home-making in a friendly local is complicated by the spiteful words of the publican, Bernie:

> Like Bernie Skinner always says – like any landlord – after the third time of calling time, "Aint none of you got homes to go to?" With that sudden fierceness, as if he's insulting his own customers, as if he really hates all boozers and loiterers and it's the worst disgrace you can throw at a person, to have no home to go to. (*LO*, 212)

Swift here explodes the stereotypical notion of the friendly, sociable pub as a fiction by emphasizing its character as a site of work, rather than recreation. In the context of the novel's explorations of home and belonging, the social space of the pub is exposed as a merely fictive home, a space characterised by relations that are more perfunctory than intimate. The connection between the pub as a fictive home and the condition-of-England novel as a fictional rendition of England is significant and will concern us centrally later. It gains an additional edge in Swift's treatment of the other pubs the men visit on their trip. They function, to varying degrees, as markers down "Memory Lane" (*LO*, 107) – either of their personal lives or, in a metafictional turn, of literary history. Thus, they visit the Bull Hotel in Rochester, which also features in Dickens's *Great Expectations* and *Pickwick Papers*. Ray's comment on spotting this pub is incisive:

> The high street dips down towards it and the main road, and if you shut your eyes and open them again you can picture how a stage-coach might once have rattled across and up the slope and swung into the yard of the Bull, with the castle looking down just like a Christmas card.
> It's an old coaching inn, tarted up and buggered about. But I don't make no jokes. (*LO*, 109)

Even before the men enter, the pub is turned into a symbol of decline and the *faux* preservation of something past its prime. The latter quality, one might also ascribe to the protagonists, their friendship, and to the England of *Last Orders*. The notion that a place might have tradition is morosely rejected as fake Christmas card nostalgia, 'tarted up and buggered about'. The place partakes of the past only in an empty, simulacral manner. In such a place, it becomes impossible to feel at home, as Ray observes when he returns from the Bull's bathroom:

> I see them at the table, with the barmaid collecting glasses, nice arse an' all, and all the bar-room clobber, brass rails, pictures on the wall, of a pub I've never been in before and won't ever be in again, it's as though I'm looking at them like I'm not here. Like it's not Jack, it's me and I'm looking on, afterwards, and they're all talking about me. [...] Like I'm not here but it's still all there, going on without me, and all it is is the scene, the place you pass through, like coachload after coachload passing through a coaching inn. (*LO*, 112-113)

In spite of the friendly company he is ostensibly in, Ray feels depersonalised and effaced. His comment on the pub as a transitory station of course reaches beyond the concrete place he talks about – prompted by the pub, he voices a view on life and on his place in society. The pub provides a potent symbol of stasis and self-numbing that applies equally to the four protagonists and to the condition of England. The sense of loss that pervades the novel undercuts the nostalgia prompted by intertextual references and visits to iconic sites: The national, as well as personal, past holds nothing that could serve for guidance or orientation.

Another pub treatment of a symbolic, but also structural nature can be found in Martin Amis's *London Fields* (1989).[26] Amis here addresses the identification of the pub with Englishness head-on: As his unhealthy and unreliable narrator Samson Young puts it, "If London's a pub and you want the whole story, then where do you go? You go to a London pub" (*LF*, 14). The pub in question is the Black Cross, a sorry place with a telling name that hints at the juxtaposition of the four (or perhaps, five) central characters from the moment of their first encounter in that very pub: "that single instant in the Black Cross set the whole story in motion" (*LF*, 14), and Samson states that "[t]his moment in the public house, this pub moment, I'm going to have to keep on coming back to it" (*LF*, 23). Like Lodge, Amis uses the pub to characterise his protagonists through their relation to the social space of the Black Cross, as the following example illustrates: Looking to buy cigarettes, Nicola Six

> entered the Black Cross. She entered the pub and its murk. She felt the place skip a beat as the door closed behind her, but she had been expecting that. Indeed, it would be a bad day (and that day would never come) when she entered a men's room, a teeming toilet such as this and turned no heads, caused no groans or whispers. (*LF*, 22)

The pub is a stereotype, but so is Nicola, and thus she can confidently predict its reaction to her entry. As a place entirely defined by its occupants and their social relations, the Black Cross is entrenched in stereotypical notions of both class and gender – 'the place' skips a beat as Nicola enters, not its customers. The pub is metonymically identified with its patrons, and since the Black Cross also defines the novel's structure, it is implied that the social make-up of this 'men's room, [this] teeming toilet' is the frame of reference by which the impending catastrophes in the dystopian vision of *London Fields* are informed and enabled: As Steven Earnshaw aptly puts it, the Black Cross is a microscopic rendition of the macrocosm in *London Fields* (London, England, the planet).[27] But the cartoonish nature of this macrocosm must be kept in mind – everything in this novel is so utterly overdone that it is impossible to take this pub, as its microcosm, at face value. Satirically, it serves to characterise the novel's protagonists in terms of their relationship to society. There is no apparent attempt to question this identification of pub with country, nation, or society, although there is evidence of ironic re-inscription: Amis's Black Cross is as hyperbolically multicultural as Swift's Bull Hotel is tired and beaten.

The simulacral aspect hinted at by both Lodge and Swift is taken to an extreme by Amis in the setting of the events leading up to the novel's catastrophic ending. Keith, darts amateur and TV connoisseur, arrives at the place where he is to play the reigning champion of London darts. From TV programmes, he knows these matches to be set in the Chuckling Sparrow pub, against a backdrop of drinkers and fans. He is confused at finding only an empty studio:

> Keith said, "Where's the pub then?"
> "Pub? What pub?" [The show's producer] Tony de Taunton looked at Keith curiously. […] "There's no *pub*. Don't you think we have enough grief already, Keith. […] All those jolly butchers and smiling grannies – that's library stuff. We use cutaways and dub the pub later."
> "Common sense," said Keith. (*LF*, 457, emphasis in the text)

The Chuckling Sparrow is a TV fiction, drawing on a gullible audience's taste for stereotypes and the illusion of sociability. Amis suggests that such spaces are only to be found in the realm of the hyperreal – if *London Fields*' England is a pub, it is half simulacrum and half sordid pisser.

The idea of England, and the pub, as simulacrum is treated with a vengeance in Julian Barnes's *England, England* (1998).[28] In this novel, a theme park is built on the Isle of Wight that offers all the attractions of 'Old England' in one convenient place and ultimately leads to the touristic and economic decline of the original.[29] The theme park's projectors determine, by global poll, what the world's citizens deem "quintessentially English": Pubs come in fifth (*EE*, 83). In discussing the marketing concept for the theme park's pub, the projectors suggest tying it in closely with other attractions:

> The lolling shepherd must later be discovered in The Old Bull and Bush [...]. The haymakers would leave off their tourney of skittles to make menu suggestions, the poacher would explain his dodges, whereupon Old Meg crouching in the inglenook would lay down her clay pipe and disburse the wisdom of generations. (*EE*, 110)

The very wording of this passage already ironises the simulacral project and the nostalgia that underlies it. One strategist, Mark, is uneasy about "figments of your imagination [showing they are] flesh and blood the same as you" (*EE*, 111):

> "That's because you're English," said Martha. "You think being touched is invasive."
> "No, it's about keeping reality and illusion separate."
> "That's very English too."
> "I fucking *am* English," said Mark.
> "Our visitors won't be." (*EE*, 111, emphasis in the text)

Like the pub which is discussed here, Englishness itself is suggested to be irrelevant as 'reality' – in the theme park designed for global appeal, it only matters as commodity. The simulacral function of the entire theme park is thus emblematically brought to a head in this debate about the pub – as it is in its very name: The Old Bull and Bush is the name of a real public house in Hampstead, documented since 1721. This pub also famously gives its name to a projected London tube station that was built in the early twentieth century but was then abandoned – it remains an abortive building site today, with steps leading down to platforms never connected to the network. The name therefore suggests the full extent of simulation inherent in the theme park pub, and hence, in the 'England' it is meant to be a quintessential feature of.

Ironically, however, the theme park's resounding success makes for a return of 'Old England' to what may be a more 'native state' in the novel's last section. This is the space, "neither idyllic nor dystopic", of "a nation fatigued by its own history" (*EE*, 252, 253). The title of the last section, "Albion" (rather than Anglia, as 'Old England' is now called), with its etymological reference to the white cliffs of Dover, suggests a clean slate, a *tabula rasa*.[30] This is bolstered by the name of the pub where the local residents now gather, the Rising Sun: It constitutes a silver streak on the horizon for the Anglians freed from their own history – a new beginning (which is also the heraldic meaning of the rising sun). This pub is a site of communal self-inspection and -negotiation:

> At first Martha [who now lives in Anglia] had been sentimental, until Ray Stout the publican […] leaned across the bar of the snug with her gin-and-tonic and the words, "I suppose you find our little community *rather amusing*?" Later she was depressed by the incuriosity and low horizons, until Ray Stout challenged her with "Missing the bright lights by now, I dare say?" (*EE*, 256-257, emphasis in the text)

Barnes seems to hint that the pub is, in fact, so quintessentially English that it survives even the death of 'Old England'. It is a space where Englishness is lived, but also examined and reflected on; and it is part of that 'reality' that reasserts itself in the novel's final scene in the shape of a confident rabbit (*EE*, 266; cf. *EE*, 133). This is a curious ending for a novel so critical of all notions of essentialism and tradition, but perhaps, it signals a move away from the experimental playfulness of postmodernism towards the 'authority and assurance' of new (albeit 'wobbly') supports, such as Klaus Stierstorfer has suggested in a different context.[31]

3. Irony, Nostalgia, and the Public House of the Contemporary Condition-of-England Novel

We have seen that through its intimate association with Englishness, the pub setting lends itself particularly well to novelists coping with the formal problem David Lodge identified for the nineteenth-century condition-of-England novel, of how to represent the state of the nation. As a stereotypical microcosm of English society, the pub is an ideal site for staging social conflicts and problems. It may be used as a 'reciprocal spatial reality' – an ostensibly neutral, shared point of reference between the intratextual and extratextual worlds.[32] Readers will immediately recognise it as a space in which social issues such as relations between genders and classes, or the negotiation and rampant commodification of collective identities, emerge most clearly. Here, existing divides are inscribed and reified prominently, as we found in most of the novels examined above. However, as we saw, contemporary condition-of-England novels tend towards an ironic view of the notion that the pub should be seen as an iconic site. They ask what the site should be iconic of, thus addressing the major challenge to the contemporary genre: In the absence of any clear notion of Englishness, they ponder the nature of the pub space. Interestingly, the authors we have considered do not question the notion that the pub is an icon of Englishness, or a microcosm of English society – instead, they render their pub spaces ironic representations of simulacral Englishness. The pub 'is' England, but since England is a mere simulacrum, so is the pub.[33] The texts exploit, rather than reject, the identification of the public house with Englishness – they use it to offer criticism of the latter.

It is not surprising that this criticism goes hand in hand with the characterization of protagonists through their relationship to the space of the pub: Space and spatial relations are intangibly connected with social relations, and when social criticism is expressed, it also manifests itself in the spatial dimension. Hence, when authors like Swift or Amis emphasise alienation and the fragmentation of the collective, their characters will be 'other' in pub spaces that may or may not define a recognizable national 'self'.[34] The position of patron vis-à-vis pub is suggested to correspond to the position of individual vis-à-vis society, and if society is problematic for the characters, so is the pub.

Renditions of the pub as simulacral imply that Englishness itself is seen as mere simulacrum by these authors – a point we may in itself safely call trivial, if not banal. Its significance stems from its common currency in the novels discussed above, which underlines that the contemporary condition-of-England novel's answer to the challenge of what to represent as 'the' condition of England is resigned – there is nothing to represent any more, there is only simulation to maintain the fiction (!) of England. Authors thus lament the state of the nation (as mere fiction) and the state of the 'state-of-the-nation novel' (as fiction about a fiction, devoid of constructive potential).[35] But the fact that the traditional genre of the condition-of-England novel persists, and that the traditional site of the pub is used in these fictions, betrays a certain nostalgia that seems to contradict the notion of the simulacrum: Why maintain either simulacrum (genre or icon), instead of offering alternatives?

The answer seems to be that there is no alternative, and that all one can do is ironise the nostalgic desire for one. Linda Hutcheon has commented on this connection of nostalgia and irony in the postmodern:

> In the postmodern, […] nostalgia itself gets both called up, exploited, *and* ironized. This is a complicated (and postmodernly paradoxical) move that is both an ironizing of nostalgia itself, of the very urge to look backward for authenticity, and, at the same moment, a sometimes shameless invoking of the visceral power that attends the fulfilment of that urge.[36]

If, in content and form, contemporary condition-of-England novels give in to the nostalgic urge to look backwards (to traditional notions of Englishness, of the genre, and of the function of literature as a means of effecting change), they do not do so in the service of re-defining Englishness. Instead, they attest to the impossibility of doing that, but at the same time thrive on the 'visceral power' that arises from looking back. This attitude, paradoxically, at the same time mocks and reinforces the importance of tradition for both signifier (novel) and signified (England). The relationship between the two thereby moves centre stage – through this meta-isation, the contemporary condition-of-England novel becomes a condition-of-the-condition-of-England-novel novel, to coin an unforgivable phrase. By focusing on representations of the pub in these novels, this development is highlighted in an emblematic way.

What inferences do these findings allow us about the social and symbolic order of contemporary English culture, and about the novel's role in commenting on it? The representative character of the social space of the pub, like the discursive space of the condition-of-England novel, is ironised, as is the nostalgic desire for 'icons'. Quite contrary to the assumption that literature, as a signifying practice, turns empty space into meaningful place, we have seen the condition-of-England novel debunk the symbolic and iconic space of the pub as a mere simulacrum without reference to anything reliably 'real'. The spatial practice we found with regard to the iconic space of the pub is the exact reverse of what might be expected: The meaning produced through pub representations is destructive of the notion that the pub should represent anything worthwhile. The idea that it forms a microcosm of English society is taken up, but mocked through the heavily ironic use of clichés with respect to gender, class, and national identity. That these aspects of the condition of England should be included, but not confronted seriously, is testament to an uncertainty of how to represent contemporary English society adequately: traditional categories are mocked and rejected as insufficient. Yet this uncertainty is turned into a virtue in that it is made to question the validity of the (similarly traditional) condition-of-England genre. The novels' iconoclasm does not halt at the pub, or the nation – it extends to their own ability to represent and to change the condition of England. The impression that emerges is that of a partly nostalgic, largely ironic, and above all, self-ironic comment on the place of literature in English culture.

Notes

1 ICONS, "The Pub – The Basics". Warde and Martens call the pub a "principal symbolic site of English recreation" and "the quintessential English institution" (2000: 85).

2 W. K. Wimsatt (1954), quoted in *OED*, s.v. "icon, 3.b", emphasis in the text. The ICONS website defines its listed icons as "uniquely important to life in England and the people who live here" and specifies them as "symbolic – they represent something in our culture, history, or way of life". They are "recognizable in a crowd", and they "have hidden depths and unexpected associations" (ICONS, "What Is an Icon?").

3 "It would be impossible even to *attempt* to understand Englishness without spending a lot of time in pubs, and it would almost be possible to achieve a good understanding of Englishness without ever leaving the pub" (Fox [2008]: 88, emphasis in the text).

4 The only monograph published on the subject of the pub in English literature lists, among the literary 'functions' of the public house, its role as "a convenient means of bringing together different levels of society […]

either to highlight existing tensions in society, or to project some idea of social harmony, or to do both," and as "the microcosm of society" (Earnshaw [2000: 13]).

5 It should be noted that two of these novels, Lodge's and Amis's, were written before the watershed year of 1989, when the so-called 'Beer Orders' legislated against breweries owning too many pubs. These orders led to the emergence of the pub chains that now dominate the scene (although the orders were revoked in 2003). One might expect that this legislation, and the market revolution it entailed, would have changed the public image of pubs – as we will see, this change is not explicitly marked in the novels I discuss here.

6 Carlyle (1840: 2-3).

7 Lodge (2002: 230).

8 *Ibid.* 234.

9 Brannigan (2003: 85). Brannigan discusses all of the novels analyzed here, except for Lodge's, in his chapter, "A Literature of Farewell: The Condition of England and the Politics of Elegy" (73-97). My reading of pub spaces in these texts yields results that agree broadly with Brannigan's assessment of the contemporary condition-of-England novel as "posing the question of non-identity, or indeed the performance of an identity which is absent or anachronistic" (97). Cf. also Connor (1996: 45-82). In examining condition-of-England novels from the 1950s to the 1980s, Connor attests to the "ambition to represent England and Englishness", which contemporary authors inherit from the nineteenth-century genre, their awareness of the genre's inadequacy for this kind of representation today, and the "residual sense of the potential of the novel to imagine, project and preserve forms of national and collective identity" (*ibid.* 47).

10 The response that nineteenth-century novelists found to their challenge is well known: It lay in the mode of writing we call realism, or perhaps more particularly, social realism. The response of contemporary authors working in this genre forms my subject in this paper.

11 On the public house and class and age, see Vasey (1975: 184-190), as well as Smith (1983: 367-385); on the pub and gender, see Hey (1986: *passim*). On the pub and ethnic identity, see also Warde & Martens (2000: 85).

12 Habermas (2009: 92-93). Habermas' 'public sphere' emerges from the exchange between aristocrats and bourgeois intellectuals – in the eighteenth century, the working classes that are to form both the main body of patrons and the subject of the condition-of-England novel are not, of course, at issue. On the synonymous use of the terms 'coffee house' and 'public house' in the early eighteenth century, cp. *OED*, "public house 2.b": "1715 *Royal Proclam.* 5 Jan. in *London Gaz.* No. 5292/2, Taverns, Chocolate Houses, Coffee Houses, or other Publick Houses".

13 The shared reception of news is a function still associated with the pub in the contemporary condition-of-England novel, with the newspapers being replaced by TV, which can be watched and responded to by all customers simultaneously. Cf. the pub The Unity in John King's *England Away*

(London, 1999). On the history of the English public house see Vasey (1975: 17-48).

14 See Cordery (2003: 3-13).

15 Dewhirst (1960: 139).

16 Joyce (1993: 178). It hardly needs to be reiterated that the pub sequences in *Ulysses* include "Laestrygonians", "Cyclops", and "Oxen of the Sun", the second being a recapitulation of English literary history – set in a pub.

17 Garvey (1995: 108).

18 This is usefully differentiated terminologically by Erica Carter *et al.*: "Place is space to which meaning has been ascribed" (Carter *et al.* [1993: xii]).

19 Urban (2007: 50-51).

20 Cf. Burden (2006: 14): "Symbolic landscapes and places have specific cultural meanings that construct, maintain, and circulate myths of a unified national identity, or whose visible ironies deconstruct those myths as we 'think of England'."

21 Winston & Marshall (2002: 15).

22 Lodge (1989). Further references in the text, abbreviated as '*NW*'. On *Nice Work* as a condition-of-England novel cf. Winston & Marshall (2002: 3-22) and Connor (1996: 73-82).

23 Swift (1996). Further references to this edition will be included in the text, abbreviated as "*LO*". On *Last Orders* as a condition-of-England novel see Cooper (2002: 80-81).

24 The bottles on the pub's bar are also compared, by Ray, to organ pipes (*LO*, 1).

25 Cf. the ogling and perhaps sexual harassment of the new barmaid in *Last Orders*, 210.

26 Amis (1990). Further references to this edition will be included in the text, abbreviated as '*LF*'. The text is discussed as a condition-of-England novel in Lea (2005: 70-81).

27 Earnshaw (2000: 267).

28 Barnes (1999). Further references to this edition will be included in the text, abbreviated as '*EE*'. The points raised in Nünning (2001) elaborate on *England, England* as a condition-of-England novel without identifying it as such explicitly.

29 The parallels to Baudrillard's comments on Disneyland are obvious and need not be reiterated here.

30 This section is entitled "Anglia" in the novel's first edition (London, 1998) but "Albion" in *EE*. On this title and the section as a whole see also Heiler (2004: 347-348), albeit with different conclusions from the reading offered here.

31 Cf. Stiersdorfer (2003: *passim*).

32 Cf. Thurgar-Dawson (2006: 35-38); quotation at 38.

33 Marketing professor Alistair Williams actually made a plea in 1998 in favour of "hyperreal pubs" to aid the industry, which "has to recognize that in contemporary western society postmodern consumers do not adopt consistent recognizable lifestyles, but opt to experiment with an eclectic

combination of goods and services in order to experience a range of, often conflicting, identities"(Williams [1998: 230]) – the novelists' assessments thus find themselves in the unlikely company of pub market research.

34 The acknowledgement of social isolation is familiar from the traditional condition-of-England novel: Cf. for instance Disraeli's assessment in *Sybil* that in cities, men "are not in a state of co-operation, but of isolation" (2008: 65). In this very passage, Disraeli attests to the indefinability of 'the nation', since there are actually two nations in England, the rich and the poor (65-66). Contemporary authors seem less concerned with enumerating the various nations living in England, but rather with ironising the notion that anyone should deem this activity worthwhile.

35 Connor's assessment is similar: "The problem of representing England, and [...] of finding a plausible or appropriate audience and form of address for such a representation, is closely related to the seemingly more parochial problem of how, if at all, the social value of literary representation itself is to be defended" (1996: 72-73).

36 Hutcheon (1998: par. 24, emphasis in the text).

Bibliography

Amis, Martin: *London Fields*, London, 1990.

Barnes, Julian: *England, England*, London, 1999 [1998].

Brannigan, John: *Orwell to the Present. Literature in England, 1945-2000*, Basingstoke, 2003.

Burden, Robert: "Englishness and Spatial Practices." – In R.B. & Stephan Kohl (Eds.): *Landscape and Englishness*, Amsterdam, 2006, pp. 13-25.

Carlyle, Thomas: *Chartism.* Boston, 1840.

Carter, Erica, Donald James & Judith Squires: "Introduction." – In E.C., D.J. & J.S. (Eds.): *Space and Place. Theories of Identity and Location*, London, 1993, pp. vii-xv.

Connor, Steven: *The English Novel in History. 1950-1995*. London, 1996.

Cooper, Pamela: *Graham Swift's* Last Orders. *A Reader's Guide*. New York, 2002.

Cordery, Gareth: "Public Houses. Spatial Instabilities in *Sketches by Boz* and *Oliver Twist* (Part One)", *Dickens Quarterly* 20:1, 2003, 3-13.

Dewhirst, Robert K.: "Saltaire", *The Town Planning Review* 31:2, 1960, 135-144.

Disraeli, Benjamin: *Sybil, or The Two Nations*, London, 2008 [1845/1981].

Earnshaw, Steven: *The Pub in Literature. England's Altered State*, Manchester, 2000.

Fox, Kate: *Watching the English. The Hidden Rules of English Behaviour*, Boston, 2008.

Garvey, Johanna X. K.: "City Limits", *Twentieth-Century Literature* 41:1, 1995, 108-123.

Habermas, Jürgen: *Strukturwandel der Öffentlichkeit. Untersuchungen zu einer Kategorie der bürgerlichen Gesellschaft*, Frankfurt am Main, 2009 [1961/1990].

Heiler, Lars: "Transformations of the Pastoral. Modernization and Regression in Jim Crace's *Arcadia* and Julian Barnes's *England, England*". – In Stefan Glomb & Stefan Horlacher (Eds.): *Beyond Extremes. Repräsentation und Reflexion von Modernisierungsprozessen im zeitgenössischen britischen Roman*, Tübingen, 2004, pp. 331-349.

Hey, Valerie: *Patriarchy and Pub Culture*, London, 1986.

Hutcheon, Linda: "Irony, Nostalgia, and the Postmodern", http://www.library.utoronto.ca/utel/criticism/hutchinp.html, 2 May 2010.

"ICONS. A Portrait of England – The Pub", http://www.icons.org.uk/theicons/collection/collection/the-pub, 2 May 2010.

"ICONS. A Portrait of England – What Is an Icon", http://www.icons.org.uk/theicons/copy_of_what-is-an-icon, 2 May 2010.

Joyce, James: *Ulysses*, Oxford, 1993 [1922].

Lea, Daniel: "One Nation, Oneself. Politics, Place and Identity in Martin Amis's Fiction". – In James Acheson & Sarah C.E. Ross (Eds.): *The Contemporary British Novel*, Edinburgh, 2005, pp. 70-81.

Lodge, David: *Nice Work*, London, 1989.

---: *Language of Fiction. Essays in Criticism and Verbal Analysis of the English Novel*, London, 2002.

Nünning, Vera: "The Invention of Cultural Traditions. The Construction and Deconstruction of Englishness and Authenticity in Julian Barnes's *England, England*", *Anglia* 119:1, 2001, 58-76.

Smith, Michael A.: "Social Usages of the Public Drinking House. Changing Aspects of Class and Leisure", *The British Journal of Sociology* 34:3, 1983, 367-385.

Stierstorfer, Klaus: "Wobbly Grounds. Postmodernism's Precarious Footholds in Novels by Malcolm Bradbury, David Parker, Salman Rushdie, Graham Swift". – In K.S. (Ed.): *Beyond Postmodernism. Reassessments in Literature, Theory, and Culture*, Berlin, 2003, pp. 213-234.

Swift, Graham: *Last Orders*, London, 1996.

Thurgar-Dawson, Chris: "Negotiating Englishness. Choropoetics, Reciprocal Spatial Realities and Holistic Spatial Semantics in William Renton's 'The Fork of the Road' (1876)". – In Robert Burden & Stephan Kohl (Eds.): *Landscape and Englishness*, Amsterdam, 2006, pp. 27-43.

Urban, Urs: *Der Raum des Anderen und andere Räume. Zur Topologie des Werkes von Jean Genet*, Würzburg, 2007.

Vasey, Daniel E.: *The Pub and English Social Change*, New York, 1975.

Warde, Alan & Lydia Martens: *Eating Out. Social Differentiation, Consumption, and Pleasure*, Cambridge, 2000.

Williams, Alistair: "The Postmodern Consumer and Hyperreal Pubs", *International Journal of Hospitality Management* 17, 1998, 221-232.

Winston, Robert P. & Timothy Marshall: "The Shadows of History. The 'Condition of England' in *Nice Work*", *Critique* 44:1, 2002, 3-22.

Sandra Heinen (Frankfurt)

Locating National Identity. The Representation of Englishness in Peter Ackroyd's *Thames. Sacred River* (2007)

Following his monumental biography of London, Peter Ackroyd's *Thames. Sacred River* (2007) again focuses on a space that has traditionally been closely linked to national identity: the river Thames, which Ackroyd introduces early on as a "token of national character".[1] Yet, while metropolitan London is in many ways a predominantly *British* space, the Thames is much more regionally grounded as the "sovereign river of England" (107) and is thus considered by Ackroyd to be "one of the sources of *English* identity and *English* power" (334).[2]

The association of landscape with national identity has a long tradition in England; "nowhere else is landscape so freighted as legacy. Nowhere else does the very term suggest not simply scenery and *genre de vie*, but quintessential national virtues".[3] Ideas of Englishness have been supported by images of "green rolling hills, shady nooks, copses, winding lanes and nestling thatched villages" and particularly by representations of the Thames in both fictional and non-fictional literature.[4] The link between the Thames and Englishness is certainly rooted in the river's actual course, which is confined to England, crossing it from West to East.[5]

If the river's spatial location is responsible for its association with England rather than Britain, it is its temporal dimension which constitutes the link between the geological aspect of the riverine landscape and a mental self-conception of collective identity. The river is deemed a "source of English identity" because it "has always been central to English life" (11).[6] As a result, Ackroyd's book is as much a *historio*graphical account of the river as it is a *topo*graphical one; and it is this conjunction between the spatial and the temporal which is central to his representation of Englishness.

Since the structure of Ackroyd's text as well as the language and rhetoric used deviate from that of standard non-fictional representations and to a large extent determine the text's signification, I will first outline the representational strategies employed by Ackroyd. In the second part of this paper I will then reconstruct the main points of Ackroyd's argument, which intensifies the traditional idea of an intrinsic connection between place and national identity by taking a performative stance and imbuing the river with auratic significance. Finally, I will briefly assess the book's role in the context of current debates about cultural memory on the one hand and British identity on the other.

1. Formal Features of Ackroyd's Text

Descriptions of the Thames – or any other river – usually follow one out of two narrative patterns: they either reconstruct the river's flow from source to mouth, thus following its spatial progression, or, alternatively, they adopt a temporal perspective and render historical events in chronological order. In either case a focus on change propels the narrative forward. Ackroyd, however, depends neither on spatial nor on temporal progress to structure his account. Instead he opts for a thematic method of organisation, which formally undercuts any sense of direction, let alone teleology. Ackroyd's textual movements back and forth in time and space have been described by several reviewers as a performative imitation of what he sees as the unpredictable movement of the book's subject. According to Jeanette Winterson, "reading this book is like being in a boat on the river itself, which never travels in a straight line, but [...] 'quixotically'",[7] while Anthony Sattin comments that the book is "as rich and meandering and wonderful as its subject".[8] These verdicts seem to me to be rather euphemistic interpretations of a text whose diverse observations are more or less loosely connected by association.

Ackroyd and his two research assistants spent much time digging up unfamiliar and surprising pieces of information connected to the Thames. The encyclopaedic effort to reproduce the vast amount of knowledge pertaining to the river has resulted in a text often resembling a compilation, which repeatedly turns – as observed by the author himself – into a "litany of names and places"

(93).[9] The main thrust of the various listings seems to be directed at highlighting the meaningfulness of the observations made, without having to be too specific about the exact nature of his meaning.

This effect is repeated on the linguistic level. Ackroyd uses many superlatives, for instance when he informs the reader right at the beginning that "The Thames is the longest river in England", but that "it must be the shortest river in the world to acquire such a famous history". In addition to such superlatives we find many unconditional, absolute statements, like "The Thames itself has always been considered holy" (79). In other places, generalisations are replaced by an openly tentative approach, revealing the thin ground upon which Ackroyd builds his argument: the speculations about the origin of the river's name, for example, are shot through with formulations which indicate a more or less "informed supposition" (23) – from the adverb "perhaps", to the modal verbs "may" and "might", to the plain admission that "no certainty can be found" (24). Another striking feature of Ackroyd's prose is its unmarked shifting between literal and metaphorical descriptions. Any form of objective metalanguage is dispensed with, in favour of an associative rhetoric which often enough leaves conventional rationality behind.[10]

In view of its stylistic idiosyncrasies, it might seem a misguided endeavour to try and reduce Ackroyd's text to a set of clearly defined argumentative points. Nevertheless I will now outline the main points advanced by Ackroyd to support his claim that there is an intrinsic link between the river and national identity.

2. Ackroyd's Alignment of Place and National Identity

Ackroyd's argument of an intrinsic connection between place and national identity is mainly based on three rhetorical strategies: (a) the way in which he relates space to time, (b) his description of the relationship between space and people and (c) the way in which he relates historical and geographical facts to mythical forms of knowledge. Although these aspects are closely interwoven in Ackroyd's text, they can be distinguished for analytical purposes as three separate claims.

Although Ackroyd avoids a chronological representation of the past and thus temporal linearity, a historical perspective is central to his representation of the Thames. He provides descriptions of the river in different eras from its geological beginning 170 million years ago to the present day, and reconstructs changing habits and technologies of transport, habitation, and cultural practice. He has a particular interest in the material traces of the past – from prehistoric daggers found by the side of the river to ancient bridges or medieval boats. These objects not only provide a window to the past which allows historical reconstructions but they also turn the Thames into a "vast compendium of history" and objectify the river's historicity.[11]

Ackroyd's description of the churches along the Thames is emblematic of his view of the Thames valley as a whole: "[i]n many of them are relics of very different styles, from the ninth to the nineteenth centuries, and this heterogeneity of periods is typical of the Thames churches. It is a place where time itself is mingled and confused." (90) In much the same way as the buildings, the landscape itself is described as having the form of a palimpsest whereby the Thames valley as a whole is shown to contain traces of various previous times; as Ackroyd maintains: "[t]he Thames contains all times." (14)[12] Ackroyd's decision not to give his book a chronological structure can be considered a formal representation of this central idea that the Thames is a place which gathers and fuses different historical periods.

Such a semantic charging of places through referral to the past is not a novelty and is particularly common whenever places are turned into symbols of a collective identity. What is unusual about Ackroyd's argument is the way in which it combines two conceptions of history which appear incompatible at first sight: In his account the river becomes, on the one hand, a witness to historical change, while on the other it is turned into a token of timeless endurance. Ackroyd puts a special emphasis on cultural artefacts and practices which are lost, "changed beyond recognition" (206), or now largely forgotten.[13] Yet this emphasis on historical change is undercut by an insistence on continuity, for instance when he states: "[t]here is an intense conservatism about the Thames" (173); or that "[t]here is a continuity, inspired and maintained by the river itself" (336).[14] Because Ackroyd highlights both historical ruptures and continuities and habitually draws generalising conclusions from specific observations, a tension between the two contrasting interpretations of historical development is kept up throughout the text.

But what at first looks like an inconsistency appears to be an intentional strategy upon closer inspection, because it parallels what Ackroyd calls the "perpetual paradox" and the "Janus-faced aspect of the river" (13). Through a metaphorical interpretation of its physical properties, the "Thames can become both an emblem of time and of eternity" (*ibid.*): While the course of the river is constant, the water in the river is never the same. The Thames thus becomes a symbol of what Ackroyd has elsewhere called "chronological resonance", the persistence of "patterns of sensibility or patterns of response",[15] which designates transhistorical connectedness, continuity despite change. This idea was translated into visual imagery for the book's cover, on which three historical representations of Thames bridges are combined to form one extended bridge.

2.2 The Relationship between Space and People

One of the assumptions underlying Ackroyd's argument is that "[t]he people, and their habitation, are in every sense determined by the neighbouring river" (182). This determination can be of a pragmatic kind as when it manifests itself in the material of people's houses or in the form of their occupations. Ackroyd enumerates, for example, families who have been working on the Thames as boatmen for many generations, coming to the conclusion that "[t]hese are continuities that the river seems to foster, patterns of labour and habitation that persisted beside the ever-flowing Thames" (177).

But the influence of the river can, according to Ackroyd, also assume a different form, such as the evocation of a mood: "[t]he true measure of the river may be found in the emotions that it summons up" (18). It is suggested that a sense of belonging and feelings of melancholy and nostalgia are the most frequent responses to the Thames and that these emotions are related to the historical dimension of the river, which invokes the past and the future, and to the river's flowing water, which indicates both change and impermanence.

As Ackroyd turns to a symbolic reading of the river here, his analysis yields no interpretation that is unique to the Thames. If his assumption about the origin of nostalgia and melancholy is correct, then every river, no matter where, should evoke the same emotions. Thus, although Ackroyd sets out to describe a specific river with a specific history, his argument frequently hinges on assumptions about rivers in general. This strategy can have two effects: either – and I assume this is the intention – all the meanings and interpretations assigned to rivers like the Nile, the Ganges, the Tiber, the Jordan or the Amazon are transferred onto the Thames – or, alternatively, the distinctiveness of the Thames is blurred.[16]

The second possibility is counteracted at various points in the argument where Ackroyd suggests that the Thames exerts a more specific influence:

> It has been claimed that there are also regional characteristics shaping, for example, those who live and work along the upper Thames and the estuary. Those who harbour a topographical imagination tend to view the various communities as in some way reflecting the characteristics of the river. The people of the Upper Thames are then considered to be calm and contemplative, almost languorous; the people of the estuary are deemed to be quick and alert, almost mischievous. (178)

Although Ackroyd distances himself here from the proposition of such an immediate correspondence of characters by calling it "perhaps fanciful" (*ibid.*), he is not generally averse to the idea that spaces influence the people inhabiting them in a very direct and material way. His assertion put forward in a newspaper article in 1993 that it seems possible to him "that a street or dwelling can materially affect the character and behaviour of the people who dwell in them" is repeated in his reflections on the composition of the soil in the Thames valley:[17]

> Those who trust the spirit of place must take account of these geological gradations and alterations. There is no reason to doubt that human consciousness is changed by the experience of living above clay, rather than above chalk, even though the nature of that change is not understood. (33)

Ackroyd's belief and interest in the effects of geographical environment on people's perception, consciousness and behaviour is firm, yet the nature of these effects remains largely nebulous.

2.3 Factual vs. Mythical Knowledge

Ackroyd describes the actual river, its length and width, its course and the surrounding landscapes, the historical events in which it has played a part and the uses to which it has been put. Factual information about all conceivable aspects of the river thus form a central part of Ackroyd's book. Yet it seems justified to say that his main interest lies in mythical forms of sense-making. Throughout the text, facts and numbers are accompanied by imaginative, speculative or suggestive passages, with no clear demarcation line between the two. As objective and non-factual knowledge are fused, the natural river and the river as a mythical construct merge.

Ackroyd not only provides his own interpretation of the river, but also refers to previous readings of it: he recounts numerous anecdotes and legends and is particularly interested in artistic representations of the river in paintings, literature and music. These works of art enable Ackroyd to trace the river's effect on the imagination and thus reconstruct what he calls the "myth of the Thames" (334). It is this imagined space which is repeatedly given centre stage and constitutes the link between place and national identity, as when Ackroyd claims that "[t]he myth of the Thames runs deeply through the national psyche." (*ibid.*).

Despite the grammatical singular, the myth of the Thames is not a stable entity, but rather conceived of as the sum of previous interpretations: "[e]ach generation has a different understanding of [the river], so that it has accumulated meaning over the centuries." (11) When he writes that "water [...] has no form of its own. It has no meaning" (*ibid.*), Ackroyd underlines that by itself, the river is not meaningful but that any meaning it may have is necessarily an attribution.

Ackroyd's work can itself be regarded as an attempt to invest the river with meaning. The book, rather than simply reconstructing previously existing meanings associated with the Thames, actively constructs its own significance by insisting on the centrality and, in particular, the sanctity of the river – its most salient attribute as the subtitle suggests.[18] Ackroyd's description of the Thames as a "holy place" (44) thus assumes a performative stance: it becomes an incantation bestowing a mythic aura upon the river in an endeavour to turn it into a commemorative landscape.[19] This procedure is one of the reasons why Ackroyd's book – like his writing in general – has repeatedly been called 'psychogeographical',[20] since psychogeography "seeks to overcome the processes of 'banalisation' by which the everyday experience of our surroundings becomes one of drab monotony".[21]

3. Whose Cultural Memory? Some Implications of Ackroyd's Argument

In Ackroyd's text the Thames is turned into a symbol of cultural unity. The river not only connects seemingly oppositional aspects – such as rural and cosmopolitan England – but also constitutes a link to the past. In the vocabulary of cultural memory studies one could therefore argue that the Thames is constructed as a *lieu de mémoire*, a site "in which a residual sense of continuity exists",[22] and that Ackroyd's text itself has become part of "that body of reusable texts, images, and rituals specific to each society in each epoch, whose 'cultivation' serves to stabilize and convey that society's self-image".[23] Like all actualisations of cultural memory, *The Thames* draws on the archive of "accumulated texts, images, and rules of conduct" in order to put the knowledge about the past "into its own perspective, giving it its own relevance".[24]

Yet, as Ian Sinclair has argued, Ackroyd's representation of the Thames is particularly problematic because of its insistence on what I have above called 'mythical forms of understanding'. Ackroyd's repeated use of "[f]ragments from mystery religions" in his attempt to "re-enchant" the landscape is regarded by Sinclair as helping to cover up existing social problems. When Sinclair therefore sets out on a "reverse Ackroyd walk", the word 'reverse' not only refers to the direction of his river walk but also to his political intention to undo Ackroyd's mystification, which he perceives to be complicit with the government's pre-Olympic attempts to "forge a computer-generated fiction of national revival". Sinclair's description counters Ackroyd's "rhetoric of regeneration, providing political opportunism with a sympathetic mythology" with illustrations of the destructive and exclusionary forces of capitalism.[25]

I would argue that Ackroyd not only turns a blind eye to the capitalist mechanisms of exclusion but also actively participates in social exclusion, even if only implicitly and possibly involuntarily. On the face of it, Ackroyd's definition of Englishness seems to be inclusive. Historical migration processes are repeatedly described and England is, therefore, indirectly depicted as a country of immigrants: "[The Thames'] history is of course that of England or, rather, of the Britons and the Romans, the Saxons and the Danes and the Normans and the other migrating groups who decided to settle somewhere along its banks." (11) Regarding more recent migratory movements Ackroyd even maintains that the Thames has become "an ancestral home for the faiths of all" (81).[26]

Yet Ackroyd's emphasis on a quasi-spiritual connection between people and place which has developed over many centuries considerably weakens ties to the country for anyone whose family has not been in Britain for "seven or eight generations" (178). Significantly, the text displays a keen interest in the traces of Roman or Anglo-Saxon culture, but almost completely bypasses more recent social changes as well as all artistic attempts "to reclaim the history of the river from the point of view of colonised and racially defined subjects".[27] When Ackroyd defines Englishness in reference to the nation's past, he ignores the fact that a conception of culture as "being rooted in space, in stable patterns of interaction of people doing the same things in the same places" has become anachronistic at a time in which "the world can no longer be so easily divided up into such clearly demarcated and spatially bounded cultural worlds".[28]

To be fair, such a lack of inclusiveness appears to be not so much a political decision on Ackroyd's part, but rather a general problem arising from the conceptualisation of collective identity as something rooted in a place and in the past. After all, most "cultures have lost their moorings in definite places" now and only a certain segment of the members of today's post-colonial,[29] globalised societies can be assumed to share the same past in the same place. Everyone else is implicitly but inevitably excluded by an identity construction based on local and historical continuity.[30]

But whatever Ackroyd's intentions might have been, the effect remains problematic – all the more so as Ackroyd chooses to deliver a performative incantation rather than a rational argument, which would be open to debate. Since *The Thames* was aimed at a broad audience and gained wide-spread visibility,[31] the book, as an instance of objectified cultural memory, now occupies a prominent (though not uncontested) position in the process of transmitting cultural knowledge about the Thames and English national identity. In the same way in which Ackroyd's representation of the Thames was shaped by the legacy of representations from Belloc to Schneer, *The Thames* is now likely to shape not only its contemporary readers' perception but also possible future representations. It may thus perpetuate assumptions that (English) cultural identity is by necessity rooted in the landscape and that collective identity can only be based on a shared past.

Notes

I would like to thank Maria Hüren and Ryan Dorr for their valuable suggestions.

1 Ackroyd (2007: 11). Further references to this edition will be included in the text. On the connection between landscape and national identity cf. also Schama (1996: 15): "National identity [...] would lose much of its ferocious enchantment without the mystique of a particular landscape tradition: its topography mapped, elaborated, and enriched as a homeland."

2 My emphasis. The references to Englishness rather than Britishness have to be considered a necessary consequence of the choice of topic: It would hardly be convincing to describe the Thames as a British river. Ackroyd's *London* (2000) already contains two chapters about the Thames ("You cannot take the Thames with you" and "Dark Thames"), which, however, focus on the river's relationship to the city and contain no references to national – British or English – identity.

3 Lowenthal (1991: 213).

4 Rose (1995: 106).

5 Cf. Schneer (2005: 289), who notes that "perhaps the Thames is more bound up with regional than national identities" and consequently calls the Thames "England's River" in the subtitle to his book. An earlier example of this tradition in non-fiction is Hilaire Belloc's *The Historic Thames. A Portrait of England's Greatest River* first published in 1909. Belloc's book was re-issued by I.B. Tauris in 2008, which is likely to be a response to the publication of Ackroyd's (and possibly Schneer's) book(s). Early examples of fictional narratives drawing a link between the Thames and English

identity can e.g. be found in the famous opening section of Joseph Conrad's *Heart of Darkness* (1899) or Kenneth Grahame's classic children's book *The Wind in the Willows* (1908).

6 Cf. Schneer (2007: 288-289): "The Thames is England's river, it is a thread woven through the tapestry of national history. [...] It has been central to English life".

7 Winterson (2007).

8 Sattin (2007).

9 Cf. Sinclair (2009), who refers to the book's opening chapter as containing a "Gradgrinding deluge of facts".

10 The following paragraph, in which a profound connection based on physical similarities between man and river is proposed, might serve as an example of the often suggestive and associative structure of Ackroyd's argument: "[t]he fact that the human body is by weight 60 per cent water may help to explain why the river has been granted human characteristics such as unpredictability and fierceness. What better way is there to symbolise purity, too, than the image of clear and limpid water? It may also help to explain the intimacy with which water is associated. The water is like blood coursing through the veins. And in that consonance between the veins of the human body and the river of the earth there is a strange pull of sympathy between the human being and the running water. Motionless waters evoke death, as the poems and stories of Edgar Allen Poe testify. When we look at our reflection in water, we are looking at ourselves in a double sense." (114)

11 Quote from 'Plate Section One' without pagination.

12 The book's review in the *Times* was accompanied by an illustration which takes up exactly this idea of the confusion and co-existence of different layers of time and the condensation of history into space. Cf. Baxter 2007.

13 Ackroyd (2007) for instance emphasises the principal nature of the described changes on the following pages in the historical section: 180 ("the traditions were lost"), 192 ("one principal change that altered the nature of the port"), 193 ("the whole landscape of the Thames at London was changed"), 194 ("changed the nature of the city itself"), 202 ("By the end of the twentieth century the docks had disappeared, vanished as they had indeed all been a dream"), 203 ("no force on earth could have withstood the change"), 208 ("the nineteenth century was the true century of change"), 230 ("the tidal river will never freeze again") or 279 ("Then everything changed.").

14 Similarly, Ackroyd (2007) points out that "[f]rom the arrival of Mesolithic settlers in 10,000 BC there has been an unbroken process of occupation and settlement in the Thames valley" (57) and that "[t]here was no crisis of survival, no gap in the historical record." (71)

15 Ackroyd (1993).

16 Ackroyd (2007) explicitly draws connections to these rivers. In particular, see chapters 4 ("Baptism") and 11 ("Holy river").

17 Ackroyd (1993).

18 The allusion to Coleridge's "Kubla Khan" in the subtitle also fits Ackroyd's visionary stance.

19 Cf. Barfield (2007b): "The Ganges is conventionally sacred within Hinduism, while the Thames has not been thought sacred in any meaningful way except by the odd Romantic, I thought, until Ackroyd's own sacralisation in the book."

20 Cf. e.g. Adams (2007) and Barfield (2007b), who, in their reviews of the *Thames*, place Ackroyd within the context of psychogeographical writing. On Ackroyd's relationship to psychogeography in general cf. Coverley (2006: 123-128).

21 Coverley (2006: 13). Guy Debord's alternative definition of psychogeography as the "study of the specific effects of the geographical environment, consciously organised or not, on the emotions and behaviour of individuals" (quoted in Coverley 2006: 10) can likewise be applied to Ackroyd's argument.

22 Nora (1996: 1). Although the concept of *lieux de mémoire* in Nora's sense does not necessarily refer to actual topographical locations or sites, such as landscapes, it can obviously be applied to them. Cf. Nora (1996: 14, 18) and for a critical evaluation of Nora's concept den Boer (2008).

23 Assmann (1995: 132).

24 *Ibid.* 130.

25 All quotations in this paragraph are taken from Sinclair (2009).

26 With this quotation Ackroyd refers to Sikh, Hindu, Buddhist and Jewish rituals performed in proximity to the Thames, but in the adjacent paragraphs he also mentions pagan and Christian religious traditions.

27 Barfield (2007a). Barfield in particular mentions several of Fred D'Aguair poems.

28 Morley (2001: 428).

29 Gupta & Ferguson (1992: 7).

30 "It might be argued that one of the principal effects of the widely perceived loss of certainty, security and safety in the destabilized 'risk societies' in which we now live, has been a widespread retreat into regressive forms of closure – whether at a national or local level." (Morley 201: 431) Following this argument, Ackroyd's representation of the Thames could of course also be regarded as part of a conservative backlash to recent debates about multicultural Britain.

31 Cf. Barfield's (2007b) comments on the "clever book design", the "lavish use of illustrations" and the text's "eminent readability", making the *Thames* "an ideal book for a holiday present". Since the book was reviewed in all the national newspapers and was in addition turned into a four-part television documentary series, the first part of which was broadcast on ITV the day after the release of the paperback edition, one can assume that it indeed reached the targeted audience.

Ackroyd, Peter: "Cockney Visionaries", *The Independent*, 18 December 1993.

---: *London. The Biography*, London, 2000.

---: *Thames. Sacred River*, London, 2007.

Adams, Tim: "Thames. Sacred River", *The Observer*, 16 September 2007.

Assmann, Jan: "Collective Memory and Cultural Identity", *New German Critique* 65, 1995, 125-133.

Barfield, Steven: "Postface. Reflections on The Literary Thames. River, City and Chronotope", *Literary London. Interdisciplinary Studies in the Representation of London* 5:1, 2007a, http://www.literarylondon.org/london-journal/march2007/Barfield.html, 28 June 2010.

---: "Peter Ackroyd. *Thames. Sacred River*", *Literary London. Interdisciplinary Studies in the Representation of London* 5:2, 2007b, http://www.literarylondon.org/london-journal/september2007/sbarfield.html, 28 June 2010.

Baxter, Katherine: "The Thames. Sacred River. Ancient and Modern" [illustrated map], *The Times*, 8 September 2007.

Belloc, Hilaire: *The Historic Thames. A Portrait of England's Greatest River*, London, 1909.

Boer, Pim den: "*Loci Memoriae – Lieux de Mémoire*". – In Astrid Erll & Ansgar Nünning (Eds.): *Cultural Memory Studies. An International and Interdisciplinary Handbook*, Berlin, 2008, pp. 19-26.

Coverley, Merlin: *Psychogeography*, Harpenden, 2006.

Erll, Astrid: "Cultural Memory Studies. An Introduction". – In A. E. & Ansgar Nünning (Eds.): *Cultural Memory Studies. An International and Interdisciplinary Handbook*, Berlin, 2008, pp. 1-18.

Gupta, Akhil & James Ferguson. "Beyond Culture. Space, Identity and the Politics of Difference", *Cultural Anthropology* 7:1, 1992, 6-23.

Lowenthal, David: "British National Identity and the English Landscape", *Rural History* 2:2, 1991, 205-230.

Morley, David: "Belongings. Place, Space and Identity in a Mediated World". *European Journal of Cultural Studies* 4, 2001, 425-448.

Nora, Pierre: "General Introduction. Between Memory and History". – In P. N. (Ed.): *Rethinking the French Past, Vol. 1. Conflicts and Divisions*. New York, 1996, pp. 1-20.
Rose, Gillian: "Places and Identity. A Sense of Place". – In Doreen Massey & Pat Jess (Eds.): *A Place in the World. Places, Cultures and Globalization*. Milton Keyes, 1995, pp. 87-118.
Sattin, Anthony: "The Best Travel Books of 2007", *The Sunday Times*, 9 December 2007.
Schama, Simon: *Landscape and Memory*, New York, 1996.
Schneer, Jonathan: *The Thames. England's River*, New Haven, 2005.
Sinclair, Iain: "Upriver". *London Review of Books*, 25 June 2009.
Winterson, Jeanette: "Tidal Forces" [review of Ackroyd's *Thames*], *Financial Times*, 29 September 2007.

Sonja Frenzel (*Cologne*)

London Identities. Gendering the Urban Body in *Fin-de-Siècle* Urban Poetry[1]

1. Introduction

What a city like London actually *is* seems a trivial question only at first glance. In fact, its manifestations are manifold: Geographical particularities describe London's position according to longitude and latitude, in the South of England with the river Thames winding through the city; architectural features include famous buildings like Buckingham Palace or 10 Downing Street, well-known squares or even common streets in residential neighbourhoods as well as Hyde Park with its Serpentine; finally, Londoners' practices of habitation embrace, quite generally speaking, discursive inscriptions of meaning upon neighbourhoods and boroughs, which have contributed to the East End's reputation as a multi-cultural area, which have rendered Soho a fashionable shopping precinct and which have made Nottinghill Carnival a tourist attraction. Arguably, thus, these elements merge into a palimpsestual identity whose many layers are intricately interwoven and, therefore, remain difficult to grasp.

London's identity – or, perhaps rather more accurately: London's identities – will be traced, in the contribution at hand, in a semiotic reading of two examples of London urban poetry dating from the *fin-de-siècle* era: Amy Levy's "London in July"[2] and Alfred Douglas's "Impression de Nuit".[3] Urban poetry seems to be the most apt genre for such an approach to unravelling London's entangled urban identities. It draws on Roland Barthes' short essay entitled "Semiology and the Urban", in which he provides a most unusual and, at the same time, insightful definition of the city.[4] He maintains that the city itself is a poem and, perhaps not all too surprisingly, he conceives of the city as a poem that inherently plays on signs. Reading London urban space(s) in line with Barthes thus means deciphering the rules of this game, i.e. the intricate relationships between urban poetry and urban space(s) that engender London's urban identities.[5]

This contribution's historical scope is based on the historical and cultural significance of late-nineteenth-century London being the largest city in the world. Indeed, the processes of industrialisation had lead to unparalleled growth of the city, as "a population of one million at the beginning of the nineteenth century increased to approximately five millions by its close. By 1911 it had risen to seven million".[6] London's newly emergent urban environment thus offered a broad range of new and hitherto undreamt-of experiences for large and ever-growing numbers of people in Great Britain. Perhaps paradoxically, it also made a pertinent subject for poetic texts, and, what is more, prepared the ground for new innovations in the poetic tradition.[7]

Gender issues, however, remained a controversial topic both in Victorian London and in *fin-de-siècle* urban poetry. Indeed, it was women who occupied a particularly contested position in the city. In the division of public and private spaces, the latter remained a predominantly female sphere, whereas the former were associated with male practices, such as finance, trade and commerce. Urban spaces were, and to some extent still are, gendered by social practices and symbolic associations. At the same time, the social, political and, above all, economic changes of the *fin-de-siècle* era granted women entry into the public domain. What is more, a newly developing urban way of life offered them not only anonymity, but also the freedom to live self-determined lives. In the light of these contradictory experiences, perceptions and performances of femininity in and of London's urban space(s), women's public appearance was frequently regarded as posing a threat to the previously 'male' social order of the city, to hitherto known gendered roles and gendered conduct.[8]

It is against this backdrop that this contribution seeks to read London urban space(s) through their representations in urban poetry at a particular historical time in British urban culture and thus to grant at least a small glimpse of London's urban identities. In a first step, this endeavour will be located within the realm of the contemporary spatial turn; in fact, an alternative approach to theorising urban space(s) at the interface of materiality and discursivity will be proposed and subsequently illustrated by a reading of Levy's London poem. In a second step, this contribution attempts at gendering its social-constructionist theory by reading urban space(s) in terms of an urban body. Douglas's poem will then illustrate the practical implications of these endeavours. Finally, these two analyses of London urban poetry will be juxtaposed in order to reveal their significance for a semiotic reading of London identities.

2. Theorising Urban Space(s)

As the spatial turn has gained ever-increasing popularity in the study of culture, many subjects in the humanities have come to adopt a wide range of new objects of study; what is more, in dealing with these new objects, they have considerably expanded their disciplinary scope to include new theories and methods from other academic fields. In other words: Space has become an empirical as well as a heuristic category in contemporary studies of culture.

This turn to space was facilitated by a mutual convergence of the academic discipline of human geography in the social sciences on the one hand and academic subjects in the humanities – mainly historical studies and literary studies – on the other. In human geography, the concept space has undergone significant changes. Along these lines, Hans Heinrich Blotevogel[9] and Benno Werlen[10] identify a cultural turn towards hermeneutics or, more generally speaking, towards interpretative methods. These promote, first and foremost, a turn from empirical studies towards constructionist approaches examining cultural aspects of human beings' living conditions and their practices. Arguably, thus, the concept of 'space' has gradually lost its material grounding. Instead, it has come to be regarded in terms of the social structures that unfold within it. In the field of urban studies, it was mainly Michel de Certeau's *The Practice of Everyday Life*[11] and Henri Lefebvre's *The Production of Space*[12] that have contributed decisively to establishing space as a relational and performative concept, hence as a concept which is enacted and perpetually re-enacted through its inhabitants' relationships and their practices of habitation.

This de-materialisation has rendered the concept of space susceptible for appropriation by other disciplines. In the humanities, historical studies chiefly examine the complex relationships between space and remembrance;[13] literary studies analyse representations of space and examine their cultural-symbolic meanings. A literary work's setting and plot, its characters and their relationships not only unfold in space, but decisively shape the readers' constructions of imagined spaces as well. In urban literature, these imagined spaces are intimately interwoven with actual life-places and the readers' experience thereof. Hence, academic practices of 'reading spaces' must take into account that urban literature does not merely *re*-produce and *re*-present a given city but – in the intricate interplay of text, context and readership – produces and presents its own version of this particular life-place.[14]

These conceptualisations of space have brought forth an abundance of inter- and transdisciplinary approaches to reading spaces. Yet, they have eschewed a crucial paradox: In spite of the conceptual de-materialisation of space, analyses of space remain inevitably grounded in the materiality of space. Any endeavour at reading (urban) spaces must therefore move beyond a concept of space as relational and performative; indeed, it must confront the contested relationship between substance and discourse. Martina Löw suggests a solution to these complex issues when she juxtaposes urban forms with human practices,[15] which jointly produce a city's intrinsic logic.[16] As urban forms include not only size, but also density and heterogeneity, they are intimately interwoven with urban practices.[17] Hence, the de-materialisation of matter resonates in Löw's readings as well.

A more valuable approach can be found in Hana Wirth-Nesher's edited collection *City Codes.*[18] The author differentiates the various elements of the urban environment into four components: the natural, the built, the human and the verbal components.[19] It is significant to observe that some of them primarily denote the city as substance (particularly the natural and built components), while others (the human and verbal components) describe the urban environment in terms of the discursive practices of urban life. At the same time, all four components are entangled in multi-faceted ways and their intersections illustrate the intricate interwovenness of substance and discourse. The following brief outline will describe these entanglements with particular reference to gendered experiences, perceptions and performances in and of urban space(s) and will thus serve as a framework for reading London urban space(s) in urban poetry.

The natural component addresses the contested relationship between nature and culture and, in fact, aims at transcending the long-standing dichotomies between these two notions. Wirth-Nesher illustrates how elements generally associated with nature – such as trees and grass, rivers and ponds – have become integral parts of urban forms and practices. London's Hyde Park may serve as a famous example, as it constitutes a well-known location within London's urban space(s) and a site for both leisurely strolls and ambitious drill trainings. The ensuing interwovenness of urban forms, urban practices and the natural component of the urban environment bears pertinent implications for gendered experiences, perceptions and performances in and of the urban environment. This may be observed, for instance, in the positioning of urban parks in relation to living and working areas and its impact upon male and female urban dwellers' particular practices within these urban space(s).

Meeting these gender differences, efforts at greening the urban environment have become increasingly popular tools for developing the city. These deliberate constructions and re-constructions of urban space(s) draw attention to overlaps between the natural and the built component of the urban environment. Both are devised in processes of urban planning and render the city a man-made habitat. Furthermore, the built component includes London's spatial structures: those formed by its tight web of urban forms, such as streets and thoroughfares, as well as of the city's network of bus routes and underground lines; but also those shaped by the gendered experience, perception and performance of practices of habitation that reflect intricate mechanisms of inclusion and exclusion.

This latter aspect also pertains to the human component of the urban environment. Most notably, Pierre Bourdieu has highlighted the significance of human practices of habitation for the construction and perpetual re-construction of urban space(s) in his notion of 'habitus'.[20] From a postcolonial stance, Bill Ashcroft spells out the intricate relationship between urban dwellers' practices of habitation and urban space(s) most succinctly:[21]

> Place is never simply location, nor is it static […] like culture itself, place is in a continual and dynamic state of formation, a process

> intimately bound up with the culture and the identity of its inhabitants. Above all, place is a result of habitation, a consequence of the ways in which people inhabit space, particularly that conception of space as universal and uncontestable that is constructed for them by imperial discourse.[22]

He postulates that urban practices may serve as tools for appropriating urban forms, in that they simultaneously reflect potentially restrictive boundary lines and bear the potential to undermine them. The ensuing tensions are a vital aspect of gendered experiences, perceptions and performances in and of London's urban spaces in the *fin-de-siècle* era. What is more, these practices thus exercise crucial influence upon processes of identity formation and upon the experience of ever more frequent encounters with strangers. From a gendered perspective, the experience and perception of the urban environment as characterized by anonymity and isolation or, from a more positive vantage point, by personal freedom must, once more, be re-considered.[23] The human component in Wirth-Nesher's model thus pertains to the social dimensions of urban ways of life, but also – and more importantly – draws attention to the necessity for gendering urban theory.

Finally, Wirth-Nesher's model introduces a verbal component into its conceptualization of the urban environment. This component includes any kind of written and spoken text found in the city: street signs, billboards or graffiti as well as conversations among urban dwellers, guidebooks and newspaper articles left on park benches. Expanding the scope of this component, Andreas Mahler, in his edited collection *Stadt-Bilder. Allegorie, Mimesis, Imagination* further adds literary renditions of the urban environment.[24] As such, the verbal component fulfills a special role in the urban environment. It is both an independent category and, simultaneously, a meta-category that (re-)produces and (re-) presents the other three components. This essay takes London urban poetry as one particular example of a city's verbal environment; it seeks to read two poetic texts as (re-)presentations of the other three components of the urban environment, i.e. the natural, the built and the human component of the city of London.

Amy Levy's poem "London in July" exemplifies the verbal component's (re)production and (re)presentation of London's urban environment. As the speaker wanders through the city in search of his or her lost lover, his or her experience of sadness and despair is deeply entangled with elements of the natural, the built and the human components. In the opening lines, already, the juxtaposition of private and public indicates the close relationship between the speaker's innermost feelings and his or her life-place: "What ails my senses thus to cheat? / What is it ails the place" (ll. 1-2). Indeed, private and public spheres coalesce when the speaker's senses and his or her surroundings are equally affected by the loss of a loved person.

This initial, though rather general reference to the speaker's life-place is further specified in terms of the human component of the urban environment, since "all the people in the street / [...] wear one woman's face" (ll. 3-4). In the urban crowd the individual is lost in a twofold sense: not only is the speaker unable to distinguish individual faces, but rather, s/he merges the faces of those s/he encounters into the one face of his or her lost love. His or her misery increases even further when s/he concedes that his or her "love dwells in London town" (l. 7), but nonetheless remains out of reach for her (cf. l. 8). The perpetual disappointment of the speaker's hope underlines the experience of anonymity in the ever-growing city of London and emphasises his or her loneliness.

It is significant to note that the human component is then compared, firstly, to the natural component and, secondly, to the built component of the urban environment. The "London trees" (l. 5) have been deprived of their lively green colour by the July sun so that the speaker perceives them as dull, lifeless and "dusty-brown" (l. 5). While these elements of the natural component already illustrate the speaker's melancholy mood, his or her growing despair is further reflected in the wanderings through London's streets, i.e. by elements of the city's built component. In the opening line of the third stanza, the urban environment is evoked as a "various and intricate maze" (l. 9). Breaking the metric rhythm of the poem, this exclamation reveals the speaker's wretchedness most concisely. S/he is lost in the "wide waste of square and street" (l. 10), in a convoluted place, where it seems impossible to find orientation. Nonetheless, s/he regains hope; after all, it is in this chaotic urban environment, too, where fate may reunite him or her with his or her lost lover: "where, missing through unnumbered days, / we twain at last may meet!" (ll. 11-12)

Throughout this poem, the speaker's practices of habitation represent a gendered experience and perception of the urban environment. For one, Amy Levy's poem inscribes one of the emerging female voices of the *fin-de-siècle* era into representations of London's urban environment. Even though, of course, the poet's gender may not be conflated with the speaker's gender, it is significant to note that the speaker's gender remains unknown, whereas the object of desire, his or her lost lover, is feminine. These observations may – albeit only tentatively – be interpreted as discursive inscriptions of gender and sexuality upon the urban environment.

Besides, the speaker's perception and experience of the urban environment as a site and symbol of his or her emotions merges private and public domains. His or her personal feelings of sadness and despair over the loss of his or her love are reflected in the public wanderings through London and, hence, in his or her experience and perception of the natural, the built and the human components of the urban environment. Accordingly, this example of the verbal component has illustrated the close relationship between all four elements of the urban environment and, what is more, it has spelled out the interrelationship between London's materiality and its discursive appropriation.

3. Gendering Theories of Urban Space(s)

Interestingly enough, the same convoluted issues of materiality and discursivity that complicate urban studies are raised in social-constructionist approaches to gender and the human body. As Judith Butler argues in her influential study *Bodies that Matter*,[25] the body does not constitute a prediscursive fact but, like the social category 'gender', it is constructed and perpetually re-constructed through discursive practices and inscriptions. Accordingly, the body *is* not, but comes into being: its substance emerges in "a process of materialization that stabilises over time to produce the effect of boundary, fixity, and surface we call matter".[26] Hence, when substance becomes matter, it attains particular meaning and may therefore be conceived of as a signifier in semiotic terms.

Likewise, in urban studies, a city's geographical and architectural substance becomes matter only in the city dwellers' practices of habitation and their discursive inscriptions of meaning. Not only are city-dwellers inevitably 'placed' within urban space(s), but it is through their human bodies that their practices of habitation are performed and that they experience and perceive the urban environment. Reading urban space(s) in terms of an urban body thus bears yet another symbolic dimension: as the discursive elements of the urban environment are enacted through the inhabitants' human bodies, these bodies are intimately entangled with the four components of the urban body.

Theorising urban space as body in this social constructionist approach bears some crucial implications.[27] Most significantly, such an endeavour is bound to raise gender issues. Gender, like space, is a relational and performative concept, which is enacted and perpetually re-enacted through (human and urban) bodies in relationships and practices. On the one hand, the city-dwellers' human bodies are gendered through their encounters with other urban dwellers and through their practices of inhabiting the urban body. The urban body, in turn, is gendered through its inhabitants' experience, perception and performance. In other words, the urban body becomes a performance context for its inhabitants' practices of habitation. As these practices generally unfold through the city-dwellers' human bodies, there emerges a crucial interdependence between urban and human bodies which shapes the urban body along such identity concepts as, for instance, gender. Fran Tonkiss illustrates these complex issues more concisely in her seminal monograph *Embodied Spaces*,[28] when she sets out to explore "the interplay between social relations, material forms and subjective positions in the city" by focusing on the meaning, the use and the shape of urban spaces.[29] When one translates these endeavours into the terminology proposed by this contribution, Tonkiss reads urban space(s) in terms of a reciprocal relationship between matter and discourse, i.e. in terms of the symbolic meanings inscribed upon the urban body through its inhabitants' practices on the one hand and the particular impact of these discursive meanings and uses upon urban substance on the other. At the interface of materiality and discursivity, gendered bodies – both human and urban – emerge in the *fin-de-siècle* era through their (re)productions and (re)presentations in London urban poetry.

In Alfred Douglas's poem "Impression de Nuit", London is described as a heavily ornamented woman's figure: "See what a mass of gems the city wears / upon her broad live bosom! Row on row / rubies and emeralds and sapphires glow. / See! that huge circle, like a necklace, stares / with thousands of bold eyes to heaven" (ll. 1-5). This personification of London's urban environment is symbolised most concisely in direct references to the city's "broad live bosom" (l. 2), which is resumed in the second stanza by "breasts" (l. 9); furthermore, the practice of wearing gems (l. 1), a necklace (l. 4) and a tiara (l. 12) associates a woman's jewellery with elements of the built component of the urban environment. Indeed, the colourful – and precious – jewellery the city is adorned with alludes to one aspect of the built environment that was of great significance in the late nineteenth century, namely to the colourful urban lights that illuminated the city at night.

Electrical street lighting had only just been introduced and did not yet cover the entire city: Some streets remained dark, others were lit by the flickering gas lamps of the early nineteenth century, while yet others already benefited from having electric lights installed. This variety of lighting rendered London an unevenly lit city;[30] indeed, as Arthur Symons outlines in his monograph *London. A Book of Aspects*: "In London we light casually, capriciously, […] and so there are blinding shafts at one step and a pit of darkness at the next".[31] Comparing these observations, once more, to a woman's body, this indicates that like a woman's jewellery, the lights are placed in strategic places to draw attention to some parts of the urban body while neglecting others. So, it is only in certain places that the colourful lights of Douglas's poem render the urban environment more beautiful and attractive. These contrasts of light and darkness are also reflected in the juxtaposition of the two stanzas of Douglas's poem: while the first stanza describes a colourful atmosphere, the second stanza paints a darker image of the city.

The woman's body is represented as so heavily ornamented that its conspicuous appearance even dares the natural environment to disappear, as the last lines of the first and second stanzas indicate. Looking in the mirror, the city is reflected as a "mire" (l. 7), a dirty and dusty place despite all its jewellery that is not even brightened by stars or the moon, both representative of the natural environment. It is the gems' "bold eyes" (l. 5) that outshine the "golden stars" (l. 6) and even the moon has deserted the city. The urban body's bright image conceals its darker side, its "lanes as dark as death" (l. 13) through which "men creep like thoughts" (l. 14).

It is significant to note that these closing lines of the poem once more allude to the initial personification of the urban body, yet to a less favourable reading of the city as gendered space. Associated with a woman's body exhibited in public, adorned with considerable amounts of jewellery, the urban body comes to symbolise a prostitute in the end. When men pursue this woman, the formerly bright lights represented by the glowing rubies, emeralds and sapphires (cf. l. 3) turn into "pale flowers" (l. 14), thus losing their promising glow and, hence, their attractiveness.

The personification of London as a female urban body draws attention to the interwovenness of materiality (i.e. the built and natural components of the urban environment) and the discursive practices that give it meaning (i.e. highlighting certain places by strategic decoration/ornamentation) and, in the poem under discussion, inscribe sexualised connotations of the city as a prostitute. In this metaphorical relationship, the initial direction runs from the built environment to the (female) urban body. Yet, when the breasts turn into "towers" (l. 9-10), while the gems of the necklace (l. 4) turn into "eyes" (l. 5), this direction is reversed. The lights do not merely emphasise the city's bright future, but at the same time its public urban body is a site of moral decline.

4. Concluding Remarks

Reading London space(s) in instances of urban poetry depends on theorising the crucial intersections of textual and contextual dimensions. After all, urban texts are deeply entangled in the semiotic play on materiality and discursivity that characterises theories of urban space. They reproduce and represent London's urban environment, but, at the same time, produce and present their own versions of the city, of its material substance and its inhabitants' discursive practices of habitation. Indeed, urban poetry thus constitutes a powerful example of the discursive appropriation of urban space(s).

In the two examples of urban poetry discussed in this paper, London's urban environment was described, first, in terms of its natural, built and human components. While a reading of Levy's poem illustrated the close relationship between person and place, an analysis of Douglas's poem took these interrelations one step further to a personification of the urban environment as a woman's body.

Reading the urban environment in terms of the body suggests an alternative approach to theorising urban space(s). Above all, it means deciphering the urban environment's semiotic meanings by taking the intricate intersections of materiality and discursivity seriously. What is more, this heuristic position sheds light on the complex processes of gendering London urban space(s). On the one hand, London's gendered identities emerge at the interface of the urban body and the city dwellers' human bodies (cf. Levy's poem "London in July") or in particular perceptions and experiences of this category at a given historical time (cf. Douglas's poem "Impression de Nuit").

What is more, poetic (re)productions and (re)presentations of urban space(s) reveal the contested significance of the category 'gender' in a particular historical time. Expanding this approach to a diachronic perspective may help to discover the significance of gender for the formation of London's urban identities. Besides, linking these urban developments to changes in gender theory through time may yield new insights into the intersections of the constructions and re-constructions of urban identities, both of London's inhabitants and of this metropolis itself.

Notes

1 This contribution is part of a larger research project developing a poetics of London. The applicability of its hypotheses has been tested, apart from the present focus on gender and the urban body, with regard to ecocritical approaches and with regard to the South African metropolis Johannesburg. These two further publications are due to appear in 2012.

2 Levy: "London in July". All line references used in this contribution were added for convenience's sake.

3 Douglas: "Impression de Nuit".

4 Barthes (1986: 97-98).

5 Taking the city as its main theme and starting point, urban poetry depends on a crucial link between poetry and its cultural circumstances, i.e. between poetic texts and their urban, but also their social, political and historical contexts. Reading London urban poetry therefore needs to place these works of art within the urban environment. For a survey of London urban

poetry from the Romantic Age to Postmodernism, please refer to Altnöder (2010).

6 Ackroyd (2000: 564).

7 See, for instance, anthologies like Barth (1988), Adams (2002), Rogerson (2003), Mergenthal (2006); cf. Williams (1985: 13, 20).

8 Tonkiss (2005: 95).

9 Blotevogel (2003).

10 Werlen (2003).

11 De Certeau (1984).

12 Lefebvre (1991 [1974]).

13 Bachmann-Medick, in her seminal *Cultural Turns. Neuorientierungen in den Kulturwissenschaften*, maintains that in the humanities, it is historical studies that have adopted the spatial turn most thoroughly. After all, the spatial turn has provided innovative theories and methods for studying the political and social implications of historical events. (2007: 312-314).

14 Mahler (1999: 12).

15 Cf. Löw (2008).

16 A city's intrinsic logic ("Eigenlogik") is a somewhat vague category that comprises a given city's particular development as well as the ensuing creative power for structuring its inhabitants' practices of habitation (*ibid.* 79).

17 It was Louis Wirth, in his essay "Urbanism as a Way of Life" (1938), who first proposed these three descriptive features that have since remained underlying constants of urban discourses.

18 Cf. Wirth-Nesher (1996).

19 Wirth-Nesher herself speaks of the natural, the built, the human and the verbal environment. For the purposes of this contribution and for clarity's sake, Wirth-Nesher's terminology will slightly be rephrased here: rather than four types of environment, this contribution assumes four components of the urban environment, thus taking 'urban environment' as an umbrella term which comprises Wirth-Nesher's types.

20 Cf. Bourdieu (1998).

21 Cf. Ashcroft (2002).

22 *Ibid.* 156.

23 For a detailed discussion of these aspects, please refer to Georg Simmel's pertinent essay "The Metropolis and Mental Life" (1950 [1903]). Even though it mainly deals with the emergent metropolis in the Modern Age, its theses are still relevant for contemporary urban studies.

24 Cf. Mahler (1999).

25 Butler (1993).

26 *Ibid.* 9.

27 It is commonplace practice in academic writings on the city to use the body as a metaphor. For instance, Richard Sennett entitled his seminal study of urban environments *Flesh and Stone. The Body and the City in Western Civilisation* (1997). Moreover, Peter Ackroyd, in his voluminous and insightful historiographical account *London. The Biography* (2000), likens

the city's byways to thin veins and its parks to lungs; in fact, he contemplates, "in the mist and rain of an urban autumn, the shining stones and cobbles of the older thoroughfares look as if they are bleeding" (Ackroyd [2000: 1]). But these approaches stop short of taking into account the interwovenness of substance and discourse which lie at the core of this contribution.

28 Cf. Tonkiss (2005).

29 *Ibid.* 94.

30 Cf. Ackroyd (2000: 440-441).

31 Quoted in *ibid.* 441.

Bibliography

Ackroyd, Peter: *London. The Biography*, London, 2000.

Adams, Anna (Ed.): *London in Poetry and Prose*, London, 2002.

Altnöder, Sonja: "Urban Poetry. History, Intertextuality and Current Developments in London Writing". – In S. A., Wolfgang Hallet & Ansgar Nünning (Eds.): *Schlüsselthemen der Anglistik und Amerikanistik / Key Topics in English and American Studies*, Trier, 2010, pp. 121-148.

Ashcroft, Bill: *Post-Colonial Transformation*. London & New York, 2002.

Bachmann-Medick, Doris: *Cultural Turns. Neuorientierungen in den Kulturwissenschaften*, Reinbek bei Hamburg, 2007.

Barth, Adolf (Ed.): *London Poems,* London, 1988.

Barthes, Roland: "Semiology and the Urban". – In Mark Gottdiener & Alexandros Ph. Lagopoulos (Eds.): *The City and the Sign. An Introduction to Urban Semiotics*, New York, 1986, pp. 87-98.

Blotevogel, Hans-Heinrich: "'Neue Kulturgeographie' – Entwicklung, Dimensionen, Potenziale und Risiken einer kulturalistischen Humangeographie", *Berichte zur deutschen Landeskunde* 77:1, 2003, 11-12.

Bourdieu, Pierre: *Praktische Vernunft. Zur Theorie des Handelns*. Frankfurt, 1998.

Butler, Judith: *Bodies that Matter. On the Discursive Limits of 'Sex'*, New York, 1993.

De Certeau, Michel: *The Practice of Everyday Life*. Trans. Steven Randall, Berkeley, 1984.

Douglas, Alfred: "Impression de Nuit". – In Barnaby Rogerson (Ed.): *London. A Collection of Poetry of Place*, London, 2003, p. 91.
Lefebvre, Henri: *The Production of Space*, Oxford & Cambridge, 1991 [1974].
Levy, Amy: "London in July", http://www.famouspoets andpoems.com/poets/amy_levy/poems/6903, 10 September 2010.
Löw, Martina: *Soziologie der Städte*, Frankfurt a.M., 2008.
Mahler, Andreas (Ed.): *Stadtbilder. Allegorie, Mimesis, Imagination*. Heidelberg, 1999.
Mergenthal, Silvia (Ed.): *Poetischer London-Führer*, Darmstadt, 2006.
Rogerson, Barnaby (Ed.): *London. A Collection of Poetry of Place*, London, 2003.
Sennett, Richard: *Flesh and Stone. The Body and the City in Western Civilisation*, New York, 1997.
Simmel, Georg: "The Metropolis and Mental Life". – In Deena Weinstein (Ed.): *The Sociology of Georg Simmel*, New York, 1950 [1903], pp. 409-424.
Tonkiss, Fran: *Space, the City and Social Theory. Social Relations and Urban Forms*. Cambridge, 2005, 95.
Werlen, Benno: "*Cultural Turn* in Humanwissenschaften und Geographie", *Berichte zur deutschen Landeskunde 77.1*, 2003, 35.
Williams, Raymond: "The Metropolis and the Emergence of Modernism". – In Edward Timms & David Kelley (Eds.): *Unreal City. Urban Experience in Modern European Literature and Art*. Manchester, 1985, pp. 13-24.
Wirth, Louis: "Urbanism as a Way of Life", *American Journal of Sociology* 44.1, 1938, 1-24.
Wirth-Nesher, Hana: *City Codes. Reading the Modern Urban Novel*. Cambridge, 1996.

Elke Schuch (Cologne)

The Importance of Geography and Space for Identity Formation. Liverpool

Recent theorising about identity and space has drawn attention to the fact that places do not have single but multiple identities, and that rather than being localised and bounded in space they are processes, unstable and performed.[1] While agreeing with this view, it would be equally misleading to conceive of mobile identities as entirely de-territorialised. Individual districts may be home to multiple populations, each with a differing sense of and attachment to place as well as differing perceptions and experiences, but they have in common the built form of their shared urban environment as a constituent of their identities. "Place identity", therefore, "is an essential part of self-identity. The places we share with others and their shared meanings help to form a collective self-identity of the community."[2] Not only do spatial borders continue as the basis of collective action, but they are also tied up in very complex ways with social boundaries, the formation of identity and the production of difference.

Liverpool's geographical position makes this city a particularly apt place to reveal the social and historical processes that produce bounded spaces and the implications of these for those who are contained and enact their identity within them. Built as an Atlantic-facing coastal settlement on the furthermost edge of the western coastline of Europe in the thirteenth century, the city has remained on the edge and set apart from Britain ever since – in terms of its spatial geography but also with regard to social and cultural space. When, at the 2007 European Champions League semi-final between Liverpool FC and Chelsea FC, a banner at the Kop end of Liverpool's ground proudly proclaimed "We're not English, we are Scouse", it was an expression of Liverpool's pride in locality as well as a sense of difference and apartness expressed through reference to the distinct Scouse identity.[3]

Figure 1: Liverpool FC supporters with a banner

1. The Influence of the River and the Sea

The river and its proximity to the sea play a significant role in the imagination of Merseysiders and in the construction of their Scouse identity. The port runs directly into the city centre and has always been part of the general downtown bustle, rather than being confined to periphereal areas, as in some other port cities, for example London. The viewpoint from the Pier Head is dominated by the sea, hence Liverpool's tendency to look westward towards the Atlantic and North America for inspiration and orientation rather than inward and towards the rest of the nation. Approaching the city from the water it becomes obvious what a "wonderfully non-English city" Liverpool is.[4]

The geographical advantage of being located on the western coastline of Europe meant that Liverpool was well-suited for overseas trade. The construction of the Old Dock in 1715, the world's first wet dock, further helped the city to rapidly develop and expand as a trading post. During the eighteenth and nineteenth centuries the city consequently grew into the second most important port in Britain and into the "gateway to Empire".[5] The proximity to the sea distinguished the city from other northern English cities in terms of its pattern of growth. Since the city's local economy was predominantly built around port activities rather than industrial activities,[6] Liverpool had few factories and, unlike other northern cotton towns inland, for example Manchester, which regularly employed factory workers, the bulk of the work force in Liverpool were casually employed. While factory work was work behind closed doors, entailing weekly wages but also the need to clock on, the climate of casual labour gave people in Liverpool the feeling of being in charge of their own destiny and owning their own time – time which people in the manufacturing industries did not have. As a result, Liverpool turned into a city that did not have to 'clock on' and with this came a sense of independence, pride and the feeling of being a step above the factory workers in most of England's manufacturing towns. Not only the dockers, but also the mercantile middle class in Liverpool, who were amongst Britain's most active and prosperous traders, felt superior to the rest of the North. There was a proud, perhaps even snobbish, saying: 'Liverpool Gentlemen, Manchester Men', which was based on the fact that Manchester was a manufacturing city with mills and smoking chimneys, whereas Liverpool was a port with clean sea air, populated by wealthy merchants who merely took a percentage cut of the manufactured goods as they passed through Liverpool to export.[7]

Nowhere could this sense of pride in difference be seen better than in the city's successful involvement in what was euphemistically called 'the African trade'. Again geographical circumstances worked in Liverpool's favour: As a west-facing port it was well-suited for overseas trade, but also in close proximity to a fast developing manufacturing hinterland which provided the goods used in the purchase of human slaves in Africa and to which it was linked by a transportation network of waterways and – after the opening of the Liverpool and Manchester Railway in 1830 – of trains. Manchester, meanwhile, had developed into an area renowned for manufacturing metal goods and textiles. With the development of the 'triangular trade' there was now an outlet for these goods, and with the influx of cotton from America the textile business boomed in the North.[8] In this triangle trade British manufactured goods from the hinterland were transported to Liverpool and loaded onto ships bound for West Africa, where they were exchanged for slaves who were then taken into forced plantation labour to the West Indies and America. In return, sugar, rum, tobacco and later cotton, from the New World were shipped back to Liverpool. With 90 per cent of Britain's slave trade clearing from its port by the beginning of the nineteenth century,[9] the city had developed into 'the capital of the slave trade', a designation which powerfully illustrates the way race and place intersected in the cultural production of 'Liverpool'. When the anti-slavery lobby was gathering momentum in British society at the end of the eighteenth century, opposition to abolition came mainly from Liverpool merchants, with 64 petitions compared to fourteen from London and twelve from Bristol.[10] Liverpool merchants defended the city's commercial success against 'outside' abolitionist opinion, praising the slave trade for bringing labour to the colonies, happiness to the slaves, and wealth to Liverpool. Debates in Parliament on the slave trade question became known as a confrontation between "Liverpool Man" and "Humanity Man".[11] Liverpool thus stood condemned for barbarism and philistine commercialism, but it also stood defiantly – even proudly – apart. Liverpool's opposition to the abolition of the slave trade has to be seen as yet another expression of self-declared political and economic 'otherness'. The feeling of being apart from the rest of Britain continued when, after abolition, the local merchant class did not suffer a loss of revenue, but adapted with remarkable rapidity to the altered situation and focussed on the burgeoning Lancashire cotton industry.

The Emancipation Proclamation throughout the British Empire in 1834 opened up the possibility of hiring cheap Black labour to work on the cargoes around the West African coast and as articled seafarers on merchant navy ships on the trading route between West Africa and Liverpool.[12] It was therefore not unusual for merchant navy ships to come to port and bring with them a "motley crew", an ethnically diverse group of sailors – including Europeans, Irishmen, Indians, Chinese, and African-Americans – who made for a very diverse social composition.[13] Many Black seamen remained transient, but others, attracted to the casual dock labour in the port, stayed and settled permanently, thereby changing the ethnic and demographic profile of the city forever. Sitting at the crossroads of routes of migration and trade Liverpool consequently became a stopping-off point for sailors, traders and tourists who – together with the port's casual labour market – created a cosmopolitan seafaring population to the extent that the port city itself embodied the concept of the 'motley crew'.[14] One area in Liverpool where this vibrant cosmopolitanism and the mixing of different cultures was more pronounced than anywhere else was the internationally famous Scotland Road or 'Scottie Road', which was close both to the back end of the city centre and the docks. The seamen who travelled the world identified with the cultural diversity of Scotland Road and considered it a 'home' to which they returned after their voyages. American author Herman Melville (1969:138), who visited the port city in 1839, observed in his novel *Redburn* that:

> sailors love this Liverpool; and upon long voyages to distant parts of the globe, will be continually dilating on its charms and attractions, and extolling it above all other sea-ports in the world. For in Liverpool they find their Paradise.[15]

On many of the giant passenger liners that sailed from Liverpool and other British ports in the nineteenth century, the longest and busiest alleyway that ran through the ship was known as Scotland Road – named after the bustling working class thoroughfare in Liverpool. Even the E-Deck on the *Titanic* had an alley called Scotland Road, which proves the extent to which Scotland Road was a 'home' for the seafaring population in the sense of an imagined location, as much fixed in a mental landscape as in actual geography.

2. Irish In-Migration in the Nineteenth Century

Another factor which contributed to Liverpool's otherness was the influx of thousands of Irish immigrants who arrived in Liverpool in the second half of the nineteenth century due to a failure of the potato crop in most parts of Ireland in the 1840s. Most of these immigrants did not plan to stay in Liverpool for any length of time, but regarded the town as a departure point to the New World of America. But once they had reached Liverpool, many were forced to stay on because the cost of the passage was often too high. By 1851, more than twenty per cent of the population of Liverpool were Irish,[16] but most of these Irish-Liverpudlians "remained segregated in their enclave",[17] seemingly immune to the normal processes of ethnic fade. During the nineteenth century Liverpool's residential areas were highly stratified with district areas taking their identity from the socioeconomic status and ethnic affiliation of their residents. While the mansions of the merchant traders and ship owners were built on the rises overlooking the water, the skilled workers (including many Welsh and Scottish migrants) tended to congregate in inner residential areas. The poorest housing was at the water's edge, with the majority of Liverpool's black community originally settled around the South Dock areas and the Chinese community a mile or two further inward. The Irish, who were escaping from the famine and who were largely unskilled, tended to congregate around the slums at the north end of town close to the waterfront and its casual labour market.

When the Irish arrived in large numbers, Liverpool became a Catholic Celtic enclave in a Protestant Anglo-Saxon kingdom. This development seemed to confirm yet again that Liverpool was a place apart, seemingly operating on different principles than the rest of the country. The Irish presence was in fact so large that it changed forever the accent and dialect of Liverpool. Before the arrival of the Irish, the Liverpool accent differed little from other northern urban varieties in Lancashire. After the 1850s, the prevalent accent developed from Irish-influenced English and the indigenous Lancashire variant and acquired its distinctive nasal Scouse inflection. As the pecularities of Scouse are almost entirely phonological, Gerald Knowles has argued that the adenoidal, nasal quality of the Scouse accent was further accentuated and shaped by Liverpool's poor public health in the nineteenth century, which had been worsened further by the great influx of Irish immigrants.[18] By the mid-nineteenth century, Liverpool was a very densely populated area. The Census records a population of 77,000 in 1801, rapidly rising to 376,000 in 1851 and to 685,000 in 1901.[19] Building could not keep up with the dramatic explosion of Liverpool's population. Many Irish immigrants were crowded into the older parts of town and an estimated 30,000 lived in damp cellars and court housing.[20] Overcrowded, damp cellared housing led to respiratory problems and the prevalence of colds. Knowles argues that an impairment of nasal resonance for many people over a long time resulted in it becoming regarded as the linguistic 'norm' and was subsequently copied by others learning the language. The Scouse accent thus became a badge of identity for the people in Liverpool or, as Du Noyer puts it: "Liverpool's uniqueness is reinforced every time a local opens his mouth."[21] The fact that most of the Irish immigrants remained in the town centre in order to be close to work opportunities – predominantly in the dockland area – meant that the resulting Scouse accent they helped to create remained firmly within the city boundaries, with the Bootle area in the north, Huyton in the east and the Wirral peninsular in the south. Theoretically, therefore, only approximately 500,000 people speak it, which adds to its exclusiveness as an accent.

3. The Twentieth Century – Place as Disgrace

Historically, the city's fortunes had been dependent on a specifically colonial mode of production. It was therefore not surprising that the decline of the British Empire in the twentieth century also became the decline of Liverpool.[22] While its geographical position ensured Liverpool's status as the British Empire's major port, with the end of empire and Britain's entry into the European Community in 1973, Liverpool's geography was about to become a liability, triggering a drastic reversal of fortune. The city was now ill-placed for European trade, whereas economic areas and ports situated on the east and south east coast of England were more suitably located for trade with members of the Common Market. In addition to the changing patterns of trade relations, the advent of mass air travel reduced the need for luxury liners and when containerisation began in 1955, the need for manual labour started to fall drastically. The former 'gateway to Empire' thus became disconnected from the very transport networks that had maintained its prominent position within the global economy. The collapse of Britain's manufacturing sector during the Thatcher years was nowhere more readily felt than in Liverpool. It resulted in mass unemployment accompanied by disinvestment, depopulation and widespread urban dereliction, reinforcing the city's political and cultural isolation.[23] The ensuing 'us against the rest of the world'-attitude was particularly virulent during the 1980s, when the Militant administration ran Liverpool City Council and harshly, albeit unsuccessfully, opposed the national government's cuts in public expenditure. The city, moreover, had a long-standing image problem, occasioned by the reputation of wheeling and dealing in local politics, labour violence, trade union militancy, drug-related crime and civil unrest. Undoubtedly the most absurd outcome of the Toxteth riots in 1981 was that the British government seemed to believe that the environment in the district Toxteth affected its residents negatively and decided that what Black people really needed was a more uplifting environment. The government launched an initiative to have trees planted up and down Princes Avenue, a major street in Toxteth. It also launched a second project: It spent £50 million on a Garden Festival Centre. The tree solution might have been a political manoeuvre, feigning interest while at the same ignoring the root causes of the race riots. Yet, there might have been more to it: According to Peter Ackroyd's study of the English imagination, trees appear again and again as the guardian spirits of the English people and English places, with greenery and gardens central to both an English sense of self and an English sense of place.[24] If the trees were meant to turn Liverpool's black population into 'pleasant' and law-abiding English people, the planting of the new flora might have intended a similar effect for Liverpool in general: to turn an essentially non-English city, which had become notorious for an obsolete and declining way of life, into a 'proper English' place, suitable for investment.

The precipitous fall from grace of this once proud industrial city encouraged narratives in other parts of Britain about this place as disgrace: "They should build a fence around [Liverpool] and charge admission", a *Daily Mirror* editorial from 1982 claimed. "For, sadly, it has become a 'showcase' of everything that has gone wrong in Britain's major cities".[25] Media reportings and comments such as these led to further stigmatisation of the city. Liverpool's otherness was reinforced in the 1980s and 1990s, when a number of events harmed its reputation still further, dislocating it even more from the rest of the UK. The Heysel stadium accident in Brussels in 1985 and the Hillsborough football tragedy in 1989 were both constructed as local to Liverpool rather than to one particular football team. The negative coverage on Liverpool football fans by the tabloid paper *The Sun* led to a boycott of that paper in Liverpool that has continued up to the present. The child murder cases of James Bulger (1993), Anthony Walker (2006) and Rhys Jones (2007) seemed to confirm yet again that one was always hearing about Liverpool for the wrong reasons. As all these events were accompanied by a public display of grief and mourning, the people from Liverpool stood accused of mawkish sentimentality, or, as Boris Johnson, the current Mayor of London, put it rather provocatively, of wallowing in their "victim status" and in the apparent desire to share "tribal grievance against the rest of society".[26] The publicity surrounding these tragedies showed that there was a certain 'outside' impatience with Liverpool's self-obsession and self-pitying insistence on its difference and particular problems.[27] When recognition of Liverpool's social and economic problems came from the European Union in 1993 as the area obtained 'Objective One Priority' for support and regeneration, the grant seemed to prove to many outside the city the special status proffered to the people of Liverpool, who seemed to consider themselves "God's Chosen People fallen upon hard times".[28] Against this backdrop of economic and political crisis and negative, even vindictive media reporting, Liverpool, as a consequence, became more and more introspective, but generally not unhappy in what seemed a secure world of isolation and difference.

4. Urban Renaissance in the Late Twentieth Century

In the 1970s and 1980s it seemed laughable to promote the city as a commodity and 'urban product' in view of its severe social and economic problems.[29] However, by the end of the millennium Liverpool, like other British cities, particularly those in the North which had suffered most severely from the effects of de-industrialisation, started to reinvent itself through culture-led urban regeneration. This was an obvious strategy given the city's reputation for cultural and creative achievement. The Albert Dock, whose refurbishment was launched in 1984 by the Merseyside Development Corporation, now combines tourist, retail and leisure facilities with private accommodation and museum space. The new Liverpool Echo Arena and Convention Centre next to Albert Dock opened in 2008, allowing artists to perform to an audience of some 11,000. In the same year, the opening of a £20 million cruise ship terminal resulted in a major boost for the region's tourism industry and has turned the Port of Liverpool once again into one of the most important UK ports. A series of other culture-led initiatives, for example the launch of the Liverpool Institute for Performing Arts (LIPA) in 1995 and of FACT, a centre for film, art and exhibitions in 2003, were likewise aimed at connecting culture with local economic growth.

Similarly, official bids for Liverpool to become European Capital of Culture in 2008 and a UNESCO World Heritage Site in 2004 showed how strongly the city authorities had come to embrace tourism and heritage as part of their programme of economic restructuring. Liverpool promoted its official bid for the European Capital of Culture competition with the slogan 'The world in one city', highlighting the blend of a highly local with a wider global identity and representing the city as socially inclusive and culturally diverse.[30] Liverpool's bid was successful not only because of its many cultural attractions and achievements, but because of the city's emphasis on local distinctiveness, inclusion and community participation or, as Sir Jeremy Isaacs, chairman of the judges' panel, put it, "the whole city [was] involved in the bid and behind the bid".[31] When one bears in mind that Liverpool's construction of a sense of identity has depended time and again on asserting its difference, the award was an important distinction which yet again seemed to recognise the apparent uniqueness of the city and helped to boost local confidence, tapping into a deep and long-standing pride in Liverpool culture and identity. When Liverpool FC won the Champions League final in 2005 against all odds, the surprise victory "instantly served as a metaphor for the city's revival and rehabilitation".[32] Another important regeneration project initiated by a Liverpool City Council under new management was the development of an underutilised inner-city area of Liverpool. It was regarded as strategically important as it lay between (and could thus help to connect) the city's central shopping street, the two universities, Chinatown and the waterfront. Completed in the Capital of Culture year 2008, the one-billion-pound retail-led regeneration project named 'Liverpool One' now naturally extends the city's existing retail area and connects the city centre back to its historic waterfront. The proximity of the docks and the Mersey required that this development should respond to the city's maritime context and should have a certain scale and grandeur. The subsequent construction of tall, majestic buildings, such as the residential building One Park West (Fig. 2), reflects the maritime heritage around them, but also the city's regained confidence and claim to past greatness.

Fig. 2: One Park West standing tall at seventeen storeys and overlooking Liverpool's historic waterfront

The most recent regeneration projects reveal a strong interest on the part of the city officials in developing and unifying an area around a coherent image and in marketing Liverpool not just as different from other cities, but also as reconnecting to its maritime and imperial past.[33] Such attempts to establish a relationship between place and identity strongly depend on nostalgia for past glories but, as Merle Tönnies has pointed out, "[h]arkening back to the past is not opposed to confronting and even taking pleasure in postmodern possibilities", in particular the possibilities of shopping and other acts of consumption.[34] Given that in the United Kingdom shopping has increasingly become a recreative pursuit, providing people with new and emancipatory forms of postmodern identity-fashioning,[35] the new shopping, residential and leisure destination 'Liverpool One', with its combination of retail units and recreational facilities, has considerably improved the quality of life of its local population by offering them the personal gratification of consumption. It has also managed to attract the suburban upper-middle class back to the city and to involve them in public culture and leisure.[36]

5. Conclusion

Liverpool's geographical location ensured that it became a key player in the global economy that grew up around the British Empire. Yet, while advancing British political and economic interests during Empire times, Liverpool paradoxically fashioned an identity for itself that disavowed Britain. Located *in* the North of England, but not *of* it, nineteenth-century Liverpool defined itself against commercial London in the South and against industrial Manchester in the North. The city differed sharply from its neighbouring regions in that it did not share the same industrial history as many other Northern towns or cities of Lancashire or Yorkshire. The local dialect Scouse is not typically north-sounding, and unlike its Northern neighbours, there was little internal migration, most of its immigrants coming from outside, in particular from Ireland. All these factors have set Liverpool apart from the rest of the North as well as from the United Kingdom as a whole. Liverpool in the twentieth century, faced with loss of Empire and de-industrialisation, found itself on the wrong side of the country as the rest of Britain founded economic ties with Europe. The way Liverpool expressed its 'otherness' – its problematic construction and projection of itself through history from an international seaport in Victorian times to the insular enclave, the "Capital of Itself"[37] in the twentieth century – has sometimes been misread in other parts of Britain, leading to further alienation. This, in turn, has fostered defensiveness and truculence on the part of the Liverpool people, who cut themselves off from the rest of the country even further. During the better part of the twentieth century the city constructed its identity out of an inverted, inward-looking history and thus fatally remained locked in self-pitying nostalgia, an attitude which actively prevented change. However, over the last twenty years Liverpool has increasingly opened up to the potential of building up its cultural capital. The many culture-led and retail-led regeneration projects have not only encouraged inward public and private investment leading to considerable economic growth, but have also improved the way the city is perceived by local residents as well as outsiders.[38] Whether the latest developments will make the social and economic difference the city has been hoping for remains as yet to be seen, but the idea of culture as a dynamic, innovative and forward-looking force for the sustainable rebranding and reinvention of Liverpool seems to be the way forward.

Notes

1 See, for example, Massey (1994, 2005).
2 Erickson and Roberts (1997: 36). Similarly, Michael Savage (1996: 69) has claimed that space provides both places – or 'habitats' – for the possible development of common life-styles and collective identities *and* opportunities for the cultivation of personal and social networks both within and across places of residence. Places thus become "not just passive backdrops to social process but are actively involved in the constitution and construction of social identities".
3 The term 'Scouse' derives from a Scandinavian dish of boiled meat and potatoes brought to the city by sailors. Scouse is today also used to refer to the distinctive Liverpool accent.
4 John Belchem on *Passport to Liverpool. The Story of a City on the Edge.* (DVD Liverpool, 2008).
5 Lane (1987).
6 *Ibid.* 35.
7 Aughton (1990: 148).
8 Cameron and Crooke (1992: 15).
9 *Ibid.* 12.
10 *Ibid.* 72.
11 *Ibid.*
12 Frost (2000: 198).
13 Aughton (1990: 177), Du Noyer (2004: 3), Cohen (2007: 12-13). African seamen are credited with giving birth to the oldest black community in the country dating back to at least the 1730s. Chinese seamen began to settle in Liverpool in the late 1860s, thus founding Europe's oldest Chinese community.
14 Recording his childhood in Liverpool at the beginning of the twentieth century, Liverpool-Irish 'slummy' Pat O'Mara describes in his autobiography how he grew up amongst "Negroes, Chinese, Mulattoes, Filipinos, almost every nationality under the sun, most of them boasting white wives and large half-caste families […] each colour laying claim to a certain street" (2007: 11).
15 Melville (1969: 138).
16 Belchem (2007a: 8).
17 Belchem (2000: 151).
18 Knowles (1973).
19 Belchem (2007a: 8).
20 Aughton (1990: 93).

21 Du Noyer (2004: 7).
22 Wilks-Hegg (2003: 47).
23 Liverpool's social dislocation caused by these economic factors can be seen in the decline of the city's population from around 870,000 just before the Second World War to 440,000 by the time of the 2001 Census (Meegan 2003: 54).
24 Ackroyd (2004: 3-7, 411-18).
25 *Daily Mirror*, 11 October 1982, quoted in Lane (1987: 11).
26 Johnson (2004). As he made these comments in the *Spectator* shortly after a Liverpool man, Kenneth Bigley, had been brutally murdered by Iraqi hostage takers, the rage in Liverpool was understandably strong. Although the *Spectator* editorial caused outrage in Liverpool, there was no shortage of people in Britain who agreed with Johnson. "What Boris was rightly attacking was the sentimental victimism, coupled with a righteous sense that they are in fact God's Chosen People fallen upon hard times". Posted by Edwin Greenwood on Civitas Blog, 19 October 2004.
27 In his critical account of Liverpudlian self-dramatisation, writer Alan Bennett (1994: 289) can barely hide his dislike for the people in Liverpool who "have a cockiness that comes from being told too often that they and their city are special." Even the Scouse accent with its rising inflection at the end of a sentence suggests to him a "built-in air of grievance" (*Ibid.* 144).
28 Civitas Blog (2004).
29 Erickson and Robert (1997: 38).
30 Once the gateway to empire and proud of its cosmopolitanism the city is now one of the least ethically diverse British cities, with those categorised in the 2001 census as Black Caribbean constituting only 0.7 per cent (compared to 4.8 per cent in London) and a Black African population of 1.2 per cent (5.3 per cent in London), (census 2001).
31 Quoted in BBC News, 2003.
32 Belchem (2007b: 231).
33 Concerns that the latest civic boosterism activities might pose a threat to authentic Liverpool identity have partially materialised in a rise in rents and property values (Norwood 2004) as well as a widespread privatisation of public space: In order to receive the one-billion-pound renovation the city had to grant the development company Grosvenor a 250-year lease which involved giving up the public rights of way. Moreover, the newly constructed buildings threatened to change and dominate the entire city centre. Another point of criticism is that much of the inward investment in Liverpool has been directed at the inner-city area, thus helping to create a rapidly regenerating and increasingly privatised centre and a derelict and marginal periphery (Meegan 2003: 72, Cohen 2007: 204-206, Belchem 2007b: 233).
34 Tönnies (2000: 149).
35 *Ibid.*

36 Littlefield (2009: 111-112), Meegan (2003: 70). A retail study conducted by Liverpool City Council in 1999 revealed that Liverpool people were far from short of money and had in fact started shopping elsewhere (Littlefield [2009: 48]). The revived spending power of local consumers as well as the possibility of attracting affluent shoppers from Liverpool's suburbs and outer fringes entailed that Liverpool needed more retail space. The cultural importance of shopping and consumption was confirmed more recently by a 2007 study into the future of retail property written for the British Council of Shopping Centres, where it says: "Shopping is the UK's national pastime. [...] It is difficult to overstate the importance of retailing to the UK's economic and social well-being, or its significance to a very wide range of public and private sector interests [...]." ("Future of Retail Property").

37 Du Noyer (2004: 5).

38 See the joint study 'Impacts 08' by the University of Liverpool and Liverpool John Moores University, which evaluates the social, cultural, economic and environmental effects of Liverpool hosting the European Capital of culture title in 2008 (impacts 08 website).

Bibliography

Ackroyd, Peter: *Albion. The Origins of the English Imagination*, London, 2004.

Aughton, Peter: *Liverpool. A People's History*, Lancaster, 1990.

Belchem, John: *Merseypride. Essays in Liverpool Exceptionalism,* Liverpool, 2000.

---: *Irish, Catholic and Scouse. The History of the Liverpool-Irish, 1800-1939*, Liverpool, 2007a.

---: "The New Liverpool. History, Culture and Identity on Merseyside". - In Christoph Ehland (Ed.): *Thinking Northern. Textures of Identity in the North of England*, Amsterdam & New York, 2007b, pp. 217-238.

Bennett, Alan: W*riting Home*, London, 1994.

British Council of Shopping Centres: "Future of Retail Property. Future Shopping Places, 2007", http://www.bcsc.org.uk/research/forp/reports/FORP_Report10_ES.pdf, 19 June 2010.

Brown, Jacqueline Nassy: *Dropping Anchor, Setting Sail. Geographies of Race in Black Liverpool*, Princeton, 2005.

Cameron, Gail & Stan Crooke: *Liverpool – Capital of the Slave Trade,* Liverpool, 1992.

http://www.statistics.gov.uk/census2001/profiles/h.asp, 19 June 2010.

Civitas Blog: "Boris Johnson should not have apologized", http://www.civitas.org/uk/blog/archives/2004/10/boris_johnson_s.html, 20 November 2008.

Cohen, Sara: *Decline, Renewal and the City in Popular Music Culture. Beyond the Beatles,* Aldershot, 2007.

Du Noyer, Paul: *Liverpool. Wondrous Place. Music from the Cavern to the Coral,* London, 2004.

Erickson, Bill & Marion Roberts: "Marketing Local Identity", *Journal of Urban Design* 2:1, 1997, 35-59.

Frost, Diane: "Ambiguous Identities. Constructing and De-constructing Black and White 'Scouse' Identities in Twentieth Century Liverpool". – In Neville Kirk (Ed.): *Northern Identities. Historical Interpretations of 'The North' and 'Northernness'*, Aldershot, 2000, pp. 195-217.

Garcia, Beatriz, Ruth Melville & Tamsin Cox: "Creating an Impact. Liverpool's Experience as European Capital of Culture", http://www.liv.ac.uk/impacts08/, 19 March 2010.

Johnson, Boris: "On Bigley's Fate", *The Spectator*, 16 October 2004.

Knowles, Gerald: *Scouse. The Urban Dialect of Liverpool*, PhD, University of Leeds, 1973.

Lane, Tony: *Liverpool. Gateway of Empire,* London, 1987.

Littlefield, David: *Liverpool One. Remaking a City Centre,* Chichester, 2009.

Massey, Doreen: *Space, Place and Gender,* Cambridge, 1994.

---: *For Space,* London, 2005.

Meegan, Richard: "Urban Regeneration, Politics and Social Cohesion. The Liverpool Case". – In Ronaldo Munck (Ed.): *Reinventing the City? Liverpool in Comparative Perspective*, Liverpool, 2003, pp. 53-79.

Melville, Herman: *Redburn. His First Voyage. Being the Sailor-boy Confessions and Reminiscences of the Son-of-a-Gentleman, in the Merchant Service*. Ed. Harrison Hayford *et al*, Evanston & Chicago, 1969 [1849].

Munck, Ronaldo: "Introduction. The City, Globalisation and Social Transformation". – In Ronaldo Munck (Ed.): *Reinventing the City? Liverpool in Comparative Perspective*, Liverpool, 2003, pp. 1-20.

Norwood, Gaham: "Mersey Rising", *The Sunday Times*, 14 November 2004.
O'Mara, Pat: *The Autobiography of a Liverpool Irish Slummy*, Liverpool, 2007 [1931].
Passport to Liverpool. The Story of a City on the Edge, DVD, Liverpool, 2008.
Savage, Michael: "Space, Networks and Clan Formation". – In Neville Kirk (Ed.): *Social Class and Marxism. Defences and Challenges*, Aldershot, 1996, pp. 58-86.
Tönnies, Merle: "Postmodern Forms of Leisure in Contemporary Britain", *Journal for the Study of British Cultures* 7:2, 2000, 141-151.
Wilks-Hegg, Stuart: "From World City to Pariah City? Liverpool and the Global Economy, 1850-2000". – In Ronaldo Munck (Ed.): *Reinventing the City? Liverpool in Comparative Perspective*, Liverpool, 2003, pp. 36-52.

Illustrations

Figure 1: Liverpool FC supporter with a banner, http://www.fmgreece.gr/phpBB3/viewtopic.php?f=141&t=20867&start=45, 20 July 2008.
Figure 2: One Park West, http://www.oneparkwest.co.uk/oneparkwest.aspx, 24 March 2010.

Ingrid von Rosenberg (Dresden/Berlin)

Changing Faces of a Region and the Growth of New Place Identities. Reflections of the Structural Change on the Land- and Cityscapes of the North East and the Effects on Its People

1. Introduction. The Meaning of Landscapes

The North East of England, the second smallest region after London in square kilometres and with a population of only 2.6 million in 2008, is nevertheless a particularly interesting part of the country: it looks back on a very special history that has helped to form its characteristic land- and cityscapes. How is 'landscape' to be defined? In an essay for the volume *Cultural Geography. A Critical Dictionary of Key Concepts* American geographer Don Mitchell distinguishes cultural from natural landscapes, defining the nature of cultural landscapes as a double one. On the one hand, he sees them as an outcome of social relations, also as a result of specific relations of production, which in western societies are capitalist and thus include a history of alienation. Those who build the landscape, often do not own it. But, on the other hand, Mitchell argues, landscape is also perceived, defined and defended in localist terms, is bound up in national and regional identity and is one of the means by which people come to "know their home".[1] Leaving aside the natural landscapes of the North East, though several are of outstanding beauty, my article will focus on its cultural landscapes. I am not so much concerned with the property relations that have been determining the face of the region, though they will be referred to, but with the significance of the changing land- and cityscapes for people's place identity. The North East is one of those British regions in which the structural economic changes of the past decades have been most drastic, and it seems worth investigating how this has affected the local population's sense of identity.

2. A Brief Economic and Cultural History of the North East with a Special Focus on County Durham

'To carry coals to Newcastle' – this old proverb, which, as everybody knows, means to do something utterly superfluous, preserves in the most condensed form the memory of the importance the region once had for the nation: up to the mid-twentieth century the North East was England's most important provider of coal, then the main source of energy. Though Newcastle itself – apart from some small mines on the outskirts – functioned only as the main port for shipping coal to London and abroad, its hinterland formed the biggest English coalfield for centuries: the counties of Durham, Tyne and Wear, Northumberland and Tees Valley. Perhaps already under the Romans, but certainly from the thirteenth century onwards coal was excavated in the region. In some places it lay near the surface, in others deep underground with some of the seams stretching far out into the North Sea. From the beginning of the Industrial Revolution more and more shafts were sunk to meet the rising demand, until the North East became the dominant coal producing area in the UK. As it is impossible to treat the whole area here, I will focus on County Durham as an exemplary part with occasional references to other areas and the region as a whole.

The heyday of the Durham collieries was in the 1910s. In 1911, the year of the highest production, 152,000 miners, 30 per cent of the local labour force, produced 56 million tons of coal from 400 pits, around half of which was exported.[2] In the 1920s there were still 150 pits and 47 cokeworks, many of them small and all privately owned, employing 150,000 men. The decline was gradual, beginning already in the 1930s as a result of the Great Depression and the plummeting international trade. Temporarily, the downturn was halted by the war demand, so that when the industry was nationalised in 1947, there were still 127 pits employing 108.000 men.[3] But between 1950 and 1970, as a consequence of changes in the global economy, around 100 pits were closed, and the closures continued in the 1980s and 1990s.[4] The dramatic last big strike of

1984-1985, which lasted a whole year but could not prevent the end of the industry, is still looming large in the local population's collective memory. In 1994 the last pit in County Durham was closed, Wearmouth Colliery in Sunderland, now the site of the football Stadium of Light, built in 1995. Meanwhile the British coal industry has revived to a certain extent, but deep mining has not. Open-cast mining, however, bitterly fought by environmentalists, is on the rise, providing now about half of the nation's demand in coal. The North East contributes 1.2 million tons per year, the largest amount outside Scotland, which produces an astonishing 5.7 million tons.[5]

While mining mostly happened in rural areas, the follow-up industries of steel making, engineering and shipbuilding were located in the urban areas near the coast. The whole of the North East is a prime example of how, as Doreen Massey has argued, "the spatial division of labour [...] structured the spatial organisation of the UK during much of the nineteenth century".[6] Of course the industries formed the landscapes. In the case of the coalfields this meant the erection of pitheads with wheels and towers, smokestacks, sheds and slagheaps, the building of mining villages with their characteristic rows of terraced cottages climbing up and down the hills, and terrible pollution of the land and the beaches, on which much of the waste was dumped until this was stopped in 1976. Work in the industry, which was fixed in place, did, however, not only mean a livelihood, but produced a particular 'way of life' in Raymond Williams's sense, a sub-culture, which in its turn produced a sense of place, a boundedness and pride despite the harsh environment and dangers of the workplace (one should not forget: disasters that cost many lives happened regularly, the last one in Easington Colliery in 1951 killed 83 men). The characteristics of the miners' lifestyle have been well documented by middle-class observers such as George Orwell and J.B. Priestley, even Virginia Woolf, but also recorded by working-class writers from the area such as Jack Common and Sid Chaplin. The confined living conditions produced close family ties, a strict gender division, camaraderie underground, community spirit and class consciousness. While women, faced with the double burden of household duties for mostly large families and work in various jobs, had hardly any time for hobbies, favourite leisure time activities were developed by the men: the allotment culture and pigeon rearing as a respite from the heat and dust of the pits, the brass bands, socialising in the working men's clubs, greyhound racing and football watching.

3. Changes in the North East from the 1950s Onwards. New Uses of the Coalfields and Economic Problems

The disappearance of the coal industry worked like a sea change in the pattern of this lifestyle. What is most important in the present context: the landscape has changed completely. If you travel to County Durham today, without any knowledge of the past, you would probably not identify the area as a former coalfield. Amazingly, only very few relics of the industry are preserved. Some communities like Shotton and Seaham have set up wheels as memorials for the industry, others like Easington keep a plaque to remember a pit disaster. Washington preserves a headgear and engine house of one of its once five pits, in Woodhorn a nineteenth-century colliery has been turned into a museum, while in the open air museum of Beamish a fake mine was constructed. The rest of the land has been transformed back into a part of England's 'green and pleasant land'.

This has mostly been due to the work of Durham County Council, which as early as the 1950s realised the need to clean up the environment.[7] In 1964 a County Council Reclamation Team was set up, which began to organise the reclamation of derelict coalmines and, in the course of time, increasingly worked in co-operation with English Partnerships (the national regeneration agency), local councils and private business. The land which had belonged to the British Coal Board, had to be sold to either business or local councils. As not many former pits were suited for 'hard-end use', i.e. new industrial purposes, most areas were put to 'soft green uses' such as public open spaces, community woodland, recreation grounds, even golf courses or agriculture. Derelict railway lines were transformed into biking or walking routes. Since 1964, 85 per cent of the costs were covered by the government, later money also came from European sources like the European Structural Fund and the Derelict Land Grant. In 1991 work was intensified by the establishment of an East Durham Task Force and the launch of the project 'Turning the Tide' in 1997. The main tasks to be tackled were the clean-up of beaches, the demolition of the slagheaps, planting trees and grass and turning land to communal or agricultural uses, though the soil is not best suited for the latter. For the Herculean work it has done, Durham County Council has been awarded several prestigious prizes from national and European private and governmental environmental organisations. Remaining problems are the mine water and sludge, which threaten to pollute the drinking water and the soil.

Fig. 1: Sherborn Hill Pit before reclamation

Fig. 2: Sherborn Hill Pit after reclamation, 1970

Narrowing the view now to individual ex-pitheads, one can observe a variety of uses which were decided by the local councils as the planning authorities. In several cases, remaining buildings have been put to community uses. In the former pit village of Washington, for example, a much frequented boxing school and a neighbouring youth club with the telling name of "Pitstop", chosen by the youngsters themselves, operate in well-preserved former pithead sheds. Nearby a similar building now houses an impressive award-winning charity, the Bridge Project, set up by local women to improve the educational and training opportunities for women by providing courses from health care and child-rearing to computer courses and personal development training. Even a crèche is available. A Millenium Project, a gym plus sportsground for communal use, was also erected on a former pithead, and one might also include the Stadium of Light in Sunderland, homeground of Sunderland AFC, as it provides possibilities for one the most popular sports. Apart from hosting games and the occasional pop concert, Sunderland AFC also runs a number of educational programmes to keep local youths off the streets.

However, not all former pitheads have been dedicated to communal purposes, some are used commercially. Several small workshops were established on old pitheads. In Seaham, for instance, a former coastal pit town, two closed mines (Dawdon and Foxcover) were turned into fairly big industrial estates. Seaham has been especially lucky as it was chosen for a flagship project of the East Durham Task Force's 'Programme for Action'. Apart from the establishment of the industrial zones the 'Seaham Regeneration Scheme' has also included a number of environmental improvements and landscape projects to increase the area's attractiveness for business and tourism. Recently a posh estate of detached houses has been erected near the seafront, and not very far away a huge shopping centre with 358 shops was opened in 2007. Ironically, to provide it with some local flavour, this 'non-place', to quote Marc Augé, is called Byron Place, because in 1814 Lord Byron married Anne Isabelle Milbanke, the daughter of a local family, in Seaham.[8] The centre, despite a smart design – the shops form a semi-circle with the middle passage covered by a series of light and white tent-like constructions –, is financially not yet very successful: too few potential customers live in the surroundings, and tourists are (still) rare. Seaham also houses the only five-star hotel and spa in the North, the converted late eighteenth-century mansion Seaham Hall. With this luxury hotel, its cleaned beaches below the cliffs and a new promenade Seaham, besides being a business location, is obviously aspiring to become a seaside resort, which in the long run might also profit Byron Place.[9]

And what has become of the miners' cottages and villages? They had to be sold, too, either to the tenants, the council or private landlords, which has caused problems. Many of the houses remain and have been renovated with public money as e.g. the village of Easington, which figured in the film *Billy Elliot*. In other cases, often after demolition, new housing has been built, modest, but comfortable bungalows with gardens and garages. Washington is such a place, and its private as well as communal lawns are groomed with such loving care that they can compete with those in the grounds of any stately home. No doubt, County Durham today offers many new attractive sights beside the traditional magnets, the ancient Cathedral and town of Durham, Barnard Castle and some beautiful spots on the coastline. One understands that tourism has become an important source of income, contributing £627 million to the local economy in 2008 and providing 11,000 jobs.[10] The foundation of interesting museums like the Bowes Museum and the open air museums Beamish and Killhope, documenting the work and culture of the past, have certainly helped to increase the region's attractiveness for both visitors from outside as well as locals, for whom they may function as institutions to support their local identity. The county now proudly advertises itself as 'The Land of the Prince Bishop', preferring a reference to the ancient history of the bishop seat in Durham city to reminding tourists of the coal mining past. But underneath the beautiful surface the people have to struggle with a number of problems, and this not only applies to the population of County Durham, but to the North East as a whole.

The economy in the North East has turned from domination by coal and other heavy industries to a diversified, mostly service-based one. After especially hard times in the 1980s and 1990s, gradually new work has been created in the area, though not enough. Manufacture (mostly of chemicals, chemical goods, man-made fibres, machinery and transport equipment) does still exist in the North East and with 17 per cent of the region's GVA even surpasses the national average of 13 per cent.[11] The export of such goods as a percentage of GVA was higher than the national average (28 per cent as compared to 19 per cent). But most jobs are in the public sector services, e.g. in local councils, hospitals, education (five universities are located in the region), even prisons, followed by call centres, tourism and work in branch plants of national and international companies such as Nissan in Sunderland. On the other hand, the entrepreneurial culture is little developed and IT, finance and other business activities are underrepresented. When the economic crisis began in 2008, commentators expected that the impact on employment would be milder than in the South precisely because of the great dependence on state-provided jobs, which seemed safe, while in the South the much larger private sector seemed more vulnerable. Yet the unemployment rate in the fourth quarter of 2009 continued to be higher at 9.3 per cent than the national average of 7.8 per cent, and the region has the highest proportion of unemployed households. The number of self-employed people is low. Out-migration surpasses in-migration, so that County Durham lost 2.9 per cent of its population between 1981 and 2004, though it has grown since then. Male employment in County Durham dropped from a high-wage profession – miners were once the most highly paid workers in the country – to low wage and insecure service jobs. Women fared better in so far as they increased their share of the working population, especially since the Miners' Strike, during which many, engaged in the 'Women against Pit-Closure' movement, learnt to act self-confidently in public. In fact, as Doreen Massey writes, "the new jobs that came to the North East, then, were mainly for women".[12]

4. *A Hypothesis. The Growth of a New 'Collective Patchwork Place Identity'*

All these changes necessarily had an impact on people's sense of identity, once so firmly work-based and place-bound. As Massey states, "'the identity of place' is much more open and provisional than most discussions allow".[13] And she continues to argue, "identities of places are inevitably unfixed [...] because the social relations out of which they are constructed are themselves by their very nature dynamic and changing".[14] It is always difficult to make precise statements about people's place identity at a particular moment in time. For the North East there are as yet no comprehensive studies including polls and representative interviews concerning people's changing attitudes to their place of home, but the observation of their behaviour seems to allow certain conclusions. The mining villages and small towns, once "coherent, bounded and settled" communities *par excellence*, have turned into what Massey calls "meeting places", where several "activity spaces" meet, i.e. neighbours go out to work in a great variety of working environments.[15] These offer a basis for personal identification only to a limited extent, especially as many jobs are no more long-term and safe but have to be changed frequently. Thus people develop what I would like to term a 'collective patchwork place identity'. On the one hand they are still bound to their familiar local environment and community. They also cling to the old pastimes; the allotment culture and the brass bands are as alive as ever. Though many expected the band culture to die with the pits or at best survive as a tourist attraction, it has remained a favourite pastime. 52 bands took part in the North England Brass Band Championship of 2009, and the Big Meeting in July, the Miners' Gala in Durham city, once the annual meeting of all the pit bands from the area, proudly displaying their elaborately stitched banners while playing and marching through the town, has remained a highlight of the local calendar. In 2009 on a particularly sunny 11 July the 125th Gala was celebrated with 46 bands playing and 100,000 visitors enjoying the spectacle. In 2010, 70 organisations took part in the 126th Big Meeting, and again over 40 bands played. What was once a demonstration of pride in a very special culture has turned into the commemoration of a tradition and a popular festival.

On the other hand, people have developed new elements of local identity. Pleasure and pride in the changed green and clean environment, which attracts tourists, are certainly part of a new place identity, as many utterances from local people reveal. Women even seem to have profited from the economic changes. No longer confined to the home, they increasingly take part in the public sphere of work, either in paid employment, in voluntary community work or in both, which undoubtedly not only raises their self-confidence, but also intensifies their sense of connectedness to the community. The women working in and for the Bridge Project are a good example. Finally, the inhabitants of Durham County, especially the young ones, have become participants in a particular consumer culture, represented by the shopping malls, local pubs and discos in the many small and bigger communities. Though consumer culture is, of course, a global phenomenon, it takes locally specific forms, and the pub and club culture with heavy drinking and sparsely dressed girls even in mid-winter are characteristic of life in the North East of England. It seems opportune to remember Stuart Hall's famous saying here: 'identity is a moveable feast'. Even the miners' strong sense of identity was not one that existed of yore, but developed slowly over the 150 years that the industry lasted. New circumstances produce new identities.

5. Economic and Architectural Changes in an Urban Environment. The Example of Newcastle upon Tyne

Turning now to the urban areas of the North East, I have selected Newcastle as my example. This ancient city on the north bank of the river Tyne, the biggest in the region with its 260,000 inhabitants, was as much affected by the structural changes as the coalfields. Gradually it lost all its key industries – coal, steel, engineering, shipbuilding and most of its manufacture, which caused great unemployment and deprivation. Since the 1950s the city and county councils, local business and property developers have made great efforts to create new employment opportunities. Though several poor and deprived areas remain, especially on the fringes of town, a new cityscape in and near the centre has come into existence, which may contribute or has already contributed to the emergence of a similar collective patchwork place identity as in the coalfields, mixed from old adherences and new elements, though different ones. In urban areas buildings and public spaces can play an important role in people's sense of belonging. Paul Jenkins, writing about place identity in cities under post-modern conditions, has stressed the chance architecture offers as a new source for identity construction after the loss of long-established work-based identities: "Definition of space through architectural urban design and development at the local level can be a key driver in the reconstruction of place identity at the level of the city or agglomeration."[16] One might assume that in a city the place identities of the citizens vary more than in the country, due to a more complex employment pattern and a more diversified class structure. Yet changes in the physical appearance of the town affect everybody.

Cities in general change their appearance much more often throughout history than rural areas, as the economic and creative forces concentrated there speed up and intensify developments.

With reference to Newcastle, sociologist Dave Byrne wrote: "The remaking of the city in the first half of the nineteenth century was so drastic and growth in the second half of the century was so massive, that it makes sense to see Edwardian Newcastle as a new place laid over an old place."[17] The equally profound change with which we are concerned here began in the 1950s and gathered momentum in the 1980s. In the first phase from the 1950s to the 1970s, mostly under Labour rule, planners of the city and county councils, engineers and bureaucrats, operated as the primary actors. Several big projects were pushed through: slum clearance in the old working-class areas west and east of the city centre to create new spaces for business and the universities of Newcastle and Northumbria, the resettlement of people in overspill housing on the Edge, and, above all, the improvement of car access to the city. In fact, it seems, cars were their prime consideration. A city on two levels was planned, comfortably broad streets including a motorway through the city, and above a pedestrian level including many foot bridges. Fortunately only parts were realised as the buildings had the charm of the then fashionable brutalist style and the traffic noise became appalling. Under the Thatcher government in the 1980s planning authority shifted from the city council to property developers, who were not concerned with the city as a whole but with the development of individual financially promising sites. In this era office parks and the huge shopping centre The Metro on the Gateshead side, at the time the largest in Europe, were built. Gradually the employment structure changed to a service-dominated one. In 1987 the QUANGO Tyne and Wear Urban Development Corporation became the chief development agency, working in partnership with the city council and private businesses. It was their joint efforts that in the following years put the final touches to the present face of the city. While the council, with the help of government funds and Lottery money, erected public buildings to improve the city's potential as a cultural centre, private investors built office blocks and leisure sites, the precondition for the creation of a variety of new service jobs. The Edge and the river were now prioritised, though some important projects like the Centre for Life, an educational and research venue for the life sciences, were also erected in the city centre. Any first-time visitor to Newcastle, will immediately be attracted to the riverside. This is not a matter of course, as the river was a stinking open sewer up to the 1970s, when an interceptor sewer scheme finally cleaned it.

Today, as in many other former ports, with Baltimore leading the way in the 1970s, the Newcastle and Gateshead riverfronts have been fundamentally regenerated. In contrast to London's South Bank, the two quaysides form a mixed business, housing and cultural centre as a result of the combination of private and public investment. Where once shabby warehouses, small workshops, poor housing and a cheap market lined the river, today broad promenades link privately owned, expensive office buildings, posh apartment blocks, restaurants and cafés with representative public buildings. The Law Courts, erected on the north side in 1990, face the Baltic on the Gateshead quayside, an exhibition venue for contemporary art housed in a converted flour mill, which opened in 2002, and the Sage, a huge and fanciful music centre designed by Sir Norman Foster (opened in 2004). The Sage was built right below the renovated fourteenth-century parish church of St Mary's, now a heritage centre documenting Gateshead's history. Between the newly designed banks the river itself offers an impressive sight with its ten bridges, the oldest dating from 1850. The latest, the Millenium Bridge of 2000, is a particularly fascinating sight. The award-winning elegant tilting footbridge designed by Wilkinson Eyre Architects and constructed by the engineering firm Gifford, both local companies, consciously refers to the past. Its construction continues Newcastle's traditional expertise in engineering and optically takes up the bow of the famous Tyne Bridge built in 1928.

Fig. 3: Millenium Bridge and View of Newcastle Quayside

All in all, Newcastle's and Gateshead's quaysides with their bold new architecture and conscious references to the local past indeed offer an aesthetically pleasing and unique vision, well-suited to supporting the growth of a new place identity. There are strong signs that the riverside has indeed become very popular and operates as an inclusive place. Though the Baltic has not become a big magnet for locals, the bridge has and so has the Sage. The bridge has become the favourite connection between the two towns and is the site of all big fireworks now. The Sage contains several concert halls where not only renowned classical orchestras and jazz bands perform, but also many local music groups. It also runs an extensive youth programme including musical education and psychological advisory programmes, and it even, in co-operation with the University of Sunderland and Gateshead College, offers the opportunity to do a BA in Community Music. During the day a affordable café attracts any number of people, who sip their coffee while enjoying the view of the river. The Sage has quickly become a favourite place with Newcastle citizens from all layers of society.

Despite the best intentions of the city planners the concrete buildings of the 1960s and 1970s could, by contrast, be located anywhere and have not developed into places people are specially attached to, though in October 2009 an exhibition honoured the town planners of this period. Other parts of town, however, may act as additional props for place identity, especially historical sites and buildings, though – as in so many other towns – many of these were demolished in the course of the various reconstruction waves. A number of medieval buildings remain, such as parts of the old castle, remnants of the old town wall and St. Nicholas Cathedral, some of the massive late nineteenth-century company buildings and, above all, the elegant classical quarter of Grainger City at the very heart of town with 244 listed buildings, built from 1835 to 1842 and, according to Nikolaus Pevsner, one of the finest classical ensembles in the country with the beautifully curving Grey Street as a special highlight.[18] The quarter was constructed as a commercial centre with shops below housing or offices, but also contains some stately public buildings like The Central Exchange Buildings, the

Theatre Royal and the Assembly Rooms. It is now a Central Conservation Area.

At the other end of the scale some places representative of today's consumer and leisure culture may also operate as elements of people's place identity, especially for young citizens. The huge Metro Centre is one of them, another is Bigg Market, the hub of Newcastle's party district situated in the oldest part of town. Newcastle has become the capital of Britain's notorious pub and club culture, and young people from all parts of the country flock there to enjoy their weekends or to celebrate their stag and hen parties. Older people might not like it, neither the excessive boozing nor the commercial aspect, but this drinking and clubbing is certainly part of a locally rooted working-class sub-culture and as such should be taken seriously by cultural studies.[19]

7. Conclusion and a View to the Future

To conclude: After the loss of the traditional work-based identities both the changed landscape of the coalfields and the new cityscape of Newcastle, built after the 1950s, have produced chances to construct new patchwork place identities which are partly inspired by an acceptance of or even pride in new developments, partly by preserving links to the local past and traditions of culture and crafts. A particular work of modern art may perhaps be seen as a symbol of this development: the Angel of the North, which has become a pillar of people's local identity, not just for Newcastle citizens, but for the whole North East. Twenty metres high, designed by Anthony Gormley and constructed from local steel between 1994 and 1998, the statue was erected on a hilltop overlooking the A 1, the A 167 and the East Coast Main Line railway, thus greeting everybody approaching the city from these sides. At first received with some scepticism, the Angel, listed as an 'Icon of England' by Icons Online, a project of the Department of Culture, Media and Sport, has long become a landmark of the area of which people are proud, as its nickname 'the Gateshead Flasher' indicates. With its strong foothold in the ground on the one hand and its wide open wings on the other, suggesting Newcastle's openness to the world and to new developments, it seems well-suited to symbolising the spirit of the city and the region.

On 6 May 2010 a new era has begun: after thirteen years of Labour government a Conservative – Liberal coalition is in power. Already in the run-up to the election Conservative leader David Cameron picked on Northern Ireland and the North East of England as the two British regions with the smallest population but the highest rate of public spending (15.3 per cent in the North East as compared to the national average of 10.9 in the period 1998/9 to 2011/12) and the highest proportion of public employment. He pronounced his firm intention to cut public spending and employment considerably and to promote more private business. One plan, which is fiercely opposed not only by Labour, but also by local business people, aims at scrapping the regional development agency One North East and replacing it by Local Enterprise Partnerships (LEPs). The fear is that, in the wake of this change, decisions over investments and business support will be removed from the local level to Whitehall. A little more than a year after the new government came to power some alarming trends can be observed. Unemployment is rising – from July to September 2011 alone it rose by 18.000 – and at 10.7 per cent is now the highest in the country, comparing to a national average of 7.9 per cent. Political journalist Richard Moss assumes that this dramatic increase is mostly due to public sector cuts.[20] Women are particularly vulnerable to job losses, and one in five young people are out of work. Especially hard hit among the work places are colleges (of around 1,500 jobs known to be at risk in 44 colleges around England, more than 800 are to be axed at the region's colleges)[21] and local councils, but also the voluntary sector and tourism are suffering from severe cuts, the latter as the government has scrapped a tourism support package for the region and additionally banned development chiefs from promoting the area.[22] It seems very doubtful whether under the present economic circumstances the private sector will be able to make up for all the job losses, as hoped by the government. How this gloomy development will affect people's lives and their place identities, which they have only fairly recently begun to construct after the collapse of the old ones formed in the nineteenth century, remains to be seen.

Notes

1 Mitchell (2007: 53).
2 Wood (1994: 83-84).
3 Simpson, "Introduction to Coal Mining and Railways".
4 *Ibid.*
5 Carrell (2009).
6 Massey (1994: 52).
7 Information about the work of Durham County Council is given in *The Greening of the County* (2004).
8 In his book *Non-Places. Introduction to an Anthropology of Supermodernity* (1995), Marc Augé distinguishes 'places', which have a particular identity created by history and relations, from 'non-places' of transience that have no special identity. Examples are airports, hotels, supermarkets, refugee camps, etc.
9 The following brief overview of the economy refers to the whole of the North East unless otherwise indicated. It is mostly based on the survey *Portrait of the North East. Regional Trends* (2010) by Allan Worthy and Ian Gouldson. Other informative websites are www.onenortheast.co.uk, www.englandsnortheast.co.uk, www.countydurhamfoundation.co.uk.
10 "Tourism Facts and Figures. Economic Impact of Tourism in Durham".
11 GVA stands for Gross Value Added and is a good measure of the economic output of a region.
12 Massey (1994: 203).
13 *Ibid.* 168.
14 *Ibid.* 169.
15 Massey (1995: 49, 57).
16 Jenkins (2005: 25).
17 Byrne (2001: 341).
18 Nikolaus Pevsner's praise, uttered in *Northumberland* (1957) of *The Buildings of England* series (1951-1974) is again and again proudly quoted in tourist information material on Newcastle.
19 Hilary Fawcett from the University of Bedforshire has written about the cultural significance of this behaviour in Cheryl Buckley & Hilary Fawcett (2002). The girls' daring dress style and heavy drinking are interpreted as acts of class-specific defiance in a situation where the world of work does not offer any real chances for self-realisation.
20 Richard Moss, "Unemployment Surges as Public Sector Cuts Hit Home". See also government statistics, broken down by regions: Labour market statistics 2011, A07: Regional labour market summary. 01 May 2011 – 31 July 2011. www.ons.gov.uk/ons/publications/re-reference-tables.html?edition=tcm%3A77-222431, 14 October 2011.
21 Stephen Exley, "North East 'Hammered' as It Bears over Half of FE Job Cuts".
22 Adrian Pearson, "North East Tourism Industry Hit by Spending Cuts".

Anonymous: *The Greening of the County. Forty Years of Reclamation by Durham County Council 1964 to 2004*, Durham, 2004.

Augé, Marc: *Non-Places. Introduction to an Anthropology of Supermodernity*, London 1995 [French original 1992].

Buckley, Cheryl & Hilary Fawcett: *Fashioning the Feminine. Representation of Women's Fashion form the Fin de Siècle to the Present*, London, 2002.

Byrne, Dave: "The Reconstruction of Newcastle. Planning since 1945". – In Robert Colls & Bill Lancaster (Eds.): *Newcastle upon Tyne. A Modern History*, Chichester, 2001, pp. 341-360.

Carrell, Severin: "Opencast coalmine surge weakens UK's authority at climate change talks", *The Guardian*, 14 August 2009, www.guardian.co.uk/environment/2009/aug/14/coal-energy/print, 11 November 2009.

http://www.countydurhamfoundation.co.uk, 11 November 2009.

Durham County Council: *The Greening of the County. Forty Years of Reclamation by Durham County Council 1964 to 2004*, Durham, 2004.

Exley, Stephen: "North East 'Hammered' as It Bears over Half of FE Job Cuts", *TES Newspaper*, 29 April 2011, http://www.tes.co.uk/article.aspx?storycode=6079660, 30 September 2011.

Jenkins, Paul: "Space, Place and Territory. An Analytical Framework". – In Cliff Hague & P. J. (Eds.): *Place Identity, Participation and Planning*, London & New York, 2005, pp. 19-38.

Massey, Doreen: *Space, Place, and Gender*, Minneapolis, 1994.

---: "The Conceptualization of Place". – In D. M. & Pat Jess (Eds.): *A Place in the World? Places, Cultures and Globalization*, Oxford, 1995, pp. 45-85.

Mitchell, Don: "Landscape". – In David Atkinson *et al.* (Eds.): *Cultural Geography. A Critical Dictionary of Key Concepts*, London & New York, 2007, pp. 49-56.

Moss, Richard: "Unemployment Surges as Public Sector Cuts Hit Home", *BBC Mobile*, 14 September 2011 http://www.bbc.co.uk/news/uk-england-14919704, 14 October 2011.

http://www.onenortheast.co.uk, 2 November 2009.

Pearson, Adrian: "North East Tourism Industry Hit by Spending Cuts", *The Journal*, 30 August 2011, http://www.journallive.co.uk/north-east-news/todays-news/2011/08/30/north-east-tourism-industry-hit-by-spending-cuts-61634-29325557/, 30 September 2011.

Pevsner, Nikolaus: *Northumberland*, The Buildings of England 15, Harmondsworth, 1957.

Simpson, David: "Introduction to Coal Mining and Railways in the North East", "http://www.englandsnortheast.co.uk/CoalminingandRailways.html, 2 November 2009.

"Tourism Facts and Figures. Economic Impact of Tourism in Durham." www.tourismnortheast.co.uk/visit-county-durham/tourism-facts-and-figures, 11 November 2009.

Wood, Gerald: *Die Umstrukturierung Nordost-Englands. Wirtschaftlicher Wandel, Alltag und Politik in einer Altindustrieregion*, Duisburger Geographische Arbeiten 13, Duisburg, 1994.

Worthy, Alan & Ian Gouldson: *Portrait of the North East*. Regional Trends 42, 2010, www.statistics.gov.uk/pdfdir/rtne0610.pdf, 15 August 2010.

Gabriele Linke (Rostock)

Subjectivity and Place in Contemporary Scottish Autobiography. The Case of Glasgow

"Perhaps we could imagine space as a simultaneity of stories-so-far."[1]

Contemporary Scottish autobiographical texts are often characterised by the strong sense of place which they convey and which is vital for the social and cultural positioning of the autobiographer. In many ways, such life stories expose the correlation between place and class, ethnicity, religion and gender. The home, the street with its shops and cinemas, parts of the city, the rural outskirts as well as places outside Scotland take on special meanings in the autobiographers' lives, but these meanings vary for different persons at different times. Furthermore, the decline of traditional industries in the second half of the twentieth century engendered social changes which have affected both the lives of the people and the spatial patterns of living all over Scotland and especially in cities such as Glasgow. Before I look at different autobiographical texts and their constructions and reconstructions of Glasgow in the twentieth century, I will examine possible links between autobiography and recent concerns in social geography.

1. Space – Subjectivity – Ideology – Autobiography

So far, autobiography has not been appreciated much for its contribution to understanding place and space while the fiction written about places such as New York and London has received ample attention by critics and scholars alike.[2] Autobiography as a type of text has often been considered an anomaly of literature and hard to classify, hovering awkwardly somewhere along the continuum between the fictional and the factual. Autobiographies tend to reflect the messy, subjective characteristics of human experience, and recent theory on space has, however reluctantly, acknowledged and considered exactly this aspect of space.[3] Revising existing approaches to understanding space, Doreen Massey offers three propositions.[4] Firstly, she claims that space is constituted through interactions, which supports an anti-essentialist conception of space. Secondly, she defines space as a sphere of coexisting heterogeneity, which implies that there is a multiplicity of stories. Thirdly, she sees space as always under construction, never finished nor closed. Others have argued along similar lines, emphasising that there is "no immutable *genius loci*" and that meanings are not inherent in any place.[5] Rather, as Barney Warf claims, places and landscapes are embedded in networks of social relations and constructed by people in a multitude of ways, from different viewpoints at different times, thus fluid, twisted and unstable.[6] This social constructionist view has informed much of the recent theorising of space as well as my own study.

With regard to autobiography, this concept of space implies that different autobiographers will construct a place in diverse, contradictory and changeable ways. Therefore, it should not be expected that a place will arise from autobiographical texts with a unified and stable meaning. Regenia Gagnier describes this – non-essentialist – position in different terms, noticing that "[i]n writing of how people situate themselves in the world, nothing is self-evident, neither the aspects of the world and Nature that one would think salient, nor the 'self' itself [...]";[7] autobiographical writing is, naturally, subjective.

In this paper, I will understand subjectivity mainly in the sense outlined by Gagnier, who finds subjectivity in different relations. Firstly, the subject is the subject to itself; secondly, it is subject to, and of others, "in fact, it is often an 'Other' to others, which also affects its own sense of subjectivity".[8] Furthermore, the subject is also the subject of knowledge, for example in the discourses of social institutions. Fourth, the subject is a separate human body which is closely dependent on its physical environment. Finally, subjectivity is opposed to objectivity, which means that the particular or partial view from an individual body is opposed to "some other (if only hypothetical) universal view [...]".[9] In self-representations like autobiography, the I is the subject of the sentence as well as 'subjected' to the symbolic order of language and (intersubjective) culture.

The close connections between such an understanding of subjectivity and the view of space as developed by Massey are easily discernable and can be found in the emphasis on social relations and interactions on the one hand and subjectivity on the other; furthermore in the rejection of essentialism and the acceptance of fluidity; and finally in the interdependence between body, geography, knowledge and discourse. In Kathleen Kirby's words, the subject could be located in the space of the body, the physical space of geography with its social and cultural dimensions, and in discursive space.[10] She stresses that space predetermines to a large portion a subject's status and, though to a lesser extent, the ideological formations subjects encounter.[11] Nevertheless, theorists such as Richard Johnson have warned that in an approach that focuses on the social production of culture (including space), the character of a cultural product cannot be inferred mechanically from the conditions of its production although it will be influenced by them.[12]

The relationship between subjectivity and ideology mentioned by Kirby requires some elaboration. As Louis Althussser pointed out, "there is no ideology except by the subject and for subjects", and "all ideology has the function (which defines it) of 'constituting' concrete individuals as subjects".[13] Subjects meet, through their particular location in space and history, certain ideological formations, in which they situate themselves. A similar dynamic relation can be found between the subject writing his/her autobiography and pre-existing models of life stories. On the one hand, autobiographical writing happens from the unique point of view of an individual body, but on the other hand, this body is part of complex social and discursive networks, and the writing of the self entails the use of pre-existing socially constructed systems of language and narrative patterns, which are often ideologically charged. Gagnier argues that

> […] hegemony appears in autobiography in the form of master, or broad cultural, 'narratives' that determine how people see their lives. For example, such narratives include ideologies of gender […] that make women and men write their lives in terms of romance and financial success, whether or not their lives are conducive to such pursuits.[14]

Such broad cultural narratives are bound to include naturalised meanings of places, but the autobiographer uses existing narrative elements and concepts creatively to construct her/his subject position in and towards places.

I will close my preliminary considerations with a brief discussion of the relevance of metaphors, which, as Warf pointed out, "are a critical means by which we understand and appreciate the importance of space and spatiality in social life".[15] Since George Lakoff and Mark Johnson's *Metaphors We Live by* came out in 1980,[16] the important role of metaphor for cognition and thus for understanding cultures has been acknowledged. In the 2000s, and especially in his *Metaphor in Culture*, Zoltán Kövecses has elaborated on the concept of metaphor and argued that metaphor occurs primarily in thought and not only in language, and that we understand the world (culture) through metaphors.[17] Metaphors are based on embodied human experience and make understandable otherwise intangible entities such as inner life, mental processes, emotions, abstract qualities, moral values and social and political institutions. The conceptual metaphor LIFE IS A JOURNEY features strongly among Kövecses' examples and links metaphor with autobiography (LIFE) and place. The abstract category of LIFE can be understood through a variety of metaphors as, for example, LIFE IS A GAME, but LIFE IS A JOURNEY represents a fundamental metaphor widely shared in western cultures.[18] This metaphor connects the body, space and time. With regard to space, it involves conceptual correspondences ('mappings') between the locations along the way and the stages of a life, the motion along the way and the leading a life / the passage of time, or the destinations and the purposes in life.[19] Thus the cognitive theory of metaphor supports the assumptions that were expounded earlier with regard to the connectedness of life, bodily experience and physical space as well as the discursive construction of space. Furthermore, cognitive linguists' understanding of metaphor as an inherited form of thinking corresponds with Elizabeth Grubgeld's idea that "inherited forms of imagining a life give design to the autobiography".[20]

Within the theoretical framework outlined above, my analysis of the construction of post-Second-World-War Glasgow in autobiographical texts, will focus on

- the way in which different subjects, different autobiographical Is, locate themselves differently in the geographical and social spaces of working-class Glasgow,
- the multiplicity and diversity of stories constituting this from various subject positions
- and the – unsystematic and shifting – connections between class, social mobility, religion, education and space. Due to limitations of space, the impact of gender cannot be treated in detail and remains to be discussed in another paper.

Through my investigation of the autobiographies, I try to assess Mary Jo Maynes's finding that "class ambiguity is, in fact, typical of worker autobiographers".[21] Before I start my analysis, I will briefly outline my understanding of autobiography and describe my textual basis.

2. The Autobiographies

With Philippe Lejeune, I understand by autobiography a "retrospective prose narrative written by a real person concerning his own existence, where the focus is his individual life, in particular the story of his personality".[22] An autobiographical text can also be seen as a "narrative [that] is a prime means of cultural bonding which we use to integrate ourselves with our culture and also to make sense of what is going on around us".[23] Autobiographical texts are the results of constructive processes in which discursively established, conventional patterns of life stories are selected, realised and enriched from a subjective position. Existing cultural patterns and concepts are employed creatively to represent subjective experience. Harold Rosen has described the large number of different autobiographical acts, which range from family anecdote to multi-volume memoir,[24] but in this study, I will restrict my material mainly to book-length published autobiographies.

In my analyses, I will examine four autobiographies by persons born and raised in Glasgow in the early to mid-twentieth century with regard to their constructions of Glasgow. The earliest autobiography was written by Ralph Glasser (b. 1920). In the first part of his Gorbals trilogy, *Growing Up in the Gorbals* (1986), he recounts how he, the son of Jewish immigrants, grew up in one of the most infamous working-class areas of Glasgow. His mother died when he was still young; he became a worker and got involved in socialist politics. In parts II and III, *Gorbals Boy at Oxford* (1988) and *Gorbals Voices, Siren Songs* (1990), he covers the time from his winning an Oxford scholarship and cycling from the Gorbals to Oxford till the 1980s.[25] In Oxford, after extended inner struggles over his Jewish and working-class identity, he became a renowned sociologist.

Robert Douglas (b. 1939) grew up in Glasgow as an only child, suffering under an abusive father and enjoying close ties with his mother. After the death of his mother when he was fifteen, he was sent to an army camp. The story of his childhood, *Night Song of the Last Tram* (2005), was followed by a second volume, *Somewhere to Lay My Head* (2007), in which Douglas recounts the various jobs he held in various places in his adolescent years.[26]

Meg Henderson (b. 1948) is the daughter of Glaswegians of Irish descent; her father held various manual jobs, her mother was a housewife. In her childhood, she was enveloped by the love of her mother and her aunt, Peggy. Nevertheless, her whole family's life darkened when her beloved Aunt Peggy died in childbirth. After leaving school, Henderson trained as a nurse, worked abroad and later became a journalist and writer. She describes how, as an adult, she embarked on a search for the truth about her aunt's death and uncovered that it had occurred due to the disregard doctors showed for working-class women.[27]

Janey Godley (b. 1961) was born into what could be called a broken family in Shettleston, a working-class area in the East End of Glasgow. Her mother was unable to maintain the family and later killed by a lover, her father was a hard-working, educated man but was an alcoholic, and Godley herself was, over years in her childhood, sexually abused by an uncle. She married young into a family of criminals, ran a pub with her husband and finally achieved considerable fame as a comedian.[28] The central theme of her life story is 'survival' of abuse, thus her story reads in parts like a 'misery memoir'.[29]

All of these autobiographies start with early childhood memories but end somewhere between entering adolescence (Douglas's *Night*

Song) and mid-life (Henderson), therefore it seems appropriate to concentrate on childhood memories. They are all set in the various working-class districts of Glasgow – the Gorbals, Balmano Brae, Blackhill, Drumchapel, Maryhill and Shettleston.

3. *Subjective Glasgows*

Class and space

I will start my analysis with the question of how the autobiographers locate themselves in Glasgow, socially and spatially, and begin with Glasser's description of the Gorbals, the most infamous working-class district of Glasgow, in the interwar years. On the first pages of his life story, he already establishes the same landmark sites of working-class life that we find in the later working class autobiographies. He mentions places such as the decaying tenement buildings with their shared lavatories, the factories, the shops, pubs, pawn shops and 'steamies', that is, the public wash houses (19). Throughout his narrative, he blends his childhood memories with commentaries which express his authorial position as a social scientist. He starts his life story not with an introduction to his home and family but with descriptions of a friend's family leaving the Gorbals for the Soviet Union, with portraits of the Gorbals men and with observations on the political activities of the Jewish workers. He assigns a prominent place to the Workers' Circle, the social and political club for Jewish immigrants which burst with socialist and anarchist papers and books as well as heated political and philosophical debates. In the following passage, Glasser describes his early contact with the Workers' Circle, characteristically blending his memories with political reflection:

> Sometimes [...] Charlie and I wandered up the reverberating wooden staircase and stood staring in at the doorway, thumb in mouth. Perhaps, with a child's fresh insight, I understood, more profoundly than they did themselves, why those men congregated there: that they found consolation, a spiritual refuge, from the struggle with the day-to-day world, a place to recharge their dreams. (10)

Through the playful use of the child's perspective, he suggests that the conditions of Glasgow's working class resulted not only in crime and alcoholism but also in socialist ideas which served as an escape. This description of the Workers' Circle in the Gorbals does not only establish a history of working-class Glasgow that defies the dominant narrative of a slum for the lowest of the low, brimming with violence and destitution, although he acknowledges the existence of all of this. Rather, by immediately focussing on the political activities in the Gorbals, he constructs this working-class area as a centre of political radicalism and (Jewish) working-class activism. Through the eyes of his childhood self, he re-creates the Gorbals as the site of a multitude of different voices, of contradictions, hope, doubt and struggle, not once giving the impression of a unified working-class and ideology.

Meg Henderson's post-Second-World-War childhood is also presented as shaped by life in the working-class tenements, but her family moves around Glasgow. She describes her few memories of Balmano Street, the old tenement district where she was born, in terms of "old buildings", "winding, narrow covered lanes, or closes", "cramped dark houses with several generations of families living in them" and "aunts, uncles and cousins living all around" so that she "could safely walk into any house in the area, because if it didn't belong to family, it belonged to a friend" (16). When the house collapsed, the family was moved to the Blackhill council estate. Henderson fills in all kinds of information on the history and the reputation of the council estate. She relates, for example, that it started in an unattractive industrial area in 1933 and that residents were renowned for their violence and degradation, the common view of the residents of Blackhill being that they "were those with no choice, no hope and no power; they were simply deposited there and abandoned" (39). Nevertheless, Henderson sets her own family apart from the average population of Blackhill, claiming that her family were "lumped in" simply because they had no other place to go to after the collapse of their tenement, but did not belong (40), and observing that there were others like them. Due to her subject position as a leftist academic with a working-class background and to the attitudes and aspirations instilled in her by her mother, she is interested in breaking up the stereotypical image of the religiously segregated city, of homogeneously 'good' or 'bad' areas and of Blackhill as a slum of the Catholic poor. When she emphasises the social diversity that is denied, or repressed, by the notoriety of Blackhill, she is also defending her own mother's respectability. Her subject position enables her to reflect explicitly on the social meanings of the place, to question its dominant meanings and acknowledge its contradictions and fragmentation. This acknowledgement of fragmentation can also be read as an attempt to resist the essentialisation of the Catholic Irish diaspora in Glasgow.

Recent studies of place have highlighted that boundaries are capable of structuring space and life. The boundaries of the housing estate, Henderson observes, also represented social boundaries. She claims that the dominant classes tried to isolate Blackhill, through which ran neither trams nor busses, and that "[...] it was generally acknowledged by those outside that those inside were a bad lot and by keeping them together the better areas of the city would be that much safer" (41). She reports that middle-class society had the boundaries of Blackhill policed, literally:

> Indeed it wasn't unusual for children who ventured the few miles to the park in Alexandra Parade, in the respectable Riddrie/Dennistoun area, to be stopped by the police and questioned before being sent back 'tae fuck where ye belong'. (42)

The absence of public transport and the policing of the estate's boundaries are interpreted by Henderson as attempts to control and contain the unruly working classes by limiting the physical spatial mobility of its inhabitants. Furthermore, when Henderson describes how her mother became a campaigner and councillor for illiterate, or less literate, people, she delivers her own interpretation almost in Marxist terms: "I was witnessing the much-denied link between wealth – or the lack of it – and education", and she continues to declare that illiteracy "came with the territory of deprivation" (44). She constructs her years in Blackhill in terms of being caught and being stuck, of being metaphorically and physically contained, and she uses a Marxist-informed model to interpret the meaning of place in terms of class and power.

Her mother is very much described as a representative of a respectable, aspiring working class which has emulated middle-class values, "always chasing her dream" (12) of a better future for her children, which she pursues through her search for better housing. Their move to Drumchapel, a modern housing estate, in 1956 heralded to her a better life for her children and almost a "utopia" (101). Unfortunately, the new housing estate was riddled with all kinds of old and new social problems from the onset and failed to fulfil the family's hopes for a better life. Her family moved again in 1964, to Maryhill, where her mother was even more isolated. Not only does Henderson in her life story comment on all the different districts of Glasgow where her family stayed – she also explicitly constructs these parts of the city as coded in terms of class and religion and as stations on her mother's attempted journey towards social rise and a better future for her children.

All in all, Henderson depicts her own family in an unstable and uncertain position between the categories of Protestant and Catholic, and between working and lower middle class, which accounts for some of the family's restlessness. Her ability of reflection on the connection between place and class, her sensitivity to the social distinctions expressed in spatial arrangements and her awareness of the varied and changeable meanings of place distinguish her life writing from many other texts.

One such text which represents a childhood in the Glasgow tenements from a different subject position with considerably less reflection is Robert Douglas's *Night Song of the Last Tram*. Douglas was born nine years before Henderson, thus he lived through the war, but like Henderson, he spent his childhood in a Glasgow tenement district, which was, in his case, the old Maryhill. In his autobiography, there is no explicit mentioning of the class connotations of places, and the various family members are hardly situated with regard to their education and social status.

The landmarks in his childhood's Glasgow are the standard locations of mid-twentieth century Glasgow working-class life, recurring in almost all autobiographical accounts of the time.[30] The children's places for play are very much like those described by Henderson and Godley, the backyards complete with middens,[31] the street, a nearby stream, a friend's house. Locations such as the tenement, the close and the pawn shop are defining parts of the prototypical working-class tenement area. Their presence thus anchors Douglas in working-class life. Nevertheless, for Douglas, these places are not associated with the negotiations of location in a social hierarchy as they are for Henderson but rather with childhood adventures, his pals, his loving mother and his suffering under a neglectful, violent father. Only through occasional references to his father's jobs, the shortage of money or the absence of Christmas presents for his mother does he hint at his family's social location in the working class. His mother is portrayed as a respectable housewife, who, nevertheless, had to take her wedding ring to the pawn shop now and then when she fell short of money, but would then buy ice cream on their way home and defend her indulgence with a "Tae hell with poverty!" (252). Beyond this, Douglas pays little attention to social status although there are occasional references to class, as, for example when he writes that his mother had to take up a charring job "at some toff's house over in Hillhead" (256), which speaks of his (working-)class consciousness as well as his awareness of the class-related territorial divisions of Glasgow. At fifteen, he left school to start an apprenticeship as a messenger boy at the North British Locomotive Company in Springfield, another working-class district of Glasgow, where he strove to become, and was socialised to be, "[j]ust like aw the other Working Men" (289). With this Douglas emphasises that at the time, a working-class life was his natural choice and that of his 'pals'. The site of his socialisation was a prototypical engineering factory, where he experienced working-class solidarity, describing his response at the time with, "'Ah think ah'm gonny like being a working man'" (296).

The reasons why Douglas's life story lacks, compared with Glasser's and Henderson's, explicit references to class may not only be found in the authors' subjectivities but also in their different handling of the narrative instances. While in Glasser's and Henderson's texts the mature, academically trained writers constantly interfere in their childhood stories, interpreting and evaluating them with the adult's understanding of the world, Douglas tries to recreate the child's perspective with its limited insight, refraining most of the time from interspersing authorial comments and interpretations among his childhood stories. Although Douglas is a well-read and skilful writer, he does not bring anything like Henderson's academic analytical impetus to his life-writing. It is, nevertheless, telling that class awareness does show in some of his references to place such as the "toff's house", from which he sets himself apart while acknowledging his mother's inferior social position.

Spaces of religion

The divisions between Protestants and Catholics, and Irish Protestants and Catholics in particular, are remembered in all childhood stories, but again, there is no clear and uniform delineation of religious-territorial boundaries that is agreed on and shared by the different writers.

Glasser acknowledges that "echoes of Ireland were strong in Glasgow" and recounts how in the interwar years "the constant obsession with Catholic and Protestant feuding" occasionally erupted in battles between the two factions; as an illustration, he relates a childhood episode that marks his location as a Jewish boy at the time. When he and his friend are challenged by a gang of boys in a playground to declare whether they are "Billies" (Protestants) or "Dans" (Catholics), his friend asks, "Whit's a Billy? An whit's a Dan?", by his ignorance sparing them a beating (5). This anecdote places the Jewish boys outside the dominant Catholic-Protestant divide and outside the ongoing battle in and over territory. Glasser comments extensively on the religious divisions in Glasgow, but he does not perceive it as a segregated city. Rather, he finds Jews preferring mixed tenements for protective reasons, although he clearly states that where Jewish and Irish immigrants lived depended on their level of poverty. He also remembers relentless, though unorganised persecution by both Protestants and, if a little less frequently, Catholics, and deliberates about the reasons for the hostilities, which involved, at different levels of intensity, all religious groups (25-26). His own childhood was shaped by his pious Jewish father and the Jewish community but also by an early questioning of his father's beliefs. Glasser's Glasgow of the interwar years is a place vibrant with religious debate, conflict and activity, already an immigrant city and place of great diversity and exchange.

Douglas hardly ever mentions religious divisions; in his most prominent anecdote about Catholics, he describes an Irish Catholic neighbour who was good-natured and generous when drunk and was greatly admired for this. Henderson, in contrast, reflects very much about the social implications of religious affiliation in her childhood and establishes connections between place, class and religion, that is Blackhill, the lower working class and Catholicism:

> The people living in Blackhill [...] were drawn chiefly from manual labourers, which meant they were either Irish Catholics or of Irish descent, Irish being synonymous with Catholic to the Glasgow of the time. There had long been a strong anti-Catholic bias in Glasgow, and for many years Catholics were not allowed to be tradesmen. (39)

She concludes that even in the 1950s the tradesmen, who were still predominantly Protestant, earned more and had better homes than Catholics (40). Nevertheless, her parents and other couples in the extended family had entered mixed marriages so that the superficial impression of a unified Catholic neighbourhood is relativised immediately. The unfavourable portrait of Blackhill as well as her – Protestant – mother's 'horror' about being stigmatised as a Blackhill resident correspond with a previous section of Henderson's story in which she presents her mother's Protestant family as having a high regard for education and aspiring to a better life for their children (18). These aspirations, it turns out, were not shared by her Catholic father, who denied her an education in a middle-class secondary school (141). Throughout Henderson's life story, the mixing of Catholics and Protestants in her family appears to be the source of conflict and instability.

Godley expresses very worldly views on the Protestant-Catholic division of the city. She interprets her Uncle's joining the Orange Order as a sign of his wanting to belong and her own attendance of Sunday School as one of the few activities available to children on Sundays at the time. She observes that religion divided and defined communities in the city and reports ideologically driven football violence, but these divisions do little to structure her own life (31-32).

Class, space and education

Education is closely connected with spatial and social mobility. In this respect, Glasser designs his life story as the exemplary story of a scholarship boy. He excelled at school and his teachers considered him university material, but his father, given to gambling, could not keep him in school. At fourteen, Glasser found himself trapped between the love of reading and learning instilled by his Jewish environment, and his father's working-class pragmatism, which required that "[y]ou must have a trade in your hands" (35) because a trade lifted a man above the common labourer; so it was that he became a presser. At sixteen, Glasser started going to Extension Courses at the University, crossing over, spatially and mentally, to middle-class spheres. Later he won an Oxford scholarship through an essay competition, accepted it and cycled to Oxford to enter a "foreign culture" (142). The working-class environment of the Gorbals is shown to dampen as well as inspire intellectual aspirations, and the city offered educational opportunities to those seeking them with sufficient determination.

Henderson's story, set 30 years later, is not totally dissimilar to Glasser's. Like him, she encountered encouragement as well as obstacles on her path to education and sought higher education after working for several years, but while Glasser's schooling was provided in the Gorbals, her family's greater spatial mobility got her in touch with middle-class educational facilities after her family's move to Drumchapel. From there she was bussed through "leafy avenues" past big houses to a Catholic school in Glasgow's West End, "an oasis of happiness and contentment" (102). The West End is perceived as the site of desirable middle-class life, as peaceful, healthy, clean and cultured, as opposed to the dirty and violent streets of Blackhill and Drumchapel. Henderson's bus rides to the West End school stand for a temporary social movement which is inseparably tied to physical and geographical mobility.

A generation later, but in similar words, Godley describes how she "travelled from the decaying old tenements of the East End to the tree-lined streets of the West End" in search of a school for her daughter, hoping that by sending her to a private West End school she would be paving her way to a comfortable middle-class life (238-239). Spatial metaphors are almost unavoidable in writing about the issue of social mobility. The metaphorical meanings of the spatial layout of the area were not lost on Godley since she explains that the school was "a big terrace of Georgian mansions leading up to Glasgow University, as if that geographical path was a predestined choice for your own wee daughter" (238). Nevertheless, Godley seems to anticipate as well as dread her daughter's upward social mobility as she thinks:

> This is where my daughter will grow up; this is where she will meet poets and educated people and folk who don't swear loudly and come from broken homes; this is where she will mix with people who are not like me. (239)

These thoughts establish a fixed link between the place of Ashley's education and her future belonging to the middle classes. Godley wants her daughter to be socialised into a secure middle-class identity through the location of her school although, at the same time, she herself feels different and excluded from this location. To some extent, her social location resembles Henderson's, that is, both were rooted in working-class areas and in families whose members differed vastly with regard to their social aspirations, which made their own social position unstable. Both remained bound to the working class as long as they stayed with their families but later in their lives worked through childhood traumas and succeeded in achieving a middle-class life style. Tellingly, Godley's story of reclaiming her past, working through the trauma of sexual abuse and making an independent life for herself, ends with her driving "all the way out of the East End of Glasgow and into the West End" (325). A geographical move once again marks the escape from the ties of the family and the working-class.

Only Robert Douglas lets his teenage self enjoy entering a working man's life at fifteen, hoping to complete an apprenticeship, proud to be a wage earner although his father did not serve as a model for this. This youthful contentment with a working man's life can be understood as contentment with the appropriation of an essential part of working-class masculinity, which is being a bread winner. As a bread winner, he enjoys respect and a relatively secure social location. This secure location, nevertheless, does not last long, and after his mother's death, he ends up in a Boys' Camp of the RAF in Wolverhampton. Afterwards, he spends time in West Lothian, Birmingham, Durham and Northumberland, working as an electricity charge hand, doing his regular service at the RAF and ending up as a prison officer.[32] His occupational career is characterised by drastic changes of place that reflect the discontinuities in his life but also the fluidity of his social position. His career is built on training rather than education, and some of his youthful enjoyment of working and being a wage earner – being a man – seems to remain with him throughout his life.

Mobility

Another theme is the role of transportation. The physical effort of Glasser's bicycle ride from Glasgow to Oxford certainly embodies the tremendous mental, emotional and intellectual energies and stamina his move and adaptation to Oxford, that is, his crossing of class boundaries, required. In Henderson's autobiography, the absence of transportation is seen as a sign of the exclusion of the Blackhill residents from participation in the city's opportunities, which distinguished it from older tenement districts. Availability of public transport is seen as a precondition for social movement and development, as in the case of the West End school. Douglas did find tram stops near his home, became a great fan of trams and tram rides and does not anywhere construct his tenement district as an isolated, confining place. Nevertheless, mobility still signalled social passage because it was, naturally, a tram that took him to work on his first day as an apprentice, and at the end of his childhood/memories, a train takes him to the Boys' Service Camp near Wolverhampton. The prominent place of trams in his memories seems to anticipate the spatial and occupational mobility that characterises his later life, but with the exception of the 'toff' in Hillhead, he does not explicitly construct his environment in terms of class.

Outside the city, out of bounds

Public transportation also plays a role for another type of place that comes up in Glasser's, Henderson's, Douglas's, and Godley's childhood memories.[33] The autobiographers remember how, on a day's outing, they encounter 'the countryside' for the first time. For Glaswegians, one of the mythical places representing the countryside was Milngavie. Glasser describes Milngavie in the 1930s as the tram terminus from which hikers set out across wasteland for the Socialist Camp in Carbeth Muir.[34] The outings to this place are given complex social meaning in all accounts. Glasser writes enthusiastically that "the track across it [the wasteland] led *out* in every sense" and made the hikers "drunk with freedom",[35] renewed, with dreams soaring (97), but it is also a site of political discussions and lived solidarity.

Henderson follows very much in Glasser's footsteps as she recounts in her usual class-conscious style how she joined a youth group which was part of the working-class movement of the 1920s to get the unemployed and poor out into the country, re-claiming the outdoors that previously "had been the preserve of the gentry" (172). She considers joining "the Crowd" by the hills and the lochs at the weekends to have been an "escape route" (cf. Glasser's "*out*") from the weekend drinking of her father, but she was also attracted by "the silence of the loch", that is, nature as the opposite of the city, and by the Crowd as a 'natural' family substitute (174).

Douglas describes his first outing with a group of boys to "the legendary village of Mulguy" in terms of difference,[36] as a place without tenements, where the "stone-built buildings were all one-

and two-storey" and "[t]he air smelled different" (147-148). Douglas, wondering if it was a park, was told that it was "'[...] jist aw natural and open. [...] jist aw countryside'"(148). He marvels at the beauty of the bluebells but otherwise restricts himself to a description of the pleasures of a day out with his 'pals'.

The interpretation of the countryside as an escape from the social tensions, or simply the limitations (Douglas) connected with the city is clearly shared across generations although the association with working-class tradition seems to depend on class consciousness and is not generally part of this shared memory of place.

4. Conclusion

First, I would like to refer back to Maynes's statement about the class ambiguities in working-class autobiography. The general impression is that there is, indeed, very much ambiguity to be found in the way the autobiographers locate themselves and their families socially. These ambiguities appear in the diversity within the families portrayed, but also at the level of representation, where we find complex and contradictory constructions of the families and the places they inhabit. In these life stories, classes and religious groups are not as separate as, and mingle more than, could be expected, considering the commonly shared images of a socially segregated Glasgow and traditional working-class districts.

Place does play a crucial role in the conventional structures of life stories but the way it is constructed is shaped by both subjectivity and widely shared conventions of signification. What Grubgeld says about life narratives in general can also be applied to the construction of place and class consciousness: "With varying degrees of self-consciousness, autobiographers embed the particularities of experience within an inherited form of life narrative".[37] Although certain sites of working-class life such as the steamie and the pawn shop feature in all autobiographies, the extent to which the lives are constructed in terms of social class varies greatly, from Glasser's and Henderson's stark interpretations in the light of class divisions to the almost complete absence of explicit references to class in Douglas's text. While Maynes claims for working-class autobiographers of an earlier period that they were "uniformly and acutely aware of class as a meaningful category through which to interpret their life experiences",[38] I would argue that the social boundaries and meanings of places in the city have been changing all the time,[39] that the subject has been encountering changing ideological formations and that there has been neither a uniform class consciousness nor a consistent change of the interpretive patterns of life and place. Rather, geographical as well as social locations have been perceived and constructed in subjectively varying and often contradictory ways throughout. The – implicit or explicit – ambiguity of the social location of the autobiographers leads to instability, fluctuation and mobility, which also find their spatial expression in all texts considered. A discussion of the space of the body and an investigation of gender issues have been prevented by the limited scope of the paper.

When we as scholars try to understand the meanings of a place, struggling to get to its implicit, shared meanings, we often get stuck with the dominant meanings and fail to account for subjectivity. Autobiography reminds us that the construction of meanings – in this case, of places – is by no means uniform and consensual. A city like Glasgow can only be understood in fragments, and through a multitude of stories.

Notes

1 Massey (2005: 9).
2 For a recent theoretical discussion of the urban space in literature, see Gilbert (2009).
3 For recent theory on space, see Philo & Söderström (2004: 12).
4 Massey (2005: 9-11).
5 Holloway & Hubbard (2001: 115).
6 Warf (2009: 74).
7 Gagnier (1991: 4).
8 *Ibid.* 8.
9 *Ibid.* See also Haraway (1997: 63).
10 Kirby (1996: 10-13).
11 *Ibid.* 10-12.
12 Johnson (1996: 91).
13 Althusser (2006: 343).
14 Gagnier (1991: 6).
15 Warf (2009: 59).

16 Lakoff & Johnson (1980).
17 Kövecses (2002), (2005: 1-2, 163).
18 Kövecses (2005: 124).
19 *Ibid.* 123.
20 Grubgeld (2004: 1); see also Gagnier (1991: 6).
21 Maynes (1995: 4).
22 Philippe Lejeune [1971] quoted in Eakin (1999: 2). At that time, Lejeune still uses the male form as a generic term, but since the early twentieth century and especially the 1980s, the number of autobiographies written by women has grown continuously and cannot be ignored.
23 John Sturrock writes about psychologist Jerome Bruner's theory of autobiography in his *The Language of Autobiography. Studies in the First Person Singular* (1993: 292).
24 Harold Rosen presents a systematic overview of written and oral autobiographical acts in his *Speaking from Memory. A Guide to Autobiographical Acts and Practices* (1998: 19-61).
25 Ralph Glasser: *The Ralph Glasser Omnibus. Growing Up in the Gorbals* [1986], *Gorbals Boy at Oxford* [1988], *Gorbals Voices, Siren Songs* [1990] (2006), references to this edition will be included in the text.
26 Robert Douglas: *Night Song of the Last Tram. A Glasgow Memoir* (2005); *Somewhere to Lay My Head* (2006), references to these editions will be included in the text.
27 Meg Henderson: *Finding Peggy. A Glasgow Childhood* (1994), references to this edition will be included in the text.
28 Janey Godley first became a celebrated comedian in her native Glasgow but went on to perform successfully in all of Britain and in the USA. Several sketches can be viewed on YouTube, and in some as, for example, "My Mammy", she recreates childhood episodes.
29 Janey Godley: *Handstands in the Dark. A True Story of Growing Up and Survival* (2005), references to this edition will be included in the text. The expression 'misery memoir' was coined in the 2000s, when – sometimes forged – autobiographical, stories about abuse flooded the U.S. and British book markets. For a pointed characterisation of misery memoirs, see Crace (2008).
30 These places do not only feature in Henderson's narrative but also, for example, in Faley (1990), Clark & Carnegie (2003) and Stewart (2009).
31 Middens are dustbins and the places where dustbins are kept. Cf. *Shorter Oxford English Dictionary* (2007).
32 Douglas (2006).
33 Godley's most memorable outing takes her with her mother to Saltcoats, Glasgow's seaside resort.
34 More information on the history of the youth camp in Carbeth, ten miles north of Glasgow, can be found in Mitchell (2001: 80-82).
35 Emphasis in the text.
36 Mulguy is a simplified spelling of Milngavie, a village north of Glasgow that became a suburb.

37 Grubgeld (2004: 1).
38 Maynes (1995: 29).
39 Drumchapel, the modern housing estate symbolising utopia to Henderson's mother, is now one of the worst areas of Glasgow for poverty and violence. The Gorbals have gone through waves of redevelopment and attempts at gentrification.

Bibliography

Althusser, Louis: "Ideology and Ideological State Apparatuses". – In John Storey (Ed.): *Cultural Theory and Popular Culture. A Reader*, third edition, Harlow, 2006 [1971], pp. 336-346.
Bidinger, Elizabeth: *The Ethics of Working Class Autobiography*. Jefferson, NC, 2006.
Clark, Helen & Elizabeth Carnegie: *She Was Aye Workin'. Memories of Tenement Women in Edinburgh and Glasgow*, Oxford, 2003.
Crace, John: "How to write a misery memoir", *The Guardian*, 6 March 2008, 10-11.
Douglas, Robert: *Night Song of the Last Tram*, London, 2005.
---: *Somewhere to Lay My Head*, London, 2006.
Eakin, Paul John: *How Our Lives Become Stories*. Ithaca, NY, 1999.
Faley, Jean: *Up Oor Close. Memories of Domestic Life in Glasgow Tenements, 1910-1945,* Glasgow, 1990.
Gagnier, Regenia: *Subjectivities. A History of Self-Representation in Britain, 1832-1920*, New York, 1991.
Gilbert, Pamela K.: "Sex and the modern city. English studies and the Spatial Turn". – In Barney Warf & Santa Arias (Eds.): *The Spatial Turn. Interdisciplinary Perspectives*, London, 2009, pp. 102-121.
Glasser, Ralph: *The Ralph Glasser Omnibus. Growing up in the Gorbals* [1986], *Gorbals Boy at Oxford* [1988], *Gorbals Voices, Siren Songs* [1990], Edinburgh, 2006.
Godley, Janey: *Handstands in the Dark. A True Story of Growing Up and Survival*, London, 2005.
---: "My Mammy", http://www.youtube.com/watch?v=AWlzFoxyDq8 [9 February 2007], 22 September 2001.

Grubgeld, Elizabeth: *Anglo-Irish Autobiography. Class, Gender, and the Forms of Narrative.* Syracuse, NY, 2004.

Haraway, Donna: "Situated Knowledges. The Science Question in Feminism and the Privilege of Partial Perspective". – In Linda McDowell (Ed.): *Place, Gender, Knowledge*, London, 1997, pp. 53-72.

Henderson, Meg: *Finding Peggy. A Glasgow Childhood,* London, 1994.

Holloway, Lewis & Phil Hubbard: *People and Places. The Extraordinary Geographies of Everyday Life*, Harlow, 2001.

Johnson, Richard: "What is Cultural Studies anyway?". – In John Storey (Ed.): *What Is Cultural Studies? A Reader,* London, 1996, pp. 75-114.

Kirby, Kathleen M.: *Indifferent Boundaries. Spatial Concepts of Human Subjectivity*, New York, 1996.

Kövecses, Zoltán: *Metaphor. A Practical Introduction,* Oxford, 2002.

---: *Metaphor in Culture. Universality and Variation*, Cambridge, 2005.

Lakoff, George & Mark Johnson: *Metaphors We Live by*, Chicago, 1980.

Massey, Doreen: *For Space*, London, 2005.

Maynes, Mary Jo: *Taking the Hard Road. Life Course in French and German Workers' Autobiographies in the Era of Industrialization*, Chapel Hill, NC, 1995.

Mitchell, Ian R.: *Walking through Scotland's History*, Edinburgh, 2001.

Philo, Chris & Ola Söderström: "Social Geography. Looking for Society in its Spaces". – In Georges Benko & Ulf Strohmayer (Eds.): *Human Geography. A History for the 21st Century.* London, 2004, pp. 105-138.

Rosen, Harold: *Speaking from Memory. A Guide to Autobiographical Acts and Practices*, Stoke on Trent, 1998.

Shorter Oxford English Dictionary, sixth edition, Oxford, 2007.

Stewart, Mae: *Dae Yeh Mind Thon Time? Tales from the Dundee Tenements*, Edinburgh, 2009.

Sturrock, John: *The Language of Autobiography. Studies in the First Person Singular,* Cambridge, 1993.

Warf, Barney: "From Surfaces to Networks". – In B. W. & Santa Arias (Eds.): *The Spatial Turn. Interdisciplinary Perspectives*. London, 2009, pp. 59-87.

Christiane Bimberg (Dortmund)

Urban Space, City Life and Identity Construction in Virginia Woolf's *Night and Day*. The Fusion of Material and Mental Landscapes

1. Introduction

Virginia Woolf's novel is set in London in the heady days of Women's Suffrage – the story time comprises the months between October 1910 and spring 1911. Important issues addressed are the values of the past, its function for the present, the correlation of tradition and innovation, classical vs. modern literature, and the emergence of a broader, non-canonical definition of culture.

The spatial grounding of identity is particularly prominent in the novel. The interpersonal relationships between Katharine Hilbery, William Rodney, Mary Dachet, Ralph Denham, and Cassandra Otway keep shifting almost until the end of the novel. The drama of their initially unacknowledged or wrongly assessed emotions unfolds against the background of places carefully selected and narratively (re-)constructed by Woolf. Place and space in Woolf become markers of identity. Place is semanticised, becomes space, a bearer of meaning. It can therefore be read in semiotic terms. Particularly Mikhail Bakhtin's term of the chronotope is very relevant here: a concept which describes the interaction of time and space in the literary representation of human experience. In Woolf's case, urban spaces and city life are closely bound up with the concept of identity.

All in all, the novel refers to more than fifty locations in the metropolis (London), its suburbs and vicinity, other cities such as Manchester, and the countryside. The largest part of the action is set in London whose characteristics are made more evident through the juxtaposition with London's vicinity, with Manchester, with the countryside and rural ways of life – representations which are beyond the scope of the present essay. The special intersection of place, character and identity through the instrumentalisation of single locations, buildings, and rooms in London for the construction of urban space is the topic of another essay.[1] The main emphasis in this essay is thus on London city life at large, the distinctive features of cityscape and urban space as factors of identity construction.

Subsequently the phenomenon of the city is explored from various perspectives which consider psychological-archetypal aspects (psychology of characters, psychic effects of life in the city, urban imagery, the city as symbol), thematic and formal-aesthetic aspects (urban vision, urban spectatorship, interaction between city experience and literary mode), and historical, social/sociological and topographical aspects (urban landscape, the city in its socio-historical contexts, interaction between character and urban milieu, the dynamics of social relations). The essay fuses methods of literary and cultural studies. Among the critical approaches employed here that of Cultural Geography is particularly meaningful – a scholarly discipline studying the connotations of places in their connection to discourses and social relations.

2. *Urban Space, City Life and Identity Construction. Light, Movement, Rhythm, Patterns of Human Life*

The centre of attention in the novel is London. Woolf re-creates the London of her time through several images, metaphors and symbols. In the consciousness of Mary Datchet for instance, who came to London from the countryside to serve as an unpaid volunteer in the Suffrage Office, it is a huge ganglion, a centre of human activity, in which many life nerves run together or get entangled, and which unites and directs masses of people in a common endeavour. She is thrilled to be at the centre of everything important for mankind, the British Empire.[2]

In addition, London is fashioned as an international spot of attraction, tourism, and cultural facilities. The impression of luxury and modern urbanity derives precisely from the availability of electric light, because in the darkness the luxury would rarely be visible. For Mary, London's electricity symbolises its political importance and mass appeal (52). Electric light, candle light and moonlight are carefully set off against each other for social, geographical and emotional differentiation: *Un*shaded electric light is an indicator of poverty in private homes, but signifies activity, business and professionalism in office surroundings. Although Cheyne Walk / Chelsea, home of the Hilberys, one of the most distinguished families in England, is fully electrified, candle light still gives a special atmosphere to meals and other social occasions and acts as a mark of refinedness. The lamplit streets accompany most of the walks and drives of Ralph Denham and Katharine Hilbery as atmospheric factors. Moonlight in the city offers the delusion of being in the countryside instead – a romantic gesture. The look of London, its visuality, is significant: Ralph, Mary, and Katharine, in spite of their diverse social backgrounds, all enjoy the view, the skyline, the sky and the river, the contrast between light and darkness, and feel closely connected to the city. The contrast between light and darkness in London is telling. People seek or evade light for reasons of mood. Woolf's descriptions of London as a city of light agree with Raymond William's social observations: From the beginning of the nineteenth century, gas-lighting had been used for utility, but also for effect and display. At the end of the century, London was lighted even at night. Light was the obvious image for the civilisation of the capital, which, in spite of the social contrast between West End and East End as expressed in terms of light and darkness, supported the traditional idea of the city as a centre of light and learning, but now on an unprecedented scale.[3] Joseph Conrad had already exploited the contrast between darkness and light as a symbol of the antagonism between appearance and reality: darkness acquires an atmospheric and symbolic meaning suggesting the loss of all values and of the reason for existence; obscurity, uncertainty, and moral evil; the negation of cognition and of the possibility of a new life.[4]

Furthermore, the traditional and current means of transport make London a place with a highly convenient infrastructure. All London-based characters use the available means of transport with casualness and contentment. Transport becomes an expression of a modern urban lifestyle and the easy and quick (outward) communication connected with it. Different means of transport have different effects on people; the correlation between distance, time, speed, thinking and mood or atmosphere is essential here. Additionally, the means of transport are instrumentalised for identity construction; they express the protagonists' personality and function as extensions of their drives and desires. The ones instrumentalised most sophisticatedly are walking, the taxicab and the motor omnibus.

Walking is still common for most of the characters. The speed affects them physically (dizziness and trance, 99; depression, hypnotisation and despondency, 287). A change of speed indicates a change of mood or thoughts. At times the movement of walking is preferred for reasons of mood or noise, or a direction is chosen because of its agreement with the mood of the characters. Walking allows for leisurely thinking, for decision-making which is the result of meandering movements, of accompanying processes of searching and coming to terms with oneself (cf. below on movement and ideas).

The subjective sense of speed felt by cab passengers implies heterogeneous connotations: convenience and efficiency for Mrs Hilbery, but stage-like unreality, extraordinariness, and too much speed for Cassandra Otway, the newcomer to the capital, to digest the fast fleeting impressions. She suffers from overstimulation, a well-known motif in city novels often symbolising disorientation and a lack of security due to the city's immensity.[5] Interestingly enough Mary, also originally from the country, does not suffer from that symptom but enjoys the advantages of the immensity of the city, the unlimited possibilities for individual development. For Katharine, the cab connotes efficiency and reality. She appreciates the movement, its speed and determination, enjoys the lamplit streets and being out of doors alone (Mary enjoys the same things during a walk). The cab is the means of transport congenially expressing her self-concept as a modern female urban citizen. It allows her to easily adopt a quicker speed in life, agreeing with her mood. She feels physically and spiritually *transported.* Her decisions to walk or take a cab depend on time, circumstance, aims, and mood. A quick change suits her and agrees with her dynamic character and flexibility.

Katharine and Ralph's walk, and later ride on a motor omnibus, make the mood factor fully evident. The first part of their movement when they leave the hall of Cheyne Walk is a walk through the streets of London, symbolising their departure from the secure, but also oppressing bourgeois home (533). In the street, they both instinctively pick the one means of transport which agrees with their desire for quicker movement, more liberty and stronger progress in their thinking (534). Stopping by Temple Bar, Katharine becomes conscious

> […] that the splendid race of lights drawn past her eyes by the superb curving and swerving of the monster on which she sat was at an end. They had followed some such course in their thoughts too; they had been borne on, victors in the forefront of some triumphal car, spectators of a pageant enacted for them, masters of life. (534)

The change of movement, their descent from a lofty position (omnibus) to one down to earth (walk) is accompanied by a change of mood: "But standing on the pavement alone, this exaltation left them; they were glad to be alone together." (534) Another change of mood is brought about during their conversation, enhanced through the movement of the bus back to Chelsea, which leads them to discuss their splendid future (539). In other words, utmost personal freedom is felt on an omnibus. It allows for visions because of the higher and broader perspective it commands and due to greater speed, bigger distances covered, larger space appropriated. It is there that Katharine enjoys freedom, individuality, self-confidence, mastery of life and female agency. She feels physically and spiritually *elevated* because of the lights, the speed, the breeze of air (100).[6] Mary's sense of omnibuses is more radical. On the one hand, she also embraces the idea of personal freedom associated with it, thinking to celebrate her personal freedom, her independence from the tyranny of love on the top of an omnibus bound for some remote place (479). On the other she is more aware of the fatal dangers of speed after she has understood that she cannot marry Ralph (276). The omnibus is associated with life-affirming or life-denying qualities, depending on her mood.

The tube is mostly used by Ralph and Katharine (though their social backgrounds are contrasting) or mentioned in connection with them (e.g. as a place of shelter for lovers on rainy days). Mary appreciates its availability, high speed and efficiency, which suit her character as a young professional though she is aware of the potential dangers of sexual harassment as well (276).

The movements and noises of the traffic and the city give life there a peculiar touch. Each character is thus characteristically surrounded by his/her individual urban microcosm of sights, sounds and noises. This is especially true for the urban rambler Ralph, the person in closest contact with the streets. But the city also reflects his emotions and sensitivities, so that a correlation between city atmosphere and human psyche is established (419). The noise of typewriters in the offices at Russell Square stands for modern business efficiency.[7] By contrast, Cheyne Walk is a place of dignified stillness in which the noises of the city only arrive in a subdued form as if to suggest the calm but firm maintenance of Victorian values as a bulwark against the outward modern turmoil in the city close by. Here no typewriter is heard – a suggestion of tradition, but also of lacking professionalism. The only important noise is the one of pleasant food, talk, conversation and entertainment over meals. Its agreeableness is a measure of social success. Moments of stillness in the city at night – so familiar in the countryside – strike the protagonists as special.

The climactically organised narrative makes the means of transport, the passengers and their movements, the speed and the noises constitute the pace and rhythm of modern city life. In the movements of the traffic, certain underlying 'patterns of human life' become visible. As in a kaleidoscope, chaos suddenly falls into order. The metropolis is like a huge living entity which offers the characters numerous occasions for perceiving others and themselves as part of larger patterns of life through the visual images of the traffic. They fascinate the observer because they allow him/her the experience of feeling a part of, or being set apart from the crowd and thus make him/her aware of two contrary universal human desires – that to belong and that to be special at the same time – and thus the tensions between the collective and the individual mode of existence.

Mary takes some pride in her work identity; she embraces the parallel of her professional existence to that of the working (office) masses which reveals itself to her in the movement on the pavement:

> Out in the street she liked to think herself one of the workers who, at this hour, take their way in rapid single file along all the broad pavements of the city, with their heads slightly lowered, as if all their effort were to follow each other as closely as might be; so that Mary used to figure to herself a straight rabbit-run worn by their unswerving feet upon the pavement. But she liked to pretend that she was undistinguishable from the rest, and that when a wet day drove her to

> the Underground or omnibus, she gave and took her share of crowd and wet with clerks and typists and commercial men, and shared with them the serious business of winding-up the world to tick for another four-and-twenty hours. (82)

The quote betrays Mary's enjoyment both of the individuality and of the anonymity of her existence in the city, her desire to blend and become one with the masses in the service for the common or some greater good. It signifies her pride in her professional efficiency, the significance work holds for her identity and self-esteem, and the economic power of the labour force at large.

The same idea of a pattern of life – an important personal identity enfolding in the city, at the centre of events – is visualised a second time through the image of the pavement. The quote accentuates the share of women in important activities, their pride in the newly conquered professional domain and public sphere: When Mary has finished her lunch with another young woman, Eleanor, they part "on the strip of pavement among the different lines of traffic with a pleasant feeling that they were stepping once more into their separate places in the great and eternally moving pattern of human life" (86). The sense of personal achievement is at times so strong in Mary that she considers herself able to reverse the process, i.e. not just to discern but to be capable herself of influencing movements, causing or steering them physically, subjecting them to a pattern of her own making and thus manipulating people's lives: After the end of a committee meeting where Mary proves herself to be especially efficient she literally and figuratively looks down on the people from the height of her office window. Again the pavement is significant:

> The street lamps were already lit; and through the mist in the square one could see little figures hurrying across the road and along the pavement, on the farther side. In her absurd mood of lustful arrogance, Mary looked at the little figures and thought, 'If I liked I could make you go in there or stop short; I could make you walk in single file or in double file; I could do what I liked with you.' (179)

This hilarious instance of an overestimation of one's own abilities (cf. the above quote from p. 82) contradicts her realistic awareness that her services "could hardly be said to wind the world up for its daily task" (82). But the vision of ordering people in a file, arranging them in a pattern in the street expresses her newly felt enjoyment of power during the meeting (178).

Contrasting scenes relating to patterns of traffic and life stress the feelings of being different or set apart from the masses (Mrs Seal at the time of the betrayal of the women's cause in Parliament, feeling her difference from the ignorant masses, 272) or of lacking or having lost the motivation of the masses (Mary at the same time, after her decision not to marry Ralph, not uncritically embracing the ideals of the Suffrage any longer, feeling like an impostor hiding among the masses, 276-277).

Katharine's perceptions of patterns are both similar and different. The streets provide her with a source of physical and psychological strength that never fails to refresh her in moments of doubt or uneasiness. With all her individuality (at times even eccentricity) the sharing of crowded streets exhilarates her to the point that she almost forgets about her companion Ralph (99). The two contrary feelings of being part of the crowd and aware of one's distance and difference are likewise known to her: When she is walking from Bond Street to the Temple, her personal situation gets interwoven with the physical impression she receives from the pedestrians passing by. Her thoughts run from the concrete and personal to the abstract and back again, starting with a reflection on Rodney's good qualities:

> And she thought of them and looked at the faces passing, and thought how much alike they were, and how distant, nobody feeling anything as she felt nothing, and distance, she thought, lay inevitably between the closest, and their intimacy was the worst pretence of all. […] 'I don't care for any of them, and I don't care for William, […]'. (287-288)

The pattern of traffic or crowds at times also indicates the danger of lacking or lost identity or individuality, of being dissolved in the masses, extinguished. Katharine has this impression when she waits for Ralph near his office and is afraid of overlooking him in the masses of men leaving for home (468). When she turns into the main road, the pattern of traffic changes, suggesting that the normality and purpose of the masses should not be questioned, with no trace left of the fear of being extinguished among them. Yet the phrasing suggests Katharine's stance as an observer – standing close by but also aloof. The question of whether she will ever be able to feel what the masses / other people feel is left undecided, but it becomes obvious that the movements of the traffic or the crowds are "a torrent of life" (99) for her, both fascinating and frightening and signifying social variety as well as multiple modes of existence:

> The great torrent of vans and carts was sweeping down Kingsway; pedestrians were streaming in two currents along the pavements. She stood fascinated at the corner. The deep roar filled her ears; the changing tumult had the inexpressible fascination of varied life pouring ceaselessly with a purpose which, as she looked, seemed to her, somehow, the normal purpose for which life was framed; its complete indifference to the individuals, whom it swallowed up and rolled onwards, filled her with at least a temporary exaltation. The blend of daylight and of lamplight made her an invisible spectator, just as it gave the people who passed her a semi-transparent quality, and left the faces pale ivory ovals in which the eyes alone were dark. They tended the enormous rush of the current – the great flow, the deep stream, the unquenchable tide. She stood unobserved and absorbed, glorying openly in the rapture that had run subterraneously all day. (468-469)

Elsewhere Katharine and Mary perceive "the diversity of human interests" (385) in the traffic pattern of omnibuses and passers-by at the main thoroughfare close to Mary's flat. It cannot be overlooked, however, that while Mary's perceptions are more pragmatic and work-oriented, Katharine's are more philosophical: The view over London at night out of her bedroom window reveals to her the texture of her life; the hum of traffic represents the complicated relationship of the sexes at large. She recognises that unlike other people's lives, her own is determined by family, tradition, and class. Ideally she wishes for some empty space or land without any such human intercourse to carve out her own space of identity, but at the same time she realistically senses that she does not live in a social vacuum (112-113). Furthermore, much more than for Mary, the search for such a pattern of life beneath a pattern of traffic is essential for Katharine. Her belief in "a spiritual light burning steadily and steadfastly behind the erratic disorder and incoherence of life" (401) has only been temporarily dimmed during tea in Highgate. The 'pattern of life' represents to her some secret order, truth or hidden motif that can and must be discovered in a life (a recurring topic in Woolf's fiction). The search for it is an important part of her personal identity. This is illustrated through two scenes: In Mary's room, when both confess their mutual envy of each other's lifestyles, Katharine openly addresses her search. She doubts the existence of affection which, to Mary, is the only reality in fact:

> "It came over me in the Tube the other day," [...] "what is it that makes these people go one way rather than the other? It's not love; it's not reason; I think it must be some idea. Perhaps, Mary, our affections are the shadow of an idea. Perhaps there isn't any such thing as affection in itself ..." (291)

In the second scene, Katharine walks to Cromwell Road. Her persistent search for personal truth in questions of love and marriage, in which family tradition does not provide her with an answer, is likened to the course of a beam of light through darkness. To passers-by, her determined eccentric appearance sticking out from the crowds evokes parallels with the suffragettes, with politically motivated anarchism, but her beauty saves her from being laughed at (334). This notion parallels the way in which women on the city streets were traditionally assigned the roles of sexual victim, temptress, or illicit partner in nineteenth-century literature.[8] Reflecting on the complexity of the feeling of love, its different meanings for different people, Katharine compares the confusion of her and her friends' lives to a variously intersected pattern of streets which her own searching and illuminating beam is cutting across. She traces the lines of a symmetrical pattern, some arrangement of life, which invests her friends with a kind of tragic beauty. The lights radiating from her friends are scattered among the crowd and weave a shifting pattern, dissolving and joining (335-336).

Ralph has his own perceptions of patterns. He does not see Katharine in danger of being dissolved in the masses (even though her taxicab might be indistinguishable), but as a strong individual. He grasps this through her movement towards him in the Strand, among the people, when she sticks out because of her height and the distinction of her dress. A moment later the pattern changes. Ralph's observation illustrates the kaleidoscope effect mentioned above: "But immediately the whole scene in the Strand wore that curious look of order and purpose which is imparted to the most heterogeneous things when music sounds; [...]" (138-139). By contrast Ralph's occasional inability to make out a pattern signifies feelings of indetermination, the lack of purpose, control, and mastery of life, being lost among the crowds. These occur in moments of despair, for instance about Katharine's engagement to Rodney, when Ralph walks along the river embankment after tea in Cheyne Walk (166-167). Additionally the passage likens the real and the imaginary world or life to a pattern of streets – of contrasting qualities. For Ralph, the substantial world used to be the imaginary world of his dreams and desires. It is more important than the real one, has prospects of avenues leading on to the invisible distance, i.e. allows for development unlimited by a horizon. Ralph believed he shared it with Katharine, but with its supposed loss, his life is impoverished. By contrast, the real, visible life with its straight and meagre path, i.e. its limited possibilities, holds no attraction for him (167-168). Another instance of his incapability of discerning a pattern is linked to his emotional indecision about marrying or leaving Mary when he looks out of the inn window at Lincoln (245-246).

3. Movement and Ideas. The Fusion of Material and Mental Landscapes

As has become obvious from the above, the cityscape is inscribed in the narrative in its physical shape, through sights, colours, sounds, and smells. On the material map of London, the reader can trace the characters' movements as if they were moves in a chess game. He gets a clear impression of the physical urban space covered and explored by the protagonists, the speed of the movements, the time needed to cross the distances between the various locations in the coordinate system of the capital. They do not seem far off from each other, so that the characters can, at least physically, communicate with each other easily – thanks also to the various means of transport. In their temporary frustration and despair, the protagonists at times conduct wild movements between various places. Especially Mary is sought after by Ralph or Katharine in moments of distress or searching. The strategically convenient position of her private place off the Strand facilitates such impulses. The walks and drives appear as crisscross movements over the material map of London. They connect places and people physically, but actually body and mind are irretrievably interlinked in the processes. The passage relating to Ralph and Katharine's ride on the omnibus tellingly illustrates the nexus between movement and ideas or material and mental movement through the correlation of the course of the *drive* and the course of *thoughts* (534, cf. above). The description of Katharine feeling herself "possessed of two bodies" (321) – walking by the river with Denham, at the same time reflecting on her true interests in life – fittingly expresses the same nexus. The movements are invested with contrasting connotations such as arbitrariness / lack of systematicity / creativity (Mrs Hilbery 42-43, 521-522) or monotony/professionality (Mary and her father 82-83, 173, 190, 197). But above all, physical movements pave the way for important ideas – insights or decisions long overdue. The change of place or physical progress occasions mental movement, changes in the walker's or passenger's consciousness. The movements mark transitions from one state of mind to another, towards a changed or new attitude. The walks are particularly apt to have this kind of effect because the speed of walking seems congenial to the movement of the mind. In addition, in the case of two people walking together or just side by side at night through lamplit streets, there is an atmosphere of intimacy and intensity.

Many examples illustrate this importance of walking the streets of London (and also paths in the countryside). The most important insights and decisions of the protagonists happen during walks (Ralph's into the variety of modes of existence in the city, the relativity of his own experience, his feelings for Katharine; Mary's into her position towards Ralph; Ralph's about his plans for life in a cottage; Mary's into the conception of her life; Katherine's into her feelings for Ralph). Katharine's question as to whether Ralph will go on dreaming and imagining and making up stories about her as he walks along the street (408) demonstrates the narrative significance of the streets of London as a space of irrationality – of dreams, imagination, illusions, emotions, desires, wild searches. The streets have to be walked (as the meals have to be cooked in *A Room of One's Own*) for people to find out about their unacknowledged or repressed emotions, the subconscious, as Mary's interior monologue illustrates: "all these different states of mind were submerged in the deep flood of desires, thoughts, perceptions, antagonisms, which washed perpetually at the base of her being, to rise into prominence in turn when the conditions of the upper world were favourable." (182) At the end of the novel, Katharine and Ralph leave the prosperity, respectability and security of Cheyne Walk to walk the streets of London and enjoy the movement and the open air (533).

Walking the streets is thus an integral part of the protagonists' modern urbanity and almost a mode of existence of its own, suiting the insecurity and disunity of the characters. Mary even discovers the positive effects of walking without an exact destination. She describes them comparatively, applying as it were Reader-Response Theory to traffic and music:

> Strange thoughts are bred in passing through crowded streets should the passenger, by chance, have no exact destination in front of him, much as the mind shapes all kinds of forms, solutions, images when listening inattentively to music. (277)

By contrast, lapses of attention, walking about aimlessly, dreamy states of absent-mindedness or unconsciousness (Katharine 62-63, 150, 262, 304, 355, 463-464, 475, 477-478, 504, 518; Mary 87; Ralph 169) connote a precarious state of mind in Woolf, the exhibition of an unseemly emotion. It is an improper state of mind, particularly for women in the eyes of men, especially of those who care about tradition or proper conduct. This 'masculine carelessness' of attitude in women makes men feel disconcerted and impotent (262, 304).

It becomes obvious that not only place affects people, but the movements between places have an impact on the characters' thinking. The vistas that the movements offer determine what a person thinks. Following Woolf's logic about material and mental movement one could say: Be careful where you walk – it might lead you to an unexpected revelation, a sudden understanding, a significant decision. Terms like 'crossroad', 'turning-point', 'crossing', 'intersection', and 'drive' and phrases like '*train* of thought', '*track* of thought', 'to feel *transported*' or '*rambling* over an infinite variety of thoughts' are highly significant in this context because they denote movement or places of transition physically, but acquire a new figurative meaning of mental transitions as well. The big streets of London can therefore full well be called "great knots of activity" (534) – not only in the literal sense of inner city transport. Traffic is a catalyst for insights in the novel. Places and movements determine ideas. What you think and when is a matter of place and time. This is also a typical principle of narrative composition in *A Room of One's Own.*[9] Behind the seeming arbitrariness of realistic occurrence or coincidence, a careful and sophisticated narrative strategy emerges which contrasts strikingly with Mrs Hilbery's perambulating method from which no productive outcome is gained.

Examples like these illustrate the connection between movement and ideas. The reader can follow the characters' thoughts together with their moves. Because of the nexus of material and mental movement, the material landscape of the city that the characters traverse is transformed into a mental landscape in the minds of both the protagonists and the reader. Material and mental landscapes become fused and interlocked, which testifies to the impact of urban space and city life on the characters' consciousness and identity.

Taking this idea to its furthest consequence, Woolf constructs various mental landscapes or 'imaginary' or 'visionary' scenes. Their principles of construction vary and so do their connotations:

- Behind a current material cityscape or landscape, its former state is recalled and visualised, suggesting socio-historical changes.
- The current material landscape may be perceived as a backcloth for present life events.
- A character surrealistically sees another imaginary cityscape or landscape behind the material one or imagines being in a different place (a double vision of two places) and attempts to establish a communication between places across space.
- Characters think and act and communicate with each other at present amid material surroundings from the past which are thus alienated from their original context but keep on affecting them. Thus a communication between the past and the present is established between various generations. The "waft over the surface of the years" (21; here, the phrase relates to Mrs Hilbery only) establishes an incongruous simultaneity: Katharine, constantly moving in Cheyne Walk amid the relics of her dead relatives, responds to the past fortunes of her ancestors from the present perspective and thus re-appropriates the past for herself (cf. Reader-Response Theory). Vice versa surrealistically seeing the present behind the scenes of the past, and her own fortune through the eyes of her dead relatives, she feels confronted with a fundamental question of identity, personal orientation in the stream of history, her own place for self-realisation and the manageability of one's life.

- At times a character in a material landscape imagines another character not actually there: Ralph sees Katharine everywhere, 'invents' her in imaginary scenes. She is a ghost-like presence in his mind, a phantom, often remote from her true identity. Characters enjoy being in their beloved's consciousness, which is regarded by Ralph as the "utmost fullness of communion" (412) possible.
- Because of their emotional closeness, one character imaginatively follows another character's physical progress through a landscape or across an imaginary map of London.
- In a surrealist gaze, a character grasps the larger significance of invisible things in the background beneath the visible surface of a material cityscape or landscape in the foreground (philosophising stance: the associations run from concrete people to humankind or link the past, present, and future).
- Amid totally different surroundings, a character recalls a scene acted out in a different landscape and understands, enlightened by that moment, his/her true emotions or rather a false pretence to emotions not really felt. While a character is physically present, another character imagines him/her, i.e. recalls him/her in other surroundings.
- A character in self-absorption thinks of something totally unrelated to her/his actual surroundings. This consciousness represents an inaccessible region in the person's mind, so that at the moment this person appears to others watching him/her as an alien element in the present surroundings.
- A mental landscape can also be a place of refuge from ardent emotions that are perceived as threatening, and offer comforting visions of solid work instead.
- It may be a map or landscape of emotions, a state of emotional sensitivities, a site of dream-like unreality and impartiality.

All in all, the material and the mental are reciprocal in Woolf: A material map, cityscape or landscape becomes an imaginary landscape in the characters' consciousness and – vice versa – a consciousness may connote a map or landscape. Eventually Woolf leaves no doubt that for a few characters the imaginary worlds can be strikingly more real than the material one, and appearance or delusion more important than reality. Ralph appreciates the imaginary world for its unlimitedness. Katharine does so because, liberated from the constraints of the real world, it allows her direct, powerful and unimpeded sensations, potential feelings, perfect happiness and beauty instead of fragments and flying glimpses only. Statements like these underline Woolf's concern with accessing the psychic quality of reality, mental reality. Running through the whole novel are extensive body-mind discussions which cannot be fully covered within the scope of this study.

4. *Woolf's Modern Feminine Urban Vision*

All these observations on urban spectatorship, streets, crowds, their movements and motifs, patterns of life and connotations of the city show the relatedness of Woolf's city narrative to other urban fiction of the nineteenth and early twentieth centuries.[10] There, the city was represented as an "image of the human condition within urban and industrial capitalism"[11] – just that these conditions had changed since the times of Dickens and with them the quality of crowds and movements. "A predictable movement, however jostling and chaotic, had replaced the sense of randomness and variety."[12] Concerning the sexual politics of urban spectatorship, one can say that the female ramblers in Woolf – Katharine and Mary – navigate the streets with mastery, with impunity, aplomb, and a penetrating gaze like the male rambler. They discover underlying models of life and society and social relations, have liberating and disturbing visions of the crowd, though not in the sense of contamination and taint. Katharine is observed; she is an objectified female figure, a spectacle, but she is also an observer and spectator. Both she and Mary exercise the privilege of gaze. Neither of them (only Cassandra) needs a pretext for walking the streets, defences against vulnerability and exposure, forms of disguising their true identity to explore the city. They undertake no efforts at concealment and camouflage and are never accused of trespasses. They do not only enjoy the lamplight in private, just from the windows of their dwellings. Female urban spectatorship in *Night and Day* is in fact more courageous than in *The Pargiters* or *Mrs Dalloway*. The city as a "locus of expansion and emancipation"[13] does not remain a possibility, but becomes narrative reality.

This modern feminine urban vision agrees with social reality as Nord demonstrates: The 1880s produced a generation of women who for a time lived out the possibility of social and economic independence. They lived outside the family, but did not form residential communities, depending on a loosely organised network of other unmarried women. The 'new women' were united by their revolt against bourgeois family life and their fascination by London as a place for intellectual, political and professional engagement, which attracted aspiring female novelists, social investigators, and political activists. This was the beginning of mixed-sex political and social clubs, of women's clubs, when dwellings for women were built and the tops of double-decker buses were open to them. London offered anonymity and community, but it also formed a contrast to the formerly protected spaces of middle-class women.[14] Woolf's illustration of both the dangerous and emancipatory sides of female life in the metropolis – revealed through women's use of the means of public transport or their living alone at the very top of a house – bears parallels to Gaskell's ruminations on "the linked potential for danger and power inherent in women's participation in the public domain of industrial life".[15]

5. *Conclusion*

The narrative thematises the benefits and disadvantages of urban life, its peculiar rhythm and speed, the pattern of human life recognisable beneath the visions of crowds or traffic. Due to the rich sensory perceptions, London is constructed as a modern cityscape through vision and sound, whose aesthetics combine effectively. The most characteristic visual and auditory images chosen by Woolf for the cityscape are the pavement, lamplit streets, crossings, the throng of people, the traffic, taxicabs and omnibuses, the roar of wheels, the skyline, and the river.

Woolf's narrative is characterised by a high degree of intertextuality pointing to urban narratives created by writers like Dickens, Gaskell, James, Gissing, Conrad, Galsworthy or Bennett. She appropriates and re-writes the existing conventions. Further growth of the city and up-dated reflections on city life and urban space affect her conception of fiction-writing. The interaction of city experience and literary mode results in an urban vision which is modernist and gendered. Underlying it is a psychological conception of reality and the individual expressed through interior monologues and modernist symbolism. Urban space and city life are constructed through outer and inner perspectives. City life is treated less as an expression of a general condition of human life or urbanism as a homogeneous lifestyle, but Woolf's writing of urban space accommodates heterogeneous social modes of being, which are placed in a critical perspective (at least for the reader, if not always for the characters) through the contrast with the countryside. The experience of social variety is an effect of the immensity and heterogeneity of the city, but also of the accessibility of contrasting rural ways of life.

Woolf's urban vision is endowed with a modern (self-) consciousness. The experience of city life and urban space is presented as a problem of perception which bears on the problem of identity. Subjective, fragmentary and heterogeneous perceptions result in unstable identities. At the same time, however, the exploration of the city illustrates what Raymond Williams has described as the reappearance of a "collective consciousness" in an altered form, "the paradoxical experience of an ultimate collectivity which is beyond and above community"[16] exemplified through the group identity of ramblers from both sexes and diverse social backgrounds.

Woolf's urban vision does not accentuate cultural decline or the death of civilisation, but the relativity of personal experience and the complementary character of urban and rural lifestyles. Urban space and city life are presented as a significant epitome of early twentieth-century life. Place is thus fashioned into physical, socio-cultural, psychological, and emotional space. The concept of identity resulting from Woolf's creation of urban space is a social constructivist one: Urban space and city life function as cultural metaphors connoting a multiple, complex, heterogeneous identity characterised by fragmentation, hybridity, twoness, in-betweenness, and instability.

Notes

1 This is the object of study in my essay on "Place, Character, and Identity. Urban Space in Virginia Woolf's *Night and Day*" (2010).

2 Woolf (1994: 52). Further references to this edition will be included in the text.

3 Williams (1993: 228-229).
4 Cf. Hertel (1997: 311, 323, 325-326).
5 Cf. Hertel (1997: 286-288).
6 A similar sense of elevation and empowerment, the culmination of feminist self-confidence as it were, is felt by another daughter, Elizabeth Dalloway in *Mrs Dalloway*, when she takes a seat on top of a bus at Victoria Street rushing up Whitehall.
7 An interesting discussion of the context of women typists working in business offices at the time when the typewriter was introduced, in the 1880s, can be found in Joan N. Burstyn (1980: 130).
8 Cf. Nord (1995: 137).
9 Cf. my essay on "The Poetics of Conversation in Virginia Woolf's *A Room of One's Own*. Constructed Arbitrariness and Thoughtful Impressionism" (2001-2002).
10 Cf. Nord (1995: 1-4, 11, 12, 14-15, 143, 167, 201-202, 206, 237-238, 241-242, 244-245, 247); Williams (1993: 217-219, 223, 225, 233-237, 239-242, 245-246), Baumgarten (2006: 72-73, 75, 77-79, 81, 85); Hertel (1997: 14, 22, 51, 227, 394).
11 Williams (1993: 216).
12 *Ibid.* 223.
13 Nord (1995: 248).
14 Cf. Nord (1995: 181-183).
15 *Ibid.* 142.
16 Williams (1993: 246).

Bibliography

Baumgarten, Murray: "Urban Labyrinths. Dickens and the Pleasures of Place". In Peter Brown & Michael Irwin (Eds.): *Literature & Place, 1800-2000*, Oxford *et al.*, 2006, pp. 69-85.

Bimberg, Christiane: "The Poetics of Conversation in Virginia Woolf's *A Room of One's Own*. Constructed Arbitrariness and Thoughtful Impressionism". *Connotations* 11:1, 2001-2002, 1-28.

---: "Place, Character, and Identity: Urban Space in Virginia Woolf's *Night and Day*". *Izvestiya Juznogo Federalnogo Universiteta. Filologicheskiye Nauki* 1 (2010), 37-50.

Burstyn, Joan N.: *Victorian Education and the Ideal of Womanhood.* London & Totowa, New Jersey, 1980.

Giles, Judy & Tim Middleton: *Studying Culture. A Practical Introduction.* Oxford & Malden, Mass., 2001 [1999].

Gunzenhäuser, Randi: "Moving Sound. The Aural as the Repressed Sense of Modernism". – In Christoph Houswitschka, Gabriele Knappe & Anja Müller (Eds.): *Proceedings of the Conference of the German Association of University Teachers of English 2005*. Trier, 2006, pp. 291-299.

Hertel, Kirsten: *London zwischen Naturalismus und Moderne. Literarische Perspektiven einer Metropole*, Anglistische Forschungen 250, Heidelberg, 1997.

Nord, Deborah Epstein: *Walking the Victorian Streets. Women, Representation, and the City*. Ithaca & London, 1995.

Williams, Raymond: *The Country and the City*. London, 1993 [1973].

Wilson, Andrew Norman: *The Victorians*. London *et al.*, 2003 [2002].

Woolf, Virginia: *Night and Day*. London: Flamingo, 1994 [1919].

Würzbach, Natascha: "Der englische Frauenroman vom Modernismus bis zur Gegenwart (1890-1990). Kanonrevision, Gattungsmodifikationen, Blickfelderweiterung". – In Ansgar Nünning (Ed.): *Eine andere Geschichte der englischen Literatur. Epochen, Gattungen und Teilgebiete im Überblick*. Trier, 1998, pp. 195-211.

Timo Lothmann and Antje Schumacher (Aachen)

Conceptual Metaphors Revisited. The Construction of Space in Nineteenth-Century British Railway Poetry

I.

Ever since its triumph in nineteenth-century Britain, the train has enabled a hitherto unparalleled acceleration of mobility. The cultural revolution of experiencing – and conquering – time and space effected a gradual remodelling of the dialectics of man and nature vis-à-vis technology. Writers were among the first to process this progress in various registers and thus contributed to our understanding of British identity and its development.

Following a standard definition by Lakoff and Turner[1] and Lakoff and Johnson,[2] conceptual metaphors are knowledge structures that are mapped from a well-known source onto a new and less tangible target domain to be grasped by the observer. As such, metaphor is therefore only secondarily a linguistic phenomenon and primarily a matter of thought processes.[3] An example, which is clearly dependent on spatial dimensions, is "GOOD IS UP and BAD IS DOWN".[4] This conceptual metaphor finds its linguistic expression in performances like "We hit a *peak* last year, but it's been *downhill* ever since."[5] Such metaphors are ubiquitous. As Lakoff and Turner put it, "metaphor suffuses our thoughts, no matter what we are thinking about".[6] Further, conceptual metaphors are not simply cognitive crutches that we may get rid of. Rather, they are "irreplaceable",[7] as they enable us to understand the world around us or even construct reality.[8]

Different stages of development – or strategies – can be discerned in the process of integrating the technological innovation of the railway into discourse. After an initial phase of attempting to come to terms with the new technology by means of mere description, the locomotive is frequently depicted as a horse or a mythical creature, for instance. Later, the machine loses its supernatural, mythical appeal and is even deliberately demystified. Finally, it may turn into a metaphor or even a collective symbol itself, thus becoming the canvas for further projections. In this regard, spatial dimensions – i.e. up vs. down and urban vs. rural in particular – prove to be pivotal in the revision of the hierarchical relationship between man, nature and technology.

This paper discusses selected poems from the nineteenth century. Like every ordinary language performer, poets use metaphorical thought, which finds linguistic expression in their texts. The genre of poetry is characterised by an abundance, even omnipresence of such linguistic metaphors. As Lakoff and Turner observe in *More than Cool Reason*: "Using the capacities we all share, poets can illuminate our experience, explore the consequences of our belief, challenge the ways we think, and criticise our ideologies."[9] In what follows, we will analyse the discursive assimilation of the railway in the selected texts, focussing on how technology is used, as Lakoff and Turner put it, to illuminate, explore, challenge and, eventually, criticise.

II.

Several Victorian poets digested the cultural evolution induced by the railway. We can observe various stages of integrating the train into poetry. Initially, there were explanatory descriptions in order to establish and develop the train as a literary topic. By the closing years of the nineteenth century, this phase gave way to accounts in which the topic is regularly treated in a rather mundane, demystified way. There, the railway technology is shown to have become more assimilated into the lives of both authors and readers.[10] Among others, the poem "The Night Express" by William Cosmo Monkhouse, first published in 1865, assumes a key role just in between these stages of discourse.[11]

The poem introduces the train as a mythical being bursting with energy. The train – as the speaker – offers us an inner viewpoint on the plot. The choice of words in the initial lines hints at Monkhouse's objective: the mythologisation of the train as a metaphorical means of digesting the technological status quo. The machine does not appear to have been fully incorporated into the everyday spheres of the author and, presumably, the readers yet. The recourse to the supernatural helps to grasp and explain the irresistible force and massive shape of the train. Thus, the labour of the locomotive, i.e. to haul a massive, infinite-seeming shape into a sinister night, is depicted as a "Titanic toil" (l. 6). Such allusions to ancient tradition are efficiently exploited in the poem.

Yet, the train, as the Titan, is subject to some higher power. Here, it is man who is identified as the train's master. The train speaks: "I seek not to divine; / At man's command I stir, / I his stern messenger!" (ll. 9-11). While man masters the train via covert, invisible-hand strategies, the machine presents itself as a dutiful, unemotional tool. As such, it is the torchbearer of man-made progress. Technology is here reduced to its essence, namely to functioning according to man's will. However, the beast is only seemingly tamed – it can still do harm.[12]

The poem continues with the train's description of its lone journey through an adversary nature which is won by boldly crossing it. Nature is no match for the machine. As it dives through rocks and hills, nature is reduced to a canvas for technology triumphant. Thereby, a hierarchy is created as a structural key feature of the poem. Monkhouse presents the levels Nature, Technology and Man in a logical, quasi-natural order. The traditional pairing Man – Nature is expanded into a trichotomy that includes the machine as a superlative entity which, in a world rearranging itself, separates and mediates at the same time.

With respect to metaphor, the author chooses an eclectic approach. For instance, the dragon taken from mythology is combined with traits of lions and horses as well as with artificial characteristics intrinsic to the machine.[13] This interweaving of layers of imagery entails an amalgamation of the natural and the supernatural with the machine. The effect on the reader is a construct that is fantastic in the truest sense of the word.

The aesthetics of the train combines brute force with excessive speed. The train facilitates, even stands for, a new accelerated way of perceiving reality. It transgresses the long-established dimensional frontiers of space and time, tradition clashes with modernity. This cultural shock shows overtly: The train of the poem derides old-fashioned means of locomotion. Streets are derogatively referred to as time-consuming and outdated (cf. l. 18). We thus encounter the additional, universal conceptual framework of the young challenging the old. While streets have to adapt to the landscape, it is now the machine that actively transforms it.

This recreation of space is described not only as morally justified, but as a particularly valuable and necessary sign of progress, which is embraced in awe. In "The Night Express", cities are the starting and the end points of the train's journey. The small villages do not directly profit from the new technology – yet. There are still rural spaces and *terrae incognitae* that the train, which stands for the expanding industrialisation in general, can claim and will claim. On its trail of success, the train performs a "race sublime" (l. 61) against time. The train rolls at night and rests during the day before it is, by some means, reborn again. The reader recognises that a technological routine ensues which mirrors and embeds itself in the life-cycle that has been established since time immemorial.

Human beings do not explicitly appear in "The Night Express". Yet, they do in "On the Engine again" (1878) by Alexander Anderson,[14] and in "The Midnight Train" (1882) by James Macfarlan.[15] There, passengers and onlookers are spellbound by a transfigured, god-like train. While the landscape moves around the train, spatial entities are broken up into fragments. Sensory stimuli are thus changed by the train – there is a novel perception of motion and space. Besides, the poems show striking compositional, i.e. conceptual, similarities. As light opposes darkness, culture opposes nature. The train is the linking element between these incompatible, yet hierarchised poles. Again, allusions to Graeco-Roman mythology are manifold. With "iron roar", the Titan train "tears along receding lands / To where the kingly city stands / Wrapt in a robe of light" (Macfarlan ll. 23, 28-30). Like Prometheus, it brings progress by fire. In fact, the description of the new, i.e. the train, in terms of the old, Titans or horses, appears to be easier than its opposite, both for author and reader.[16] Thus, myth, inexplicable by definition, is welcome to poetically guise the still uncanny and elusive railway technology. The train is depicted as the supreme mechanical tool of man's strength of mind, thus advertising a technological imperative which is inevitable. It enables man to overcome stagnating nature together with its traditional, rigid patterns of space and time.

III.

The mainly technology-friendly stance in the poems discussed so far is rooted in a firm belief in the superiority of the new technology. This world-view is definitely a sign of the *Zeitgeist*. It then gave way for more sceptical views on the effects of the railway on culture as a whole. Before, in 1847, Tennyson had commented on the railway in his preface to "The Princess": "Strange was the sight and smacking of the time".[17] As a matter of fact, this resulted in a metaphorical challenge for the poet, which Monkhouse, Anderson and Macfarlan accepted. They positioned themselves in a limbo state between the novelty of technology and its growing absorption. In this process, however, the above-mentioned technological imperative is taken as an indisputable, axiomatic basis of argumentation in their works.

The poets under consideration portray several approaches to weave technological innovation into the cultural fabric. They offer ontological and evolutionary perspectives as well as a mythological and, last but not least, a spatial perspective on the matter. In doing so, they make use of different, multi-layered sets of imagery. In terms of conceptual metaphors, it is particularly the disappearance of the mythological constituent that marks the next step of constructing cultural space via the railway. Indeed, it was not before the end of the Victorian era that the train machine lost the supernatural and magical aspects that had veiled a possible lack of understanding of its technology. One generation after the composition of "The Night Express", "On the Engine again", and "The Midnight Train",[18] trains were hardly depicted in poetry as arcane, dangerous beasts or enigmatic demigods any more. This paradigm shift was rather characterised by practical approaches to the interlacing of technological and social effects in particular. It thus reflected the advanced assimilation of the railway into daily cultural routines.

In general, the high semiotic load of the railroad in nineteenth-century British literature is incontrovertible. Pertaining to this, the mixtures of culture-specific and human-universal elements of collective symbolism render the authors' efforts relevant, yet momentary testimonies to the processing of technology in poetry. Victorian authors like Monkhouse, Anderson and Macfarlan have been categorised as representatives of an in-between stage here. By using diversified imagery, they established the railroad itself as a genuine cultural metaphor. At the time, this new metaphor represented, as a wildcard, the unknown and dangerous, but also the promising and salutary aspects of dynamic progress.[19] In the event, this progress was idealised as an advantageous factor in terms of a redefinition of time and space. What is more, it became the catalyst of British civilisation and identity.

IV.

At this point, we may include Romantic poetry in the discussion. It is an unjustified prejudice that the Romantics were outright enemies of science and technological progress.[20] While this cliché does indeed hold some truth in the case of a small number of notable Romantics, others reacted much more positively to these developments. For example, William Wordsworth's sonnet "Steamboats, Viaducts, and Railways", composed in 1833,[21] shows that the speaker is fully aware of the "contrast between technological progress on the one and 'old poetic feeling' and 'Nature' on the other hand".[22] The overall judgement of the advantages of new technology is positive here, even though reservations about the aesthetic value of technological inventions like the railway are clearly expressed. Addressing the three technologies mentioned in the title directly, the voice reassures them: "Nor shall your presence, howsoe'er it mar / The loveliness of Nature, prove a bar / To the Mind's gaining that prophetic sense / Of future change, that point of vision, whence / May be discovered what in soul ye are" (ll. 4-8). Fully aware of the "enormous potential for development and transformation",[23] the speaker nonetheless admits that nature is defaced by technological progress.

In an attempt to come to terms with the status of these innovations, however, he considers them nature's "lawful offspring in Man's art" (l. 11). He thus resorts "to the traditional notion that science is a mere sub-system of art, and art in turn a mirror of nature".[24] Metaphorically speaking, technology becomes nature's child in this speaker's conceptualisation. He uses the conceptual metaphor of the family to describe the relationship between nature and technology.

The final thought voiced in the poem puts the notions of time and space in opposition to each other: "and Time, / Pleased with your triumphs o'er his brother Space, / Accepts from your bold hands the proffered crown / Of hope, and smiles on you with cheer sublime" (ll. 11-14). The speaker clearly refers to the changing perception of spatial dimensions, the seemingly fading distances. Technology's conquest of space is measured in units of time.

Thanks to technology, time wins the upper hand in its everlasting struggle with space.

However, this technological conquest of space is not always evaluated positively by Wordsworth. Eleven years later, he speaks of "a just disdain" of the railway.[25] Yet, as Wenzel rightly points out, we have to be careful not to interpret his sonnets "On the Projected Kendal and Windermere Railway" as a complete renunciation of his previous positive stance.[26] Considering them in detail, we may arrive at the conclusion that these are veritable harangues against the "rash assault" (sonnet 1, l. 2) and the "blight" (sonnet 1, l. 5) of the railway. However, as Wenzel suggests, we have to keep in mind the very specific situation in which they were composed. These two texts are not to be considered abstract, general reflections on the dichotomy of nature and technology.[27] Rather, they should be read as

> a concrete part of his embittered, almost militant action against an actively promoted project for an extension of the Kendal and Windermere Railway along the eastern shore of Windermere Lake, with implication of a farther reach northward through the vales of Ambleside and Grasmere, where Wordsworth was living.[28]

Wordsworth joined the public protests against this project by writing open letters and addressing members of Parliament directly.[29] One of his main reasons to take action himself were his aforementioned aesthetic objections to the railway:

> since there was no demand from industry for the line, its purpose must be to exploit the area's one staple, its beauty, for tourism. But the incursion of the railway and the development that would follow would only destroy the beauty and peace the tourists were coming to enjoy.[30]

Suddenly, the destruction of nature is no longer regarded as an acceptable negative side effect of progress, which is to be neglected in favour of mankind's conquest of space. It rather becomes the main reason for opposing spatial expansion. In general terms, Wordsworth clearly favours the conquest of space made possible by the railway. However, as soon as a specific space, namely his own geographical, social and cultural space, is to be invaded by what he, somewhat condescendingly, deems "the humbler ranks of society",[31] his attitude changes.[32] Now, the formerly negligible evil of a disfigured landscape becomes his main argument against the project. In terms of the discursive assimilation of the railway, these rather political poems – in what seems a prototypical case of NIMBY, i.e. 'not in my backyard' – show a total lack of metaphorisation, let alone mystification. Wordsworth's speaker exposes only the railway's negative side effects for the declared purpose of natural preservation and – presumably though not overtly so in these texts – social segregation.

After a time lapse of almost forty years, James Kenneth Stephen, again one of the so-called lesser poets of the Victorian age, felt compelled to reply to Wordsworth's attacks. Stephen's poem "Poetic Lamentation on the Insufficiency of Steam Locomotion in the Lake District" (1882) targets rather than eulogises the railway and the harm it does to nature by very ironically stating the exact opposite of what is really meant.[33] Literally described as the acme of human progress in the poem, the railway is actually portrayed as the very epitome of technology's destructive potential. For this purpose, the speaker first mystifies and then demystifies the railway. In fact, even the mystification is counterbalanced by the use of striking irony and thus – seemingly paradoxically – serves the aim of demystification as well.

The voice at first claims to find natural space "pleasant" (l. 11), but – considered in isolation – defective. This suggests that, to the speaker, only those spaces are worth praising that have been conquered (or ennobled) by technology. The railway is subsequently metaphorised (or mystified) according to its supposed superior position in the world: "But oh! what poet would not sing / That heaven-kissing rocky cone, / On whose steep side the railway king / Shall set his smoky throne?" (ll. 13-16) Sublime nature has left its mark on the landscape, the mountain seems high enough to reach heaven. The train is able to climb the mountain and therefore comes closer to heaven than nature, i.e. God's creation, itself. Man-made technology rules over natural space like a monarch rules over his subjects.

Yet, as the speaker does not depict the space on which technology has left its clearly visible mark as beautiful at all, the effects of this conquest clearly demystify the technical innovation immediately: "Helvellyn in those happy days / With tunnelled base and grimy peak" (ll. 17-18). The positive "happy" stands in stark contrast to the rather negative "grimy". So the voice does not sincerely lament the absence of steam locomotion in this area, but paints an ironically distorted negative picture of what the Lake District would look like if the railway was allowed to conquer this space. Landmarks like Helvellyn would be destroyed in manifold ways, one of which would be the pollution caused by the fumes emitted.

Finally, the speaker makes abundantly clear that man is superior to nature. Nature is accused of impudently overestimating its own abilities and – surprisingly – of trying to imitate man. While humans change the world systematically, nature has no concept and no plan but scatters, as it were, its features randomly in space. It is man's destiny to surpass nature with his creations and replace it. Not only creation's crowning glory, man is eventually also the Lord of creation himself and thus the ruler over space. In this final stanza, dripping with irony, the speaker clearly criticises human hubris, which has caused an unquestioned belief in technological progress so far.

V.

To conclude: The integration of the railway into discourse in nineteenth-century English poetry does not take place at once, but in clearly discernible stages. Since these stages partially overlap and do not necessarily follow one another in chronological order, they may also be considered as strategies rather than stages of discursive assimilation. The conceptualisation of sets of metaphors is pivotal in this process.

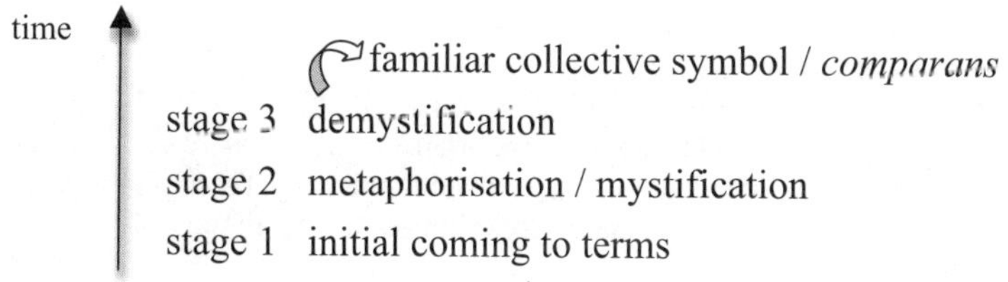

Fig. 1: Overlapping stages of literary discourse

What, then, happens after the stage of demystification? Subsequently, the technology may evolve from the *comparandum* into the *comparans* (cf. Fig. 1). To take an example from American literature, Lawrence Ferlinghetti uses the railway as a metaphor for aging in his poem "Just as I Used to Say" (1955). The same strategies of integration can be observed in texts featuring other mobility technologies, like the automobile or the aeroplane.[34]

If we assume that space does not simply exist, but that space – as well as time – is constituted by movement, then it is obvious that the acceleration as facilitated by the locomotive, the automobile and later the aeroplane has an impact on how space is (re)constituted.[35] Mobility technologies have thus become crucial transformers of space. Here, we have dealt with a selection of texts the authors of which are first-hand witnesses of this transformational process. In their poems, they employ new as well as conventional metaphors. These metaphors, *comme d'habitude*, help to define and structure our reality.

Notes

1 Lakoff & Turner (1989).
2 Lakoff & Johnson (2003).
3 Cf. *ibid.* 6.
4 Cf. *ibid.* 16, emphasis in the text.
5 *Ibid.*, emphasis in the text.
6 Lakoff & Turner (1989: xi).
7 *Ibid.*
8 Cf. Lakoff & Johnson (2003: 159).
9 Lakoff & Turner (1989: xi).
10 With respect to the stages of integrating technology into discourse, Heinimann (1992) makes use of a similar categorisation.
11 Monkhouse (1865: 65-69). The following line references included in the text refer to this edition. William Cosmo Monkhouse (1840-1901) ranks among the so-called lesser Victorian poets. His early *oeuvre* is unmistakably influenced, both in style and topics, by Tennyson. "The Night Express" is Monkhouse's main contribution to the literary discourse that features the railway as a major issue of interest.
12 The seemingly tamed beast may turn its vehement force against its master. This idea, skilfully embodied in Shelley's *Frankenstein* (1818), is implicitly present in the background of the setting of the poem.
13 Cf. "great snorts" (l. 1); "mighty mane" (l. 56); "thews of iron" (l. 63).
14 Anderson (1878: 105-109).
15 Macfarlan (1882: 102-103). Further references to this edition will be included in the text.
16 Cf. Warburg (1958: 167).
17 Tennyson (1969: 746).

18 Cf. Wenzel & Strasen (2010) for a more detailed account of the poems under concern as well as for the metaphorical processing of the railway motif by post-Victorian generations of poets.

19 The train machine served as the "tri-dimensional representation of the sensorial cacophonies of modernity, with all its certainties and doubts", Jones in Saggini (2006: 404).

20 What follows on Wordsworth's railway poetry is much indebted to Wenzel's essay "'Weighing the Mischief with the Promised Gain': The Two-sided Attitude to Technological Progress in William Wordsworth's Railway Sonnets" in Wenzel & Strasen (2010).

21 Wordsworth (1947: 47). Further references to this edition will be included in the text.

22 Wenzel (2010: 25).

23 *Ibid.*

24 *Ibid.*

25 Wordsworth (1946: 62, l. 14). Wordsworth wrote two untitled sonnets "On the Projected Kendal and Windermere Railway". The first begins with the line "Is then no nook of English ground secure…" (Wordsworth 1946: 61-62); we will refer to it as "sonnet 1" in the line references included in the text. The second begins with "Proud were ye, Mountains…" (Wordsworth 1946: 62); we will refer to this as "sonnet 2". This quote is from sonnet 2.

26 Cf. *ibid.* Wenzel argues against Heinimann's "conclusion that these two sonnets […] mark 'a complete reversal' of Wordsworth's earlier attitudes" (2010: 28).

27 Cf. *ibid.*

28 *Ibid.*

29 *Ibid.*

30 Gill (1989: 413).

31 Wordsworth (1844: 157). This is taken from a letter "To the Editor of the Morning Post" written in 1844.

32 Wenzel points out that "[t]hese arguments triggered a huge controversial debate on the legitimate defense of nature, selfishness and condescension to the poor, which has continued in Wordsworth criticism up to the present day" (2010: 29). He provides an overview of critical views on these issues.

33 The analysis and interpretation presented here is developed in greater detail in Schumacher's essay entitled "A Reply to William Wordsworth's Railway Sonnets? J.K. Stephen's 'Poetic Lamentation on the Insufficiency of Steam Locomotion in the Lake District'" in Wenzel & Strasen (2010). According to Heinimann, this "Lamentation" may be read as a parody of Wordsworth's sonnets (cf. 1992: 110) as Stephen's poem demands further expansion of the railway network in order to finally subdue nature (cf. *ibid.*). In fact, there is some evidence that Stephen parodied Wordsworth elsewhere. "A Sonnet" (1891) is partially an attack directed explicitly at Wordsworth's style and themes. In the first quatrain, Stephen lauds the depth of Wordsworth's tone (cf. ll. 1-4). Yet, in the second quatrain, he accuses Wordsworth of having the voice "of an old half-witted sheep / Which bleats articulate monotony, /

And indicates that two and one are three, / That grass is green, lakes damp, and mountains steep" (ll. 5-8). In brief: Wordsworth occasionally writes pointless and boring poetry. Incidentally, the bleating sheep linked to Wordsworth are also mentioned in Stephen's "Lamentation". Even though the speaker then admits that "at certain times / Forth from the heart of thy melodious rhymes, / The form and pressure of high thoughts will burst" (ll. 9-11), the concluding three lines are devastating: "At other times – good Lord! I'd rather be / Quite unacquainted with the A B C / Than write such hopeless rubbish as thy worst" (ll. 12-14). Thus Stephen does not entirely depreciates Wordsworth's work, but certainly regards his *oeuvre* as heterogeneous in quality.

34 Cf. Wenzel & Strasen (2010).

35 With respect to the revolution of the regime of space and time vis-à-vis motion as the guiding principle of modernity cf. Kaschuba (2004), Rosa (2005).

Bibliography

Anderson, Alexander: *Songs of the Rail*, London *et al.*, 1878.

http://gerald-massey.org.uk/anderson/b_songs.htm, 26 June 2010.

Ferlinghetti, Lawrence: *Pictures of the Gone World*, San Francisco, 1955.

Gill, Stephen: *William Wordsworth. A Life*, Oxford, 1989.

Heinimann, Alfred C.: *Technische Innovation und literarische Aneignung. Die Eisenbahn in der deutschen und englischen Literatur des 19. Jahrhunderts*, Basler Studien zur deutschen Sprache und Literatur 63, Bern, 1992.

Kaschuba, Wolfgang: *Die Überwindung der Distanz. Zeit und Raum in der europäischen Moderne*, Frankfurt a. M., 2004.

Lakoff, George & Mark Johnson: *Metaphors We Live by*, Chicago *et al.*, 2003 [1980].

Lakoff, George & Mark Turner: *More than Cool Reason. A Field Guide to Poetic Metaphor*, Chicago *et al.*, 1989.

Macfarlan, James: *The Poetical Works of James Macfarlan*, Glasgow, 1882.

http://gerald-massey.org.uk/macfarlan/b_poems_index.htm, 26 June 2010.

Merk, Aljoscha: "Titan Train with Demon Light. On the Ambivalent Relation between Nature and Culture in James Macfarlan's 'The Midnight Train'". – In Peter Wenzel & Sven

Strasen (Eds.): *Discourses of Mobility – Mobility of Discourses. The Metaphorical Conceptualisation of Trains, Cars, and Aeroplanes in Poetry*, Trier, 2010, pp. 43-48.
Monkhouse, William C.: *A Dream of Idleness, and Other Poems*, London, 1865.
Rosa, Hartmut: *Beschleunigung. Die Veränderung der Zeitstrukturen in der Moderne*, Frankfurt a. M., 2005.
Saggini, Francesca: "Transporting Scenes. Motion and Sensation on the Victorian Stage". – In Mariaconcetta Costantini *et al.* (Eds.): *La letteratura vittoriana e i mezzi di trasporto. Dalla nave all'astronave*, Studi di Anglistica 3, Rome, 2006, pp. 387-405.
Seeber, Hans-Ulrich: *Mobilität und Moderne. Studien zur englischen Literatur des 19. und 20. Jahrhunderts*, Anglistische Forschungen 371, Heidelberg, 2007.
Shelley, Mary: *Frankenstein. Or, The Modern Prometheus*, London *et al.*, 1994 [1818].
Stephen, James K.: *Lapsus Calami and Other Verses*, Cambridge, 1912 [1891].
Tennyson, Alfred: *The Poems of Tennyson*. Ed. Christopher Ricks, London *et al.*, 1969.
Warburg, Jeremy: "Poetry and Industrialism. Some Refractory Material in Nineteenth-Century and Later English Verse", *The Modern Language Review* 53:2, 1958, 161-170.
Wenzel, Peter: "'Weighing the Mischief with the Promised Gain': The Two-sided Attitude to Technological Progress in William Wordsworth's Railway Sonnets". – In P.W. & Sven Strasen (Eds.): *Discourses of Mobility – Mobility of Discourses. The Metaphorical Conceptualisation of Trains, Cars, and Aeroplanes in Poetry*, Trier, 2010, pp. 25-32.
--- & Sven Strasen (Eds.): *Discourses of Mobility – Mobility of Discourses. The Metaphorical Conceptualisation of Trains, Cars, and Aeroplanes in Poetry*, Trier, 2010.
Wordsworth, William: *Guide to the Lakes*. Ed. Ernest de Selincourt, Oxford, 1977 [1844].
---: *The Poetical Works of William Wordsworth*. Ed. Ernest de Selincourt, & Helen Darbishire, Oxford, 1966 & 1968 [1946 & 1947], vols. 3-4.

Yousef Awad (Amman)

"The Other-Others? Hidden Arabs". Fadia Faqir's *My Name is Salma* and the Experiences of Arab Women Immigrants to Britain

The purpose of this paper is to shed light on the literary representation of the experiences of Arab female immigrants to Britain through discussing Jordanian British author Fadia Faqir's recent novel *My Name is Salma* (2007). The quotation in the title of the paper alludes to the ethnic heading under which nearly 300,000 persons, mainly Arabs, were grouped in the 1991 Census in Britain.[1] Salma's experience, I argue, represents that of many Arab grassroots who have arrived at the British shores in successive waves but remained veiled. Salma's restricted interaction with the few Arabs she meets in Britain, compared to her well-built connections with women from other ethnic and racial backgrounds, points to the novel's underlying transcultural agenda. Unlike other ethnic groups in Britain, and even unlike the Arab community in the US, Arabs in Britain are tremendously invisible as they occupy an ambiguous position in the British ethnic landscape. While the novel tries to explore this zone, it also underscores the significance of going beyond the language barrier, entering the ethnic borderland and opening corridors of talks with other minorities. In *My Name is Salma*, Faqir creates a fertile ethnic arena through which Salma, the once helpless refugee, breathes, survives and thrives.

Fadia Faqir was born in Jordan and moved to live in Britain after she had finished her postgraduate degree. Prior to *My Name is Salma*, Faqir wrote two novels: *Nisanit* (1988) and *Pillars of Salt* (1998). Of the three texts, *My Name is Salma* is the only one that is set in Britain. However, all three novels are written in English. Faqir's works are part of a wider phenomenon that has become more noticeable since the 1980s. Specifically, Faqir can be seen as a member of a group of Arab writers who write in English.

Although this trend was initiated by Arab immigrants to the US at the end of the nineteenth century, as Geoffrey Nash explains in his book *The Anglo-Arab Encounter. Fiction and Autobiography by Arab Writers in English*, Faqir's works are better located within the more recent contexts of postcolonialism, diaspora and globalisation. In addition to Faqir, Arab writers who write in English and live in Britain (or between Britain and the Arab world) include: Ahdaf Soueif, Leila Aboulela, Sabiha Al Khemir, Jamal Mahjoub and Robin Yassin-Kassab.

The number of Arab women writers in this list considerably exceeds that of male Arab writers. This phenomenon invites us to further investigate the intersectionality of language, themes, gender, representation, ideological affiliation and other socio-political aspects. What distinguishes *My Name is Salma* from other 'Arab British' novels is Faqir's attempt to represent an unprivileged Arab female immigrant. Unlike, Soueif and Aboulela, whose heroines are usually upper-middle class educated women, Faqir depicts the (mis)fortunes of an invisible character who is not usually accounted for in the academic and ethnographic studies on Arabs in Britain.

My Name is Salma tells the story of Salma, a teenage Bedouin girl who lives with her family in the mud village of Hima in the Levant. Salma meets Hamdan, a handsome Bedouin from her tribe. Shortly afterwards Salma gets pregnant from Hamdan. When Salma's mother learns about it, she tells her daughter that her brother will kill her. Horrified, Salma runs to her schoolteacher, who arranges to place her under protective detention in the police station to prevent her brother from murdering her. In prison, Salma shares the stories with other women and learns how to sew. She gives birth to a baby girl, but the girl is taken from her immediately. Impressed by her tailoring skills, a Lebanese nun arranges to smuggle Salma to a convent to the north of Beirut where she acquires further sewing and social skills. Miss Asher, a British nun, adopts Salma, changes her name to Sally and arranges to take her to the UK. The British immigration authorities question the authenticity of Salma's papers but after a two-month detention, Salma sets foot on British soil. Minister Mahoney arranges for her to live in a hostel in Exeter where she meets Parvin, a second-generation Asian British girl on the run from an arranged marriage. A relationship based on solidarity and sisterhood brings the two together. Parvin raises a consciousness in Salma that she is a British citizen and that she is eligible to the rights of a good British citizen.

Salma finds a job as a seamstress and she also rents a room in a cottage owned by Liz, a drunkard descendant of a former imperialist family. Salma also makes friends with Gwen, a retired Welsh headmistress. She enrolls at the Open University for a degree in English literature. Her tutor, Dr. John Robinson, a dislocated northerner, falls in love with her and they agree to get married. She gives birth to a baby boy, but her sense of guilt for abandoning her daughter increasingly haunts her. Finally, Salma decides to go back to her village to be united with her daughter. Her mother tells her that Mahmoud, Salma's only brother, has murdered her daughter by drowning her in the well because, he believes, like her mother, the girl will bring shame to the family and tribe. Salma's senile father fishes the girl from the well and lays her to rest against the wishes of the tribe. As Salma visits her daughter's grave, Mahmoud shoots her dead.

Research studies on Arabs in Britain are at best scarce. In "Arab Communities in Britain. Cleavages and Commonalities", Camillia Fawzi El-Solh laments the lack of interest in the Arab community in Britain in published studies on race relations, racism and multiculturalism. When they are included in quantitative studies, El-Solh argues, Arabs are looked at "as an undifferentiated category, thus overlooking the heterogeneity in their national origin".[2] El-Solh maintains that Arabs living in Britain are continually affected by the complex and the fluctuating diplomatic relations between Western and Arab governments. Since the Middle East is one of the most politically volatile regions in the world, Arabs in Britain are usually targeted by anti-terrorism policies.[3]

El-Solh explains that the earliest wave of immigrants originating from the Arab world are believed to have arrived on Britain's shores during the second half of the nineteenth century, perhaps even earlier. By the late 1940s / early 1950s Arabs in Britain had begun to include more nationalities such as Egyptians, Sudanese and Iraqis, many of whom remained after completing their studies. There was also an influx of Palestinians after the creation of the state of Israel in 1948. However, by all accounts, El-Solh asserts, Arab immigrants "were numerically too insignificant to form distinct ethnic communities based on national origin" (240). In addition, their spatial dispersal, as well as the fact that they were not clustered in specific job categories, very probably also played a part in discouraging a trend similar to that discernible among the Yemeni and the Somali seafaring communities, where ethnic boundaries had clearly begun to be demarcated. The post-war economic boom enabled Arab immigrants to gain access to the British labour market, though in significantly lower numbers than economic migrants from Asia and the West Indies.

El-Solh distinguishes between "a more or less random and a chain migration".[4] The first pattern, she maintains, applies, for example, to skilled and semi-skilled Egyptians who came to Britain "as individual economic migrants" (240).[5] Many secured a permanent residence status or British citizenship through employment and/or marrying British women. By all accounts, this also applied to some Iraqi and Sudanese economic migrants. Chain migration, on the other hand, applies to Moroccans recruited from rural areas in northern Morocco for employment in the hotel and catering industries in the British capital, and to some extent in the National Health Service. They were generally confined to menial jobs with little prospect of career mobility. In the 1960s / early 1970s many of them brought their families over to Britain, thus transforming what was originally intended as a temporary migration into a longer-term settlement.

The declining fortunes of the British Merchant Navy, in conjunction with the expanding British economy, encouraged increasing numbers of seamen to take up employment in industrial and manufacturing sectors. Here, El-Solh describes chain migration, since the demand for labour encouraged more Yemenis and Somalis to join their kith and kin in Britain, eventually leading to the emergence of additional Yemeni and Somali communities in manufacturing centres such as Sheffield.[6]

The civil war in Lebanon and the economic boom in the aftermath of the 1973 oil crisis, coupled with economic and political instability in some parts of the Arab region, encouraged an Arab "brain drain as well as a flight of Arab capital in search of investment opportunities" in Britain.[7] Middle- and upper-class Lebanese, Syrian and Palestinian families moved into Britain. The "exodus" of the Lebanese-based Arab press mainly to London also provided an important employment niche for a number of male and female Arabs with the appropriate qualifications.[8] There are also those who set up their own Arab businesses in the UK, ranging from real estate and import/export ventures, to consultancy and leisure services, travel agencies and small-scale commercial enterprises. By the late 1970s and during the 1980s, the diversity of Arab communities in Britain was further reinforced by "the increasing influx of refugees fleeing persecution from areas such as Iraq and Somalia".[9]

The Arab existence in Britain is most visible in Edgware Road in London, where Arabs own and run a number of small businesses. Community leaders estimate the number of Arabs in Britain to be between 500,000 and 1,000,000 people. The lack of an exact figure is due mainly to the ambiguous categorisation of the Arabs in the census. In "The Other-Others. Hidden Arabs", Madawi Al-Rasheed argues that the 'Other-Others' in the 1991 Census is the nearest approximation that is available for the Arab population in Britain, although it is very much more heterogeneous than such a title would suggest.[10] Al-Rasheed notes that the proportion of "educationally qualified" people in this group is double that for the population as a whole.[11] Female employment, like male employment for this group, shows a higher representation in white-collar jobs and a lower proportion in the manual groups.[12] Al-Rasheed concludes that this category "remains something of an enigma on which much more work needs to be done".[13]

By the same token, in British popular culture, Arabs remain an enigma. In *My Name is Salma*, Max, Salma's boss, has preconceived images about the Arabs that range from moodiness to being extremely rich. On one occasion, Salma overhears him saying: "'Sally is in one of her moods. Arabs are obsessed with sadness.'"[14] On the other hand, Max believes that Arabs are extremely rich and they come to the UK to make more money:

> "You know what bugs me about them [Arabs]. They come here like an army, buy houses and cars then sell their houses and cars without us hard-working English people making a sodding penny out of it. They don't go to estate agents or dealers, no, they buy off each other." (152)

For the British, El-Solh argues, the term 'Arabs' is likely to "conjure up images of affluence spiced, with the exotic", overlooking substantial numbers of Arabs trapped in menial employment, or subject to the insecurity associated with their asylum status in the UK.[15]

El-Solh rightly points out that the term 'Arabs' is often used synonymously with the term 'Muslim', thereby overlooking Arabs of other religious affiliations, such as Christian Arabs, settled in Britain. For instance, an article published on 17 September 1988 in *The Economist* argues that "[t]he Arabs, happy to live in their self-contained world, have felt little need to enlighten" the British about Arabic culture, of which mosques are "[t]he most visible signs".[16] In fact, the article renders the existence of the Arabs in Britain in a most exotic way. The columnist equates Arabs with Muslims by asserting that mosques are the most visible signs of Arabs. While 'Arab' is an ethnic identity, 'Muslim' is a religious affiliation. Consequently, neither all Arabs are Muslims, nor all Muslims Arabs. The article, I believe, attempts to reduce a long history of misrepresentation and marginalisation of Arabs by accusing them of lacking the interest in explaining their culture to the British.

In fact, the Arabs have been strongly demonised in the West through newspapers, films and TV shows.[17] In the novel, when Parvin is admitted to the hostel and is assigned to share a room with Salma, she strongly resists it. The porter has a vague idea that Arabs live in the Middle East. He subscribes to orientalist representations that place Arabs outside modernity:

> "Where does she come from?" [Parvin asks].
> "Somewhere in the Middle East. Fucking *A-rabic! She rode a camel all the way from Arabia to this dump in Exeter*," he said and laughed.
> "*I am not going to share the room with an Arab*," she spat. (14)[18]

Within a context of misrepresentations and hostilities, the task to explain to Britons the tenets of the Arabic culture becomes difficult. In fact, an essay published on 11 March 1991 in *The Nation* explains some of the hardships that face Arabs in Britain. The essay was written during the 1991 Gulf War and it focuses on a decision by Britain's Court of Appeal to reject a "judicial review of the grounds for the internment and deportation of Palestinians, Iraqis and others of Arab descent living in Britain".[19] The Court's decision was based on the idea that "the evidence of wrongdoing was not necessary in their case because 'those who are able most effectively to undermine national security are those who least appear to constitute any risk to it'".[20]

The article, I would argue, shows that the Arabs occupy a vague position in the British polity. This ambiguity is caused by the

British government's attitudes and stances towards Arabs and the Arab world. These stances become clearly aggressive and hostile at times of wars and crises that involve Arab countries. It is not that Arabs lack the interest in explaining their culture to the British people, as *The Economist* article claims; it is the institutional prejudice against Arabs, turning them into suspects and potential enemies, that hinders the efforts of Arabs to explicate their culture.

My Name is Salma brilliantly depicts this paradox. Salma rushes to the kebab van run by Algerians to sniff the smell of home. Nevertheless, the owners are suspicious of her:

> "*Balak*: is that girl MI5?" the old man said.
> "What's wrong with you? Agents don't go around dressed like Arab tramps. They wear big hats like Philsy, innit? White, blond, with a cigar in their mouth," said the young man.
> "You mean Philby, you idiot. And these days agents look like anything, look like Jesus Christ himself. How do I know?" said the old man in a North African accent.
> "You are paranoid and all. At night when the leaves sway you think an American satellite is taking shots of you," said the young man. (30)[21]

At the same time, the novel attempts to highlight the heterogeneity of the experiences of Arabs in Britain. While some are paranoid and prefer to keep to themselves, others want to melt into the mainstream culture like the Algerian waiter who pretends to be French. In "The Egyptians of Britain. A Migrant Community in Transition", Ghada Karmi draws attention to a number of issues that Arabs in Britain need to address adequately:

> The important question that must now face Egyptians and other Arabs in the same situation is how long they wish to remain separate, non-participatory cultural entities within the larger society in Britain. (25-26)

Karmi's claim that Arabs in Britain prefer to remain separate from the rest of the nation is partly correct. However, her stipulation ignores the anti-Arab institutional prejudice in British polity. How can a person identify with the nation when he/she is categorised as an 'other-other' in the census? How can a person be an active member of the larger society when he/she is pushed to the margin and placed outside the borders of the nation?

The novel seems to engage with xenophobic attitudes that render Arabs, as well as other immigrants, as racialised subjects and exclude them from the body of the nation. While Salma wants to integrate into British society, the mainstream refuses to include her by continuing to remind her that she is an alien, a foreigner. There is a persistent resentment towards accepting and acknowledging the non-white within the British social fabric. The immigration *A-Z Guide* advises Salma to be passive and just follow the current. Her sense of exclusion, lack of belonging becomes clear in the following paragraph in which she identifies with other marginalised people:

> In the early evening the city belonged to us, the homeless, drug addicts, alcoholics and immigrants, to those who were either without a family or were trying to blot out their history. In this space between five and seven we would spread and conquer like moss that grows between the cracks in the pavement. (25)

In addition to identifying with the marginalised and the disenfranchised, Salma tries to penetrate English society by frequenting bars and expanding her social networks. She knows that she is in a state of perennial inbetweenness. She does not fear anymore being asked where she is from. After all, her answer to this question varies, depending on the situation. Sometimes, she does not answer. On other occasions, she pretends to be Spanish. She is quite aware of the malleability of her identity and the inconclusiveness of her phenotype. When she asks the bar manager at the Royal Hotel for a night shift job, she does not hesitate to reveal her real origin, probably because she thinks that working in menial jobs is an immigrant-controlled domain:

> "I am looking for evening job."
> "Are you registered with a job agency, the job centre?" he asked.
> I shook my head.
> He was about to dismiss me, then he changed his mind. "You don't sound English."
> "I am British of Arab origins."
> "Aha!" (131)

But when she starts her university education and meets her tutor, she insists that she is English, most probably because she equates Englishness with being educated and highly cultivated.

However, Faqir's representation of Salma as a self-confident character may remind us of Gayatri Chakravorty Spivak's argument about the subaltern. In fact, the above passage is in agreement with a response pattern which is dominant among Arab *activists* in one of the studies conducted by Caroline Nagel in 2002. Focusing on 'middle class, educated and activist Arabs in London', Nagel highlights the politics of sameness and difference in the Arab communities in Britain:

> Members of London's Arab community engage in numerous practices, politics and discourses through which they may ultimately reconfigure the terms on which the dominant group is defined. Assimilatory practices and discourses vary with groups, reflecting class and generational differences and distinct conceptions of group categories and identities like Arab, British, Black and Muslim. (279-280)

In "Can the Subaltern Speak?" Spivak criticises Foucault and Deleuze for their claim that the oppressed can know and speak their own conditions and circumstances. She critiques conflating the desire of the oppressed and marginalised with the interests of the radical intellectual to construct an undivided political subject. Spivak concludes:[22]

> The subaltern cannot speak. There is no virtue in global laundry lists with 'woman' as a pious item. Representation has not withered away. The female intellectual as intellectual has a circumscribed task which she must not disown with a flourish.[23]

Faqir can be easily accused of conflating her own interests with the desires of Salma. Is it possible that the immigration experience has given Salma a high level of awareness and attentiveness? Is the development of Salma's character logical and convincing?

To further complicate these questions, Salma is depicted as having developed an interest in British politics. She tries to "decode the latest poll in the paper", whereby Labour is leading the Conservatives by five per cent (23). She watches TV with the intention of understanding British politics:

> It was a rare occasion when I was watching television with Liz.
> "Was that the shadow Chancellor?" I asked Liz.
> "No, the Prime Minister. The Chancellor does not spit," she answered and looked at the television screen, not wanting to be interrupted.
> "Who are these puppets?" I asked.
> "Foreigners! Aliens like you," she said and smiled. (24)

Liz wants to convey the message that Salma has no right to discuss British politics because she is a foreigner. Similarly, Max insists on excluding Salma from belonging to British culture. Looking at a photo of Princess Diana wearing a swimming suit, Max expresses his anger and dissatisfaction. When Salma tries to give her opinion, Max interrupts her: "'Sal, you don't know anything about us, the British, do you?'" (241) Liz and Max's attitudes reflect xenophobic perspectives that British politics and culture is white-exclusive.

An exploratory survey by the Atlantic Forum under the title "British Arabs: Identity, Politics and Community" was published in 2009. In spite of the inherent representational biases in any survey, the report contradicts a previous "largely anecdotal" assumption "that there is a low level of participation" of the Arab British community in UK politics.[24] The report finds around 47.6 per cent of the sample positively disposed towards politics as a means of addressing social issues and problems.[25] More interestingly, the survey shows that of the 210 respondents who were eligible to vote in the last UK general election, two-thirds had exercised this right, "a percentage that is slightly higher" than the parallel figure for the UK's general population.[26]

Despite Salma's recurrent efforts to be part of the mainstream, she is continually repulsed and reminded that she is out of place.In fact, the idea of displacement is introduced early in the novel. Salma tells us:

> A few years ago, I had tasted my first fish and chips, but my mountainous Arab stomach could not digest the fat, which floated in my tummy for days. Salma resisted, but Sally must adapt. I kept looking up *adapt* in the *Oxford English Dictionary: Adapt: fit, adjust, change.* Apparently in England the police stop you in the street and check your papers and sense of belonging regularly. An immigration officer might decide to use my ability to digest fish as a test for my loyalty to the Queen. (9)[27]

The novel is deeply concerned with issues of marginalisation, integration and displacement. Faqir adds a new dimension to marginalisation because the subject of the novel is a displaced female subaltern. The novel actually gives different examples of the subaltern: Gwen, a Welsh old lady living in Exeter, Parvin, a second-generation Asian-British on the run from an arranged marriage, paranoid Algerian male immigrants etc. While these different examples of the marginalised reflect the heterogeneity of this group, the novel also attempts to explore how these characters interact and negotiate their spaces.

Upon entering the UK, the immigration officer has grilled Salma. Though she is adopted by Miss Asher, the immigration officer is not quite happy with this arrangement:

> "Are you seeking political asylum?"
> I tried to remember what Miss Asher had instructed me to say. All the trivial 'good morning's and 'enjoy your meal' were readily available, but I could not recall the exact word she had asked me to use. "Adapted," I finally said.
> "Adopted?" he said while flicking through reams of paper.
> "Yes. Yes. Adopted, Miss Asher." (134-135)

Salma's adoption papers are in order but the immigration authorities question their authenticity. Minister Mahoney exposes the authorities' apprehension towards "creat[ing] a precedent" (142) by giving Salma the right to live in the UK.

In the introduction to their book *Displacement, Diaspora, and Geographies of Identity*, Smadar Lavie and Ted Swedenburg argue that the West has responded to new waves of migration from the former colonised territories in a repressive style:

> The repressive style of response is exemplified in the hysterical talk in Western Europe about the "invasion" and the "flood" of immigrants, refugees, Muslims, and foreigners, and the concerted and ever escalating official efforts to stem the flow, to erect the ramparts of "Fortress Europe," to refuse residence to asylum seekers, to deny full citizenship rights to second- and third-generation resident "others," and to marginalise, criminalise, and exploit the labor of undocumented Third World residents. (3)

The government's discourse to curb immigration trickles down to the layman. Anti-immigration policies take a local form on the bus, in the street and in public spaces. The public are interpellated by the discourses employed by the government about how immigrants are changing British values and concepts. In the pub, the skinheads shout at Salma: "'Hey, alien! You, freak! Why don't you go back to the jungle? Go climb some coconut trees! Fuck off! Go Home!'" (34) For the skinheads, the aliens are all the same: they all come from the jungle.

When first published in 2007, the novel was received differently. Some reviewers were fascinated by the narrative techniques employed by the novelist, describing it as a mosaic in which each tile is lovely in itself but helps to create a whole that is breathtaking. Others have focused on the fatal repercussions of the tribal code-of-honour killing which forces Salma to flee from her village. In this paper I have concentrated on Salma as an example of a subaltern subject rendered doubly invisible as a result of the intersectionality of race, ethnicity, nationality, gender, religion and class. The novel, I have argued, demonstrates that by penetrating the ethnic borderland, the subaltern can find a stand from which to speak.

The Arab community in Britain is extremely heterogeneous. Its structure reflects the various waves of Arab immigration to the UK since the second half of the nineteenth century. Unfortunately, academic research on this group has tended to give attention to upper- and middle-class immigrants, partly because of the limited data available for researchers. The ambiguous position that Arabs occupy in British ethnographic discourses renders some categories of this big community, such as asylum seekers, indiscernible. While *My Name is Salma* is not meant to be read as a surrogate sociological study of the dynamics of the Arab community in Britain, it, nevertheless, contributes to unveiling this hidden group. It offers the reader a vantage point for seeing, from an unprivileged location, a harsh experience that characterises a world ruled by globalisation and advanced capitalism.

Notes

1 In the 2011 Census, the category 'Arab' is added as an ethnic group. It is true that recognising Arabs as a separate ethnic entity culminates the efforts of Arab activists who have been campaigning and lobbying for a better representation of this big community, but this categorisation might have been prompted by a growing pressure by immigration and security authorities as a result of mounting security threats since 9/11 and 7/7.

2 El-Solh (1992: 236).

3 While targeting Arabs (and Muslims) has noticeably increased in the wake of the deadly events of 9/11, prosecuting Arabs as potential terrorists predates 9/11. The article published on 11 March 1991 in *The Nation* discusses the case of a Palestinian researcher who was detained and then

released. Abbas Shiblak, born in Haifa, has been lived in Britain for sixteen years. His children are British citizens. The article argues that a crucial factor in his release was the 'Jewish lobby' because Shiblak is a friend of Simon Louvish, a British-Israeli novelist who wrote a book on the migration of the Iraqi Jews to Israel and is an advocate of Palestinian-Jewish dialogue. Louvish, the article argues, launched a campaigned that ultimately resulted in the release of Shiblak (Neier [1991: 295]).

4 El-Solh (1992: 240).

5 *Ibid.*

6 El-Solh (1992: 241).

7 *Ibid.*

8 *Ibid.*

9 *Ibid.* 242.

10 Al-Rasheed (1996: 206).

11 *Ibid.* 216.

12 *Ibid.* 218.

13 *Ibid.* 219.

14 Faquir (2007: 37). Further references to this edition will be included in the text.

15 El-Solh (1992: 237).

16 *Economist* (1988: 47).

17 For a profound discussion of how filmmakers have demonised Arabs see Shaheen (2000: 22-42) and Shaheen (2003: 171-193).

18 My emphasis.

19 Neier (1991: 295).

20 *Ibid.*

21 Emphasis in the text.

22 For different opinions on Spivak's argument on the subaltern see Morton (2007), Parry (2004) and Moore-Gilbert (1997).

23 Spivak (1988:308).

24 Atlantic Forum (2009: 21).

25 *Ibid.* 25.

26 *Ibid.* 24.

27 Emphasis in the text.

Bibliography

Al-Rasheed, Madawi: "The Other-Others. Hidden Arabs". – In Peach Ceri (Ed.): *Ethnicity in the 1991 Census*, London, 1996, pp. 206-220.

Anonymous: "In a World of Their Own", *The Economist*, 17 September 1988, 47.

The Atlantic Forum: "British Arabs. Identity, Politics and Community. Results of an Explanatory Survey by the Atlantic Forum", http://www.naba.org.uk/CONTENT/articles/Studies/

El-Solh, Camillia Fawzi: "Arab Communities in Britain. Cleavages and Commonalities", *Islam and Christian-Muslim Relations* 3:2, 1992, 236-258.

Faqir, Fadia: *My Name is Salma*, London, 2007.

Halliday, Fred: *Arabs in Exile. Yemeni Migrants in Urban Britain*, London,1992.

Karmi, Ghada: "The Egyptians of Britain. A Migrant Community in Transition", http://dro.dur.ac.uk/116/1/57CMEIS.pdf, 20 October 2009.

Lavie, Smadar & Ted Swedenburg (Eds.): *Displacement, Diaspora, and Geographies of Identity*, Durham, NC, 1996.

Loomba, Ania: *Colonialism / Postcolonialism*, London, 1998.

Moore-Gilbert, Bart: *Postcolonial Theory*, London, 1997.

Morton, Stephen: *Gayatri Spivak. Ethics, Subalternity, and the Critique of Postcolonial Reason*, Cambridge, 2007.

Nagel, Caroline. "Hidden Minorities and the Politics of 'Race'. The Case of British Arab Activists in London", *Journal of Ethnic and Migration Studies* 27:3, 2001, 381-400.

---: "Constructing Difference and Sameness. The Politics of Assimilation in London's Arab Communities." *Ethnic and Racial Studies* 25:2, 2002, 258-287.

Nash, Geoffrey: *The Anglo-Arab Encounter. Fiction and Autobiography by Arab Writers in English*, Bern & Oxford, 2007a.

---: "Review of *My Name is Salma*", *Wasfiri* 24:2, 2007b, 91-93.

Neier, Aryeh: "Watching Rights", *The Nation*, 11 March 1991, 295.

Parry, Benita: *Postcolonial Studies. A Materialist Critique*, London, 2004.

Salhi, Zahia & Ian Richard Netton (Eds.): *The Arab Diaspora. Voices of an Anguished Scream*. London & New York, 2006.

Shaheen, Jack: "Hollywood's Muslim Arabs", *The Muslim World* 90, 2000, 22-42.

---: "Reel Bad Arabs. How Hollywood Vilifies a People", *Annals of the American Academy* 558, 2003, 171-193.

Spivak, Gayatri Chakravorty: "Can the Subaltern Speak?". – In Cary Nelson & Lawrence Grossberg (Eds.): *Marxism and the Interpretation of Culture,* Basingstoke, 1988, pp. 271-313.

Staeheli, Lynn A. & Caroline R. Nagel: "Rethinking Security. Perspectives from Arab-American and British Arab Activists", *Antipode* 40:5, 2008: 780-801.

Valassopoulos, Anastasia: *Contemporary Arab Women Writers. Cultural Expression in Context*, London & New York, 2007.

Elahe Haschemi Yekani (Berlin)

Gay Melancholy.
Lost Spaces in Alan Hollinghurst's *The Line of Beauty*

> He took a copy upstairs to the flat, and opened it at random several times – to find that its splendour had a glint to it, a glassy malignity. No, it was very good. It was lustrous. The lustre was perfect and intense – it was the shine of marble and varnish. It was the gleam of something that was over.[1]

These are the thoughts of Nick Guest, the gay protagonist of Alan Hollinghurst's *The Line of Beauty*, when he looks at the only ever copy of *Ogee*, an art magazine he edited. Hollinghurst does not convey a coming-out story in which a protagonist claims a gay identity that rests on a conception of futurity. This novel with its focus on melancholy and nostalgia does not present something that is to come but distinctly 'something that was over' that has not been, but needs to be grieved.

Melancholy is conceptualised by Sigmund Freud as exactly this kind of unacknowledged and pathological mourning. Judith Butler takes this conceptualisation as her premise to explain how homosexuality becomes the constitutive outside in the heterosexual matrix. As has often been noted, Butler's performative understanding of gender identity is based on the assumption that gender is a continuous process of laboriously working through processes of normalisation, an iterative citation rather than a given entity. According to Butler, there exists a triangulation of sex, gender and desire. Heterosexual culture cannot grieve the primary same-sex love object – which in Freud's psychoanalytic theory is the parent of the same sex – and homosexuality is thus turned into "the love that is neither acknowledged nor grieved".[2] Butler elaborates that "heterosexual melancholy is culturally instituted and maintained as the price of stable gender identities".[3] Therefore, heterosexual melancholy is ingrained in the process of claiming a gender identity – a process of disavowal that is never really acknowledged. In this way, for heterosexuality to function, it demands the notion of homosexuality, which remains prohibited but necessarily within the bounds of culture. While homosexuality is indispensable to maintain the norm, it must also be excluded from the realm of the liveable – it must become the "constitutive outside".[4]

In the following, I want to analyse how Hollinghurst employs what I propose to call 'gay melancholy' as an explicit aesthetic strategy to excavate lost gay lives that have been disavowed by the normative gender order. At the same time, I will also discuss the ensuing ambivalences in this process. 'Gay melancholy' results from a double melancholy: the same-sex love object is that which heterosexuality refuses to mourn and becomes that which is not accepted as a proper object of mourning. In the novel, gay melancholy claims heterosexual melancholy and points to the double heteronormative disavowal by mourning places that have been lost but never acknowledged. In this way, melancholy is transferred to specific sites that are tied to the performativity of identity. Hollinghurst constructs and aesthetisises these places as belonging to a gay culture of the 1980s that is no more. In the novel published in 2004, it is precisely this retrospective look, I argue, that is part of Hollinghurst's aesthetic incorporation of mourning on several levels.

The Line of Beauty charts the conflicting landscapes of cruising and money making in Thatcher's England. The novel tells the story of Nick Guest: his infatuation with his 'exotic' lovers, his financial rise but also his hard downfall connected to restrictive sexual mores and the devastating effect of the so-called AIDS crisis. Nick Guest's narrative is closely linked to his inclusion into the Fedden family and their "big white Notting Hill house" (4), from which he is banned in the end. He is literally a *guest* at the family mansion and on a more symbolic level he is a guest in this heteronormative upper-class family. At the beginning of the novel, in the first part called "The Love-Chord" set in 1983, Nick is invited to stay, as a friend of the family son, Toby, but also as a kind of guardian for the suicidal daughter Catherine. Within the metropolis London, Nick can develop his tastes and gets to explore gay subculture. As a specific site in the city, the Fedden house clearly marks a first space of class distinction, and immediately this distinction is linked to

Nick's sexual orientation as another barrier that keeps him away from the kind of beauty that he is infatuated with. Nick fantasises about a possible future before his initial date with his first lover, Leo, a young Black British gay man who is to die of AIDS in the course of events:

> And Nick was in residence, and almost, he felt, in possession. He loved coming home to Kensington Park Gardens in the early evening […]. He loved letting himself in at the three-locked green front door, and locking it again behind him, and feeling the still security of the house as he looked into the red-walled dining room, or climbed the stairs to the double drawing room, and up again past the half-open doors of the white bedrooms. […] He saw himself leading someone up them, showing the house to a new friend, to Leo perhaps, as if it was really his own, or would be one day: the pictures, the porcelain, the curvy French furniture so different from what he'd been brought up with. (5)

In this detailed description of the house and furniture, the novel offers an almost fetishist appraisal of the beautiful that is always ephemeral, as are the gay spaces that Nick comes to explore. He has access to beauty, but it does not belong to him. After his first date with Leo, they decide to leave together but neither of them can offer a flat to go to; Leo lives with his mother for financial reasons, and Nick dares not bring his Black male lover to the Fedden house. As a consequence, Nick is to have his first sexual encounter with a man in the communal gardens to which the Fedden family holds a key, and again the enchantment with a specific geography is palpable.

> The communal gardens were as much a part of Nick's romance of London as the house itself: big as the central park of some old European city, but private, and densely hedged on three sides with holly and shrubbery behind high Victorian railings. (15)

In combination with the pleasure of his first sexual encounter the dichotomy of public and private space collapses:

> Nick was more and more seriously absorbed, but then just before he came he had a brief vision of himself, as if the trees and bushes had rolled away and all the lights of London shone on him: little Nick Guest from Barwick […] fucking a stranger in a Notting Hill garden at night. (40)

Later when Nick and Leo leave the park and a suspicious neighbour approaches them – with Leo's skin colour 'naturally' adding to suspicion in such restricted surroundings – Nick can produce the family key and claim the privilege to access this space on the threshold between public and private.

Social privilege and the geography of the city are closely interwoven. The Henry James scholar Nick is introduced to the social circles of the head of the family,[5] Gerald Fedden, Conservative Member of Parliament. Nick meets Lords and Ladies as well as politicians, learns about risky investments and enjoys the budding relationship with Leo. In the novel, moments of the stabilisation and destabilisation of identity coincide, and it is this ambivalence, I would argue, that often shapes narratives of queer white masculinities. This fluidity is connected to concerns around dis/empowerment. Although his sexuality is not really a secret from the Feddens, Nick's gayness is accepted only as long as it stays private, highlighting a conception of inclusion (tolerance toward homosexual people) that is, in effect, based on a kind of exclusion (aversion to homosexual sexuality).

Lisa Duggan has introduced the term 'homonormativity' to describe a "politics that does not contest dominant heteronormative assumptions and institutions but upholds and sustains them".[6] Although Duggan refers to a specific neoliberal inclusion of gay lifestyles, especially concerning the debates on so-called gay marriage, that came into effect only in a later period of time, Nick Guest to a certain extent also craves an inclusion that can be seen as anticipating homonormativity. Nonetheless, in the 1980s this desire for inclusion is not yet met by the state. In contradictory ways, gay white subjectivities can be both disempowered through exclusion via heteronormativity *and* empowered through collusion via homonormativity, producing an atmosphere of social mobility and mourning at the same time. Nick can initially be part of the upper class circles precisely because his existence as a gay man does not yet challenge certain structures of privilege. He is neither forced to live in 'the closet', a concept that we connect to earlier expressions of gay subjectivity and which has, of course, most famously been linked to Henry James's short story "The Beast in the Jungle" by Eve Kosofsky Sedgwick.[7] Nor can he 'yet' attain a fully homonormative identity that would simply mirror heteronormative norms, such as marriage.

As a consequence, Nick struggles to belong. On the one hand, he enjoys certain markers of privilege, such as whiteness, education and masculinity, while, on the other hand, he is adamantly denied others by being cast as the sexual outsider. These categorisations are at work interdependently, which also means that gay masculinity as the 'wrong' kind of masculinity always remains in a subordinate position to its hegemonic counterpart. Nonetheless, as Raewyn Connell has explained, even men in a subordinate position can at times profit from what has been called the "patriarchal dividend".[8] Sara Ahmed explains that in this kind of process "you are identifying precisely with what repudiates you",[9] and this identification shapes the gay melancholy of the novel. Nick Guest, as I have mentioned, is aspiring to a norm at a time when the kind of inclusivity towards homosexuality that we know today was not in effect and the stigma about HIV/AIDS, that was directed specifically at gay men (and IV drug users), was at its peak.

Consequently, the second half of the book, "To Whom do you beautifully belong," set in 1986, becomes a tale of the disintegration of beauty associated with the devastating effects of the incipient AIDS crisis but also with the crash of the markets that destabilised the Thatcherite dream of a never-ending financial boom. The slightly older and sexually more experienced Nick is secretly dating his second lover, Wani Ouradi, the closeted son and heir of a Lebanese supermarket-chain owner and newly rich. Wani has an alibi fiancée and is working with Nick on building the aforementioned magazine *Ogee*, referring to William Hogarth's title-giving 'Line of Beauty'. In the context of the vulgar culture of the newly rich with their casual spending habits and drug abuse, this is also linked to the constant intake of cocaine by Wani and Nick.

This section of the novel is set at the precise moment in time when the AIDS epidemic suddenly makes people more aware of homosexual existences. Coming out and mourning in this context become inextricably linked. This also affects the question of the closet which, as has been noted, no longer works as the model to narrate gay lives, given the increasing visibility of homosexuals. While Nick would want to be more public with Wani, the distinction of private versus public sexuality is no longer easily maintainable. Confronted about his closeted lifestyle, Wani says to Nick: "'I've never pretended not to be gay, it's you that's doing that, my dear. This is 1986. Things have changed.'" To which Nick responds: "'Yes. All the poofs are dropping like flies.'" (254)

In this utterance the absurdity of the situation of many young gay men in the 1980s becomes evident. While there is indeed more gay visibility and maybe even more acceptance, this coincides with an impending shadow of death that is always present. In this context the recourse to beauty is Nick's consolation as he delves into the beauty of a lifestyle of spending and travelling over the summer with Wani and the Feddens. When the extremely rich and conservative Tippers visit the Feddens in the South of France, the families learn about the death of Catherine's godfather, Pat Grayson, a gay actor who has died of AIDS, which the Feddens try to conceal at first by referring to pneumonia in front of their guests. Nick finds himself in a strange situation as the, by then, only openly gay man. On this occasion, Catherine suddenly bursts into tears and exclaims: "'Mum, for Christ's sake! […] He had AIDS!' – with a phlegmy catch in her voice, which her anger fought with. 'He was gay … he liked anonymous sex … he liked …' […] said Catherine, whose view of gay sex was both tragic and cartoonlike." (335) Catherine tries to be an ally to her gay friend and reacts angrily to the denial of her parents. At the same time, she presents a distorted image that highlights the 'Otherness' of gay sexuality. The tragic deaths of gay men affect the lives of everyone but there is hardly any recognition of the everyday lives of the gay men who are part of that society. Gay life and death are either denied or become 'cartoonish'.

This climate of either denial or paternalism sparked gay anger which found expression in gay and lesbian activism around groups such as ACT UP in the United States and OutRage! in Britain in the late 1980s and early 1990s. It also gave rise to a growing number of gay self-help groups advocating awareness concerning sex education, prevention and the media hysteria around gay sexuality. Academically, this, among other kinds of social activisms, produced what we know today as Queer Theory. Douglas Crimp utilises the phrase 'mourning and militancy' as a way to describe this mobilisation and politicisation around grief:

> The violence we encounter is relentless, the violence of silence and omission almost as impossible to endure as the violence of unleashed hatred and outright murder. Because this violence also desecrates the

memories of our dead, we rise in anger to vindicate them. For many of us, mourning *becomes* militancy.[10]

However, Nick is far from political mobilisation. His existence is sheltered by the access to money and mobility, but he is also painfully aware of the fact that he and his friends are not likely to live very long lives. Wani has random and anonymous sex partners, enjoys drugs and pornography, and it is this surrender to desire that makes him beautiful in Nick's eyes. Nick does not confront his situation with anger but with recourse to aesthetics and beauty. He constantly reflects on Henry James, and his own social life is shaped by bursts of "vicious nostalgia" (263), "a descent into his own melancholy" (310) and later, when he thinks of his initial time with Leo, a "flash of acute nostalgia" (349).

The second part of the book ends with the climactic visit of the Prime Minister at the party for the 25th wedding anniversary of the Feddens. While Nick even takes the Lady for a spin, the façade seems to crumble more and more. Nick and Wani get lost in drugs and sex with one of the waiters. The image of Wani bleeding from the nose and simultaneously performing oral sex on the waiter becomes the emblem of the crash that finds expression in the last part of the book, "The End of the Street", set in 1987.

This final section starts with the election which the Conservatives, of course, win but Gerald's results are below average and disappointing, so that the general mood is low. On the following day, Nick is informed about Leo's death a year ago and this sets him thinking about the time he met him:

> He caught the beautiful rawness of those days again, the life of instinct opening in front of him, the pleasure of the streets and London itself unfolding in the autumn chill. […] He saw Leo crossing this room, the scene brilliant and dwindling, as if watched in a convex mirror. It was the night he had stepped warily, with many ironic looks, into Nick's deeper fantasy of possession: his lover in his house, Nick owning them both by right of taste and longing. (415)

Again, space, time and affect are interwoven and Hollinghurst focuses on the emerging nostalgia surrounding Nick's loss that is described in quite materialistic terms of possession as 'his lover in his house'. Nick glamorises London and a time before AIDS that so harshly entered his reality and disrupted the sentiment of joyous sexual adventure.[11] However, *The Line of Beauty* sheds light on the fact that this nostalgia is always centred on that which has been disavowed from the beginning. Nick knows from the outset that, as a gay man, he is excluded from the places he cherishes. Loss functions as the precondition of romanticising and mourning beauty.

On a personal level, Nick has to come to terms with his own cowardice the last time that he saw Leo in a London pub. Already marked by the disease, Leo looks aged and withered and Nick dares not approach him. As I mentioned, Nick is a figure who somehow wavers between keeping his poise and disintegrating. In the end, Nick awaits the result of his own HIV test which, at that time, could easily equal a death sentence. Nonetheless, the representation of both Leo and Wani remains problematic since they first become the fantasmatic possession of Nick and then the emblematic victims of the disease represented in the novel. Consequently, Dennis Flannery argues that "both Nick and Hollinghurst's novel troublingly owe their futurity and their impact to the sacrifice of a black man".[12] Here we see once more that marginality and hegemony are conflictingly related rather than positioned in a binary opposition to one another in this novel. Nostalgia is a discourse that is linked to the conservative impetus of restoring something to the way it was before. Hollinghurst's depiction of white men's erotic obsession with racialised 'Otherness' that is intertwined with Britain's colonial past (as is even more problematically apparent in his earlier novel *The Swimming Pool Library*) must be seen as the neuralgic point in this context. The 'sacrifice' of both Leo and Wani repeats a form of disavowal that has a distinctly racialised aspect. Authors like Achille Mbembe have shown that dying has its own kind of politics, and accordingly Mbembe speaks of "necropolitics".[13] Hence, it is, of course, not only gay lives whose loss is not grievable. Mbembe describes various regimes, such as slavery or colonial occupation, in which the control over bodies links not only life and freedom but also death and freedom, as in the case of slave suicides. Therefore, we must not forget that it is often racialised 'Otherness' that defines the boundaries not only of which life is grievable but also and, more fundamentally, which life is liveable. This fact creates unease when in Hollinghurst's account it is predominantly queer characters of colour who vanish. Consequently, it is all the more important to (re)translate the psychoanalytic language of melancholy and mourning back into the realm of the political. This is a development we can also trace in Butler's more recent work. In *Precarious Life. The Powers of Mourning and Violence* (2004) and *Frames of War. When is Life Grievable* (2009) she highlights the fact that in the current wars we repeatedly find references to some lives (often non-Western / Muslim) as less valuable than others as a means to justify war and violence. A radical ethics would need to acknowledge all lives as equally grievable. Therefore, somewhat paradoxically, we have to take all deaths equally seriously if we are to value life.

At the end of *The Line of Beauty*, Gerald Fedden is caught in a financial scandal due to illegal business transactions with the Tippers, and on top of that his ongoing affair with his secretary Penny becomes a news item to his shocked family as well as the yellow press. From this point onwards, the house is constantly surrounded by journalists and even the communal gardens are invaded. When Wani's AIDS infection becomes public news, Nick's presence in the house turns into a problem, and the press is only too keen to connect what they call a "gay sex romp" (469) to the Conservative MP. Consequently, Nick is expelled from the house for good by an outraged Gerald. The following day he says goodbye to his dying lover, who is sheltered by his family, only to witness the arrival of the first and only ever issue of their joint project *Ogee* minutes later. As the opening quote emphasised, Nick is enamoured with their work of aestheticism that has no other end than to be beautiful and that will vanish with only this one issue. Beauty becomes irresistible – Julie Rivkin calls this "the impossibility of aesthetic detachment" – and possibly fatal for Nick.[14]

The Line of Beauty provides a retrospective look at 1980s Britain that combines decadence and beauty, but also charts the changing perceptions of space. This becomes most evident in the shifting meaning of the communal gardens, first, as the place of Nick's initiation to gay sex, then as a venue for cruising and anonymous sex, and eventually, as a lost space of gay melancholy. Nick's lost place is indeed a privileged site and could for gay men from different class backgrounds be matched by the lost places of cruising in public parks and toilets, pubs, clubs and saunas, many of which initially vanished as a result of the AIDS epidemic. By losing specific gay places, gay space as a site of possibility is also diminished. After the public scandal and Nick's exclusion from the house, there is one final look back:

> The one [key] he was most reluctant about was the sleek bronze Yale for the communal gardens; it had a look of secrets to it. He could probably keep it, no one would remember; it would be nice to be still in fact, if not by rights, a keyholder. […] The tall white house-fronts had a muted gleam. It came over him that the test result would be positive. […] He stared back at the house, and then turned and drifted on. He looked in bewilderment at number 24, the final house with its regalia of stucco swags and bows. It wasn't just this street corner but the fact of a street corner at all that seemed, in the light of the moment, so beautiful. (500-501)

Andrew Eastham links this scene to Nick's aestheticism that is heightened by the recognition of mortality. He describes the consequent emotion as "made up of […] nostalgia and unconditional affirmation".[15] Hollinghurst transfers gay melancholy to spaces that are ephemeral and have never been 'owned'. By writing beautifully about the loss of beauty, Hollinghurst mourns and acknowledges it, and in this way, his aesthetic strategy of gay melancholy can be linked to initial AIDS activism as a way to combine politics and mourning.

> And yet death itself can never finally not be accepted. We have to accept death to continue to live. But the difference, and the resulting ambivalence, is precisely this: the difference between those of us who must learn to accept these deaths and those who still find these deaths acceptable,[16]

writes Douglas Crimp in 1991 on the occasion of the Names Project quilt. Hollinghurst turns melancholy into an aesthetic principle and re-claims the process of mourning as a way of acknowledging shifting and vanishing gay lives and gay spaces. In this manner, gay melancholy in the year 2004 becomes a re-appropriation of a still largely unacknowledged loss. However, it proves to be a loss that centres somewhat too negligently on a specific aestheticised conception of racialised difference as erotic spectacle. Hence, in his politicised strategy of gay melancholy, Hollinghurst risks evoking a nostalgic and at times conservative image of gay culture that privileges a distinctly white perspective. These ambivalences constitute a continuous challenge to a queer culture which needs to stay alert in order to broaden the scope of which lives can, indeed, become grievable.

Notes

1 Hollinghurst (2005: 489). Further references to this edition will be given in the text.
2 Butler (1999: 89).
3 *Ibid.*
4 Butler (1993: 3).
5 Logically, Henry James is a constant intertextual and aesthetic reference point in this novel. This relationship has become the primary focus of the critical reception of the novel to date (see for instance Eastham 2006; Flannery 2005; Hannah 2007 and Rivkin 2005). I will therefore pay less attention to this facet in my reading.
6 Duggan (2002: 179).
7 Sedgwick (1990).
8 Connell (1995: 79).
9 Ahmed (2006: 174).
10 Crimp (2002: 137), emphasis in the text.
11 Hollinghurst also focused on these matters in his first novel *The Swimming Pool Library* (1988), which ends in the summer before AIDS becomes a public issue.
12 Flannery (2005: 302).
13 Mbembe (2003).
14 Rivkin (2005: 289).
15 Eastham (2006: 524-525).
16 Crimp (2002: 202).

Bibliography

Ahmed, Sara: *Queer Phenomenology. Orientations, Objects, Others*, Durham, 2006.

Alderson, David: "Desire as Nostalgia. The Novels of Alan Hollinghurst". – In David Alderson & Linda R. Anderson (Eds.): *Territories of Desire in Queer Culture. Refiguring Contemporary Boundaries*, Manchester & New York, 2000, pp. 29-48.

Butler, Judith: *Bodies That Matter. On the Discursive Limits of "Sex"*, New York & London, 1993.

---: *Gender Trouble. Feminism and the Subversion of Identity*, 10th anniversary edition, New York & London, 1999.

---: *Precarious Life. The Powers of Mourning and Violence*, London & New York, 2004.

---: *Frames of War. When is Life Grievable?*, London, 2009.

Connell, R.W.: *Masculinities*, Cambridge, 1995.

Crimp, Douglas: *Melancholia and Moralism. Essays on AIDS and Queer Politics*, Cambridge, 2002.

Duggan, Lisa: "The New Homonormativity. The Sexual Politics of Neoliberalism." – In Russ Castronovo & Dana D. Nelson (Eds.): *Materializing Democracy. Toward a Revitalized Cultural Politics*, Durham & London, 2002, pp. 175-194.

Eastham, Andrew: "Inoperative Ironies. Jamesian Aestheticism and Post-Modern Culture in Alan Hollinghurst's *The Line of Beauty*", *Textual Practice* 20:3, 2006, 509-527.

Flannery, Denis: "The Powers of Apostrophe and the Boundaries of Mourning. Henry James, Alan Hollinghurst, and Toby Litt", *Henry James Review* 26:3, 2005, 293-305.

Freud, Sigmund: "Trauer und Melancholie". – In S. F.: *Gesammelte Werke. Band X: Werke aus den Jahren 1913-1917*, Frankfurt a.M., 1999, pp. 428-446.

Hannah, Daniel K.: "The Private Life, the Public Stage. Henry James in Recent Fiction", *Journal of Modern Literature* 30:3, 2007, 70-94.

Hollinghurst, Alan: *The Swimming Pool Library*, London, 1988.

---: *The Line of Beauty*, London, 2004.

Mbembe, Achille: "Necropolitics", *Public Culture* 15:1, 2003, 11-40.

Rivkin, Julie: "Writing the Gay '80s with Henry James. David Leavitt's *A Place I've Never Been* and Alan Hollinghurst's *The Line of Beauty*", *Henry James Review* 26:3, 2005, 282-292.

Sedgwick, Eve Kosofsky: "The Beast in the Closet. James and the Writing of Homosexual Panic". – In E. K. S.: *Epistemology of the Closet*, Berkeley, 1990, pp. 182-212.

Simon Dickel (Bochum)

Do the Queer Thing. Redefining Contested Spaces in Isaac Julien's *Young Soul Rebels* and *The Attendant*

Made in the wake of the new queer cinema and funded by the British Film Institute, Isaac Julien's feature film *Young Soul Rebels* (1991) aimed at a larger audience than his previous and more experimental production *Looking for Langston* (1989). Despite its political outlook *Young Soul Rebels* can be seen and enjoyed as a movie with a crime plot and a seductive soundtrack. Still, belonging to the black British cultural studies discourse of the 1980s and 1990s, *Young Soul Rebels* deals with issues such as race and representation and the correlations of race, sexuality, and desire. This fact becomes most obvious if one pays attention to the way specific spaces are depicted in the film. Some spaces, such as the pirate radio station Soul Patrol, can be read as a response and in opposition to those in Spike Lee's influential film *Do the Right Thing* (1989). Others, such as Metro Radio and a street fair, aim at dismantling white British hegemony. Still others, such as a gay bar and a garage, refer to discussions about interracial gay desire that were prominent within the black gay culture of the 1980s and 1990s.

In 1993, one year after the release of *Young Soul Rebels*, Julien made the short film *The Attendant* about an imagined interracial gay sexual encounter between a black museum attendant and a white visitor within the rooms of a museum. The way the museum is depicted in the film can be read as a complex comment on how sexual desires are irrevocably connected to Britain's colonial past. The particular portrayal of these spaces makes it possible to read both films not only as contributions to a transnational debate about interracial queer desires but also as aiming at the redefinition of the hegemonic concept of white Britishness.

1. Radio TJ

At the beginning of the 1990s, there was a heated academic debate about *Do the Right Thing*, with a focus on questions of race and representation, stereotypes, and the legitimacy of violence. Asking whether the main protagonist Mookie does the right thing, many critics discussed if his decision to start a riot by throwing a garbage can into the window of Sal's famous pizzeria was a legitimate political act of self-defence or morally wrong. The positions in the debate about Lee's political and aesthetic approach ranged from praise for the empowering depiction of black resistance against institutionalised racism to Stanley Crouch's identification of Lee's aesthetic with 'afro-fascism'.[1] Within this debate Wahneema Lubiano and others formulated a feminist position and questioned whether Lee's approach to the categories of race, gender, class and sexuality in *Do the Right Thing* is as radical and progressive as the discourse around this film suggests.[2] Julien's *Young Soul Rebels* can be regarded as a filmic reaction to Lee's political outlook.

Those who saw *Do the Right Thing* will probably remember the character Radio Raheem and his huge boom box. Raheem is depicted as an urban black male whom Victoria Johnson describes as "visually and dialogically constructed as strong, quiet, and commanding".[3] The film inextricably links this character to Public Enemy's track "Fight the Power". Each time Raheem appears on screen, we initially hear the "Fight" of "Fight the Power", and then we see Radio Raheem's boom box in a close-up and Raheem himself filmed from a canted low angle to make his appearance more impressive.[4] His clothes, Nike's, large golden knuckle rings, and his T-Shirt with the slogan 'Bed Stuy – Do or Die' referring to Brooklyn's Bedford-Stuyvesant neighbourhood, match the music we hear because they connote urban hip hop culture. The radical lyrics of "Fight the Power" suggest a black nationalist political agenda. Raheem's golden knuckle rings form the words 'love' and 'hate', a motif taken from Charles Laughton's 1955 film *Night of the Hunter*, in which the protagonist Harry Powell has these words tattooed on his knuckles.[5] Radio Raheem's appearances are limited to public spaces. We see him walking down the block or inside one of the neighbourhood's shops and restaurants. His clothes are colourful, and he is depicted as huge and loud.

Julien starts his film *Young Soul Rebels* by visually quoting Raheem and his boom box. In the very first sequence of *Young Soul Rebels*, after the opening titles and a shot of antennae transmitting the diegetic music we then hear from a radio in the next shot, we see a black man with a radio-recorder strolling through a public park at night. This explicit reference invites the viewer to read *Young Soul Rebels* as a direct response to *Do the Right Thing*. More parallels become evident in the course of the two films: Both men will become victims of racist murders and their radio recorders will be destroyed by fire. At the same time, the difference between the characters is made clear right from the start.

TJ is listening to soul music and is wearing a smart suit. Instead of "Fight the Power" we hear Roy Ayer's song "Running Away". The title and the lyrics are introspective and emotional rather than aggressive and politically outspoken. It soon becomes clear that he is in a cruising area looking for anonymous gay sex. TJ jumps across a fence and enters the park. The fence and the nightly scene underline the impression of the park as a dark, quiet, and secluded space which stands in stark opposition to the bright, hot, and noisy Bedford Stuyvesant neighbourhood in *Do the Right Thing*.

It seems that the similarities between both characters are introduced to make the different aesthetic and political approach of *Young Soul Rebels* and its alternative construction of black masculinity visible from the beginning. TJ's character can be read as a critique of the masculine and black nationalist image of Radio Raheem. Radio Raheem is a representative of Black Power and an aggressive masculinity, whereas TJ represents an alternative masculinity which is black and gay. In a conversation with bell hooks, Julien argues that

> in black popular culture [...], a black masculinist, hard representation is what's important in articulating polemics against racism and institutionalised racism. But if we are actually trying to create a discussion among ourselves or trying to show another kind of representation, it's important to portray the kind of construction of black masculinity which is something that is very fragile and vulnerable.[6]

The character TJ is an example of Julien's project of showing an alternative construction of black masculinity which is 'fragile and vulnerable' – as opposed to a pop-cultural 'black masculinist, hard representation', for which Radio Raheem can serve as an example.

Julien's rather indirect strategy differs from that employed by the black gay filmmaker Marlon Riggs. Riggs used a sequence from Lee's 1988 film *School Daze* in his 1989 film *Tongues Untied*, the first US-film to address black gay identity, as a direct proof of homophobia within works by black straight filmmakers in the US.[7]

2. The Writings on the Walls

Lee's and Julien's films have an additional visual-textual dimension of meaning that comments on the filmic action. In many scenes of *Do the Right Thing*, graffiti, posters, or street art can be seen in the background. Likewise, in *Young Soul Rebels*, numerous graffiti and posters comment on the filmic action. As is the case with the critique of an affirmative representation of black masculinity, the political messages written on the walls shown in *Young Soul Rebels* contest those of *Do the Right Thing*.

In *Do the Right Thing*, a conversation between Mookie and his sister takes place in front of a wall with the slogan 'Tawana told the truth', referring to the controversial case of the black teenager Tawana Brawley, who accused six white men of rape in 1987. In the dialogue with his sister, Mookie warns her about what he perceives as Sal's sexual interests and forbids her to enter Sal's pizzeria. The writing on the wall supports the action on screen. It suggests that Sal really has a sexual interest in Mookie's sister and implicitly connects interracial desire with violence.[8]

In *Young Soul Rebels*, Caz and Billibudd drive past a wall with the slogan 'Black and White Unite and Fight' in their car at night. It is a call for political coalitions and a comment on Caz and Billibudd, the gay interracial couple. They will form a political coalition and support a concert against the Queen's jubilee organised by leftist groups, but the slogan also has a sexual dimension made quite explicit by Billibudd who reads out the slogan changing the last word from 'fight' to 'fuck'.[9]

In both cases, the writing on the wall comments on the filmic action and adds an additional layer of meaning. In *Young Soul Rebels*, the slogan can be read as a comment in favour of interracial desire and sexuality contesting the one in *Do the Right Thing*, which throws a negative light on interracial sexuality. It can also be seen as a comment on the political debate about interracial gay sexuality prominent among many black gay activists during the 1980s both in the USA and the UK.[10] Whereas in *Do the Right Thing* the slogan is never explained or mentioned by the characters, those in *Young Soul Rebels* comment on it and thus bring it to the attention of the viewers. And whereas in *Do the Right Thing* the murals, posters and slogans in the background mainly address issues of black politics and support black pride, in *Young Soul Rebels* we also see graffiti displaying a swastika and the initials 'NF' for National Front. At the end of the film, black and white protestors opposed to the Queen's jubilee are attacked by right-wing groups and fight back. Rather than fighting against each other like their counterparts in *Do the Right Thing*, the characters in *Young Soul Rebels* form political coalitions and oppose nationalism. Similarly to the question of the representation of black masculinity, the above example points at Julien's different political paradigm concerning interracial (gay) sexuality and the forming of political coalitions.

3. Radio Waves

Young Soul Rebels starts with an extremely long shot of the city of London at sunset with the outer boroughs spilling over the edges of the screen. Through the opening titles, the city is shown in three more shots. The soundtrack consists of an announcement of a radio speaker and different music tracks all transmitted by Soul Patrol, the pirate radio station run by the film's protagonists Caz and Chris. In the second shot, receiving antennae are visible on the skyline, and the third shot shows a large antenna in the foreground indicating the transmitter of the radio station. The fourth shot shows London at night.[11]

The vast space of the city of London is then juxtaposed to the extremely small and crowded space of the radio station itself, which is hidden in the backroom of a black-owned garage. The size and location of the radio station make clear that Caz and Chris are only allowed a marginalised space. They are black, and, as we later learn, have no jobs. Chris is still living with his sister and mother in a small flat in a housing project, and both of them do not have any perspective for the future. However, the montage of the first sequences of the film shows that rather than accepting a marginalised position in society, Chris and Caz occupy the whole of the city of London with their pirate radio station playing funk and soul music. Thus they broaden their assigned space and contest the official program of the BBC.

Next to the radio-recorder of TJ, Soul Patrol is another obvious allusion to *Do the Right Thing*. Both Soul Patrol and DJ Mister Senor Love Daddy's We Love Radio, which is located behind a storefront window in Brooklyn's Bedford Stuyvesant neighbourhood, are sources of diegetic music that is broadcast to the numerous radios in the film, contributing to the continuity of the narratives. But whereas the listeners of We Love Radio are limited to those living in the neighbourhood, Soul Patrol reaches a wider audience.

These first minutes of the film are typical of the different aesthetic approaches between *Young Soul Rebels* on the one hand and earlier black British films such as Horace Ové's *Pressure* (1976) and Menelik Shabazz's *Burning an Illusion* (1981) on the other. Similarly to the critique of US society in the African American protest literature of the 1940s, both films depict Britain as a racist society and show how black immigrants are confined to marginal spaces within it. The young protagonists are literally denied access to spaces controlled by whites. They develop a political outlook but remain confined to marginalised spaces. Both pioneering films are didactic and depict the anti-racist struggle as a reaction and in opposition to white supremacy.

Rather than focusing on the confrontation between the white racist society and a black opposition, Julien shows how hegemonic spaces are irrevocably changed and redefined through the presence of black and queer subjects. This different approach to race and representation stems from Julien's involvement with the Sankofa film collective. In the 1980s, collectives such as Sankofa and the Black Audio Collective established new ways of representing the intersections of race, class, gender, and sexuality and took a political approach that went further than the didacticism of earlier protest films, of which *Pressure* and *Burning an Illusion* are two examples.

In *Young Soul Rebels*, this contestation of hegemonic spaces works mainly through the use of colours. One of the film's most striking features is the interplay between the colours the protagonists are wearing and the spaces they are in. As it is the

Queen's silver jubilee, London is full of Union Jack flags symbolising traditional British nationalism, and throughout the film the colours red, white, and blue are dominant in almost every single shot. The way the Union Jack and its colours are used in Julien's film contests traditional notions of Englishness to the effect that Englishness itself can be perceived as an ethnicity rather than the unmarked and uncontested hegemonic norm. In his paper "New Ethnicities" presented at the Black Film / British Cinema conference in London in 1988, Stuart Hall addresses the consequences an antiessentialist approach towards blackness has for representational politics and strategies of resistance. He emphasises the need to think of the differences *within* the category black and specifically refers to the subject positions of black gay men and black lesbians. He also addresses the consequences an anti-essentialist approach has for the use of the concept of ethnicity. Hall states that

> we are beginning to think about how to represent a non-coercive and more diverse conception of ethnicity, to set against the embattled, hegemonic conception of 'Englishness' which [...] stabilises so much of the dominant political and cultural discourses, and which, because it is hegemonic, does not present itself as an ethnicity at all.[12]

Young Soul Rebels was made directly after this seminal British conference and it reveals Englishness as an ethnicity. This argument can be made on the basis of many scenes and most settings of the film. Here, it will be supported by a short description of Chris's and Billibudd's rooms and the analysis of two film sequences, Chris's first visit to Metro Radio and the depiction of a street fair celebrated in honour of the queen's silver jubilee.

4. *Red, White, Blue*

Numerous settings in the film, among them both Chris's and Billibudd's rooms, are depicted in red, white and blue. The walls of Chris's room are designed in red, white, and blue with the pattern on the wall reminiscent of the design on a sleeve of a soul music record. The outfits of Caz and Chris, red scarf, white muscle shirt, bluish suit match the three colours on the walls of the room. Because of the display of soul music items, the room can immediately be identified as a countercultural space. The lighting of Billibudd's room is bluish, in the background we see a painting in which red is the main colour. Billibudd's shirt adds white to the red and the blue. On his shirt there is a portrait of the Queen with piercings and the sentence "God save the Queen" as a reference to the song by the Sex Pistols, and he is wearing red vinyl pants. Despite these colours, which encode British national identity, his room can also be identified as a countercultural space.

At the same time, Chris and Caz's pirate radio station Soul Patrol is depicted as contesting the cultural hegemony of Metro Radio. At Metro, Jeff is the only token black radio DJ, who is allowed to play one hour of soul every week. The marginalised position of this radio DJ is made quite clear later in the film, again through the depiction of space. All of his equipment and belongings fit into one small cardboard box, which is in fact his whole office space at Metro.[13]

When Chris enters the lobby of Metro Radio, a white man walks past a guard in a uniform. It is clear, however, that Chris is not allowed to enter, and he turns left to the reception. The main part of the conversation between Jeff and Chris takes place in front of a giant crown, an interior decoration in honour of the Queen's silver jubilee. Chris and Jeff are the only black persons in the lobby, and at least three white persons push them out of their way. When they change their position, Jeff is standing in front of a life-size cardboard figure of the Queen, which is waving its arm. Their conversation matches the information one gets from reading the space they are in. They talk about limited access for black persons to clubs, the marginal importance soul music has in Metro's program, and the negative reaction of what Jeff calls "patriotic listeners".[14] The juxtaposition of Jeff and Chris with the giant crown and the waving Queen are strong markers of irony. The interplay of Chris's clothes (red bandanna and belt, white string vest) with the bluish colours in the room demonstrates how this guarded space of traditional white Britishness is in the process of being redefined by the black presence in Britain because the combination of the red and white of Chris's clothes with the blue walls and curtains adds up to the colours of the Union Jack.[15]

At the neighbourhood festival to celebrate the Queen's silver jubilee Union Jacks and other nationalist symbols are displayed, and most of the white British characters are wearing traditional costumes. The emphasis on the folkloristic elements might remind some viewers of ethnographic films documenting rituals of indigenous communities. The way in which the black characters occupy the space of the street fair indicates that white British traditions are contested and finally redefined through the presence of black characters. Some of the black children, who belong to a new generation, are wearing souvenir-crowns and Jubilee-T-shirts, thus underlining their British belonging.[16]

After a racist remark by her white elderly female neighbour, Ann, Chris's and Trish's white mother, first tears up a copy of the *National Front News* and then destroys the Union Jack her black daughter Trish has attached to her radio, denouncing the old nationalist understanding of British national identity.[17] This old understanding is replaced by the new way the colours red, white, and blue are combined and displayed against the background of the street fair. The red, white, and blue of Ann's and Trish's clothes contests the old form of Englishness represented by the majority of those attending the festival and by the flag Ann destroys. When Caz enters the scene, he is also wearing red, white, and blue clothes, but his colours are darker than those of the Union Jack. This approach to Englishness stands in contrast to the folkloristic affirmation of the old hegemonic form of British national identity in the background.[18]

Similarly to the first sequence in the lobby of the BBC, on the surface, black subjects seem to be excluded from a white hegemonic space. However, the film suggests that black people are already contesting the definitions of these spaces. Again, the display of colours implies a redefinition of traditional notions of national identity.

5. *Space/Desire*

At the entrance of the street fair, a white drag queen walks past the interracial gay couple Caz and Billibudd, looking at them in a demeaning way.[19] Similarly to Billibudd's comment on the slogan 'black and white unite fight', this short sequence once again directs the viewer's attention to debates about interracial gay sexuality. The short encounter shows the drag queen's contempt. Despite her nonconformity as a cross dresser, she sides with the majority as she enters the street fair matter-of-factly, whereas Caz and Billibudd are depicted as feeling alienated from the festival space.[20]

The sequences depicting a gay bar and the garage where Soul Patrol is located in *Young Soul Rebels* as well as the setting of the museum in the *The Attendant* can be read as comments on the debate about interracial gay sexuality, a topic that was strongly discussed among black gay men at the end of the 1980s. With the positive representation of the love affair between Caz and Billibudd and that of an imagined gay sadomasochistic sexual encounter between the black museum attendant and a white visitor, Julien takes a then unpopular side in this debate. At the time, many black gay activists supported the slogan 'black men loving black men is the revolutionary act', which was originally coined by Joseph Beam.[21]

Much of this discussion centred on the slang terms 'snow queen' and 'dinge queens', which are used within the gay subculture. They refer to white men who choose black men as sex partners and black men who have sex with white men respectively. In his essay "Confessions of a Snow Queen: Notes on Making the Attendant", Julien himself embraces the denigrating term 'snow queen'. He argues that "the out black snow queen draws attention to the fact of black desire for the white subject and contests pathologised racial identities, the products of afrocentric readings".[22] Julien regards interracial desire as positive and transgressive.[23]

Young Soul Rebels explicates this debate through the depiction of a mainly white gay club and a black-owned garage. The gay club has a racist door policy to the effect that a group of black gay men is denied entrance, whereas white men can just pass by the two bouncers. It is only because of Billibudd's membership (as a white gay man, he is a member of the club) that the group and Caz are allowed to enter as his guests. The bar is depicted as a space dominated by white gay men. They guard the borders of this space and treat black men like objects. Inside the club, Caz is touched by a white gay man:[24]

> But for all the mix it [the club] is almost entirely male and almost entirely white.
> A GAY GUY eyes CAZ up, as he walks past he strokes CAZ's arm, brushes against him. The gay guy's FRIEND notices…
> FRIEND: Mary, you are such a dinge queen…
> BILLIBUDD catches the comment and grabs the FRIEND's arm.

BILLIBUDD: Oi you, fuck off…
CAZ takes BILLI's hand off the man. CAZ turns to leave the club. BILLIBUDD follows.[25]

This sequence depicts the objectification and denigration of black men within the white dominated gay subculture. It also evokes the controversial debate about Robert Mapplethorpe's photos of black men, which is also alluded to in Julien's *Looking for Langston* (1989).[26]

The radio station Soul Patrol is located in the backroom of a garage owned and run by black men. The musical style introducing the black men working at the garage is reggae, alluding to the homophobic battyman tunes on which Julien focuses in his documentary *The Darker Side of Black* (1993). Moreover, the Rastafarian colours red, yellow, and green are on display in the garage. Similarly to the sequence in the gay club, an argument evolves. This time Caz is confronted with the black men's homophobia:[27]

CARLTON: Caz, the trouble with you, right – can't always tell which side you on.
CAZ: Now what ya sayin'? What, 'cos Chris is my mate? Or cos I mix with peop…
DAVIS: MAN! White MAN!... Nastiness!
CAZ: So dat's wot it's about, yeah? I mix with white man… I *fuck* with white men!
DAVIS: Jesus!
CAZ and DAVIS are near to blows. CARLTON intervenes, steering CAZ away.
CARLTON: Long as you doin' it to them. Min' the rod a correction no fuck up dem…
CAZ turns on DAVIS
CAZ: You're fulla shit Davis. The bruvva dat got killed in the park – he was what you call an anti-man, a bwatty boy. Dat make it alright now? You concerned 'bout who did it now?[28]

The film connects Caz's experiences of racism and homophobia with two specific settings – the gay club and the garage. Since he is placed in these settings, the viewers understand both sides of his situation. As a black gay man he is confronted with racism in the mainly white gay community and with homophobia in parts of the black community. The soul club where Caz and Chris work as DJ's is opposed to these spaces. Here, "the unique and extraordinary mix of the seventies' soul clubs emerges – girls dance with girls, boys with boys, punk with soul, black with white".[29] The club is depicted as a queer and hybrid space where race, gender, sexuality, and musical styles are mixed. Because of the exceptional interplay of these differences and in contrast to the other settings in the film, the club can be described with Michel Foucault's term 'heterotopia'. In a 1967 lecture, which was later published under the title "Different Spaces", Foucault defines heterotopias as

> real places, actual places that are designed into the very institution of society, which are sorts of actually realised utopias in which the real emplacements, all the other real emplacements that can be found within the culture are, at the same time, represented, contested, and reversed, sorts of places that are outside all places, although they are actually localizable. Because they are different from all the emplacements that they reflect or refer to, I shall call these places 'heterotopias', as opposed to utopias.[30]

With *The Attendant*, Julien establishes a broader context for the debate about interracial gay desire. By choosing the space of the museum, which David Deitcher describes as "a neoclassical bastion of Western high culture and a repository of colonial artifacts",[31] Julien can show – in a single space – the complex ways in which desire is connected to societal discourses and to Britain's colonial past.

In the museum, the present (the visitors) and the past (the artworks) are juxtaposed within one building.[32] The film reveals that colonialism is not a closed chapter that can be put safely away inside the walls of museums. The fantasies of the museum attendant are obviously triggered by the paintings, particularly by the [c.] 1833 painting *Slaves on the West Coast of Africa* by Francois-Auguste Biard. Even though the aim of the painting was to support the abolition of slavery, Deitcher states that

> Biard's work cannot conceal a more deeply rooted ambivalence, which is evident at the precise point where Biard's manifest abhorrence of slavery intersects with the ample representational evidence in the painting of his latent fascination with the black body and its brutalization.[33]

In the mind of the attendant, this painting comes very much alive and fuels his erotic fantasies. The way it is transformed into a sadomasochistic *tableau vivant* shows the active and actual influence of colonialism on present-day sexual desires. The characters in the *tableau vivant*, black and white men engaged in a sadomasochistic scene, are actively looking at the attendant.[34]

In a later scene, the framed *tableaux vivants* are replaced by drawings of Tom of Finland, and the imagined SM-encounter takes place in front of these drawings. Tom of Finland's drawings from the 1970s and 1980s exploit racist and sexualised stereotypes of black men to depict gay sexuality. The juxtaposition of the attendant's fantasies with these drawings and the replacement of Biard's painting with the drawings of Tom of Finland clarify the continuity and power racist images have for sexual desire and the depiction of sexual fantasies. By using the space of the museum as a setting for the film, it becomes possible to broaden the discussion about interracial gay sexuality. Julien transcends the personal and psychological level and connects the debate to the continuing story of the relation between sexual desire and racialised bodies.

Julien's approach to interracial gay sexuality was taken up in Cheryl Dunye's 1996 mockumentary *The Watermelon Woman*. In one sequence, a group of black lesbian friends discuss the interracial love affair between Cheryl and Diana, a black and a white woman. Just like the whole film, their dialogue is full of irony. It takes place at a kitchen table, and on the wall behind the group of lesbians a film poster of *The Attendant* is on display.[35] This shows a large portrait of the attendant who seems to observe the conversation about the political implications of homosexual interracial desire sympathetically. Both Julien's reaction to Spike Lee and Dunye's reference to Julien are proof of a transnational debate within the works of black filmmakers in the USA and Britain, negotiating the politics of race, gender, sexuality, desire, and nation.

Notes

1 Crouch (1989).
2 Lubiano (1991).
3 Johnson (1997: 64).
4 *Ibid.*
5 Julien uses golden knuckle rings that form the words 'love' and 'hate' in his split-screen video installation called *Paradise/Omeros*, which was shown at Documenta 11 in Kassel in 2003 and at the Black Atlantic exhibition in Berlin in 2004.
6 Julien & hooks (1991: 131-132).
7 Bambara (2007: 13).
8 Lee (2001, 1:11:22-1:11:33).
9 Julien (1993, 1:11:41-1:11:58).
10 See also Scott (1994).
11 Julien (1993, 00:00-00:02).
12 Hall (1988: 29).
13 Hallam, McClintock & Julien (1991: 174).
14 *Ibid.* 147-48.
15 Julien (1993, 11:07-13:09).
16 *Ibid.* 1:17:02-1:18:43.
17 Hallam, McClintock & Julien (1991: 194).
18 Julien (1993, 1:20:29-1:21:48).
19 Hallam, McClintock & Julien (1991: 191).
20 Julien (1993, 1:15:25-1:16:13).
21 Beam (1985).
22 Julien (2000: 82).
23 *Ibid.*
24 Julien (1993, 1:08:08-1:09:30).
25 Hallam, McClintock & Julien (1991: 187).
26 Mercer (1994).
27 Julien (1993, 58:59-1:01:14).
28 Hallam, McClintock & Julien (1991: 180), emphasis in the text.
29 *Ibid.* 161.
30 Foucault (1998: 178).
31 Deitcher (2000: 18).
32 *The Attendant* also alludes to the theoretical framework of black British cultural studies, because we see Hanif Kureishi and Stuart Hall among the visitors of the museum. Both of them seem to study the colonial artefacts in order to make sense of their own subject positions and, the viewer can assume, to formulate a critical view on the power relations within British society.
33 Deitcher (2000: 18).
34 Julien (2006, 02:44-03:43).
35 Dunye (2006, 47:32-50:09).

Bambara, Toni Cade: "Programming with *School Daze*". – In Paula J. Massood (Ed.): *The Spike Lee Reader*, Philadelphia, 2007, pp.10-22.

Beam, Joseph: "Black Men Loving Black Men. The Revolutionary Act of the 1980s", *Gay Community News*, 1985, 5.

Crouch, Stanley: "Do the Race Thing. Spike Lee's Afro-Fascist Chic", *Village Voice*, 20 June 1989, n.p.

Deitcher, David: "A Lovesome Thing. The Film Art of Isaac Julien". – In Amada Cruz (Ed.): *The Film Art of Isaac Julien*, Annandaleon-Hudson, 2000, pp. 11-23.

Dunye, Cheryl (Dir.): *The Watermelon Woman*, DVD, 2006.

Foucault, Michel: "Different Spaces". – In M. F. & James D. Faubion (Eds.): *Aesthetics, Method, and Epistemology*, New York, 1998, pp. 175-185.

Hall, Stuart: "New Ethnicities". – In Institute of Contemporary Arts (Ed.): *Black Film, British Cinema*, London, 1988, pp. 27-30.

Hallam, Paul, Derrick Saldaan McClintock & Isaac Julien: "Film Script". In I. J. & Colin McCabe (Eds.): *Diary of a Young Soul Rebel*, London, 1991, pp. 141-217.

Johnson, Victoria E.: "Polyphony and Cultural Expression. Interpreting Musical Traditions in *Do the Right Thing*". – In Mark A. Reid (Ed.): *Spike Lee's* Do the Right Thing, Cambridge, 1997, pp. 50-72.

Julien, Isaac (Dir.): *Young Soul Rebels*, DVD, 1993.

---: "Confessions of a Snow Queen. Notes on Making *The Attendant*". In Amada Cruz (Ed.): *The Film Art of Isaac Julien*, Annandale-on-Hudson, 2000, pp. 79-83.

--- (Dir.): *The Attendant*, DVD, 2006.

Julien, Isaac & bell hooks: "States of Desire". – In I. J. & Colin McCabe (Eds.): *Diary of a Young Soul Rebel*, London, 1991, pp. 125-40.

Lee, Spike (Dir.): *Do the Right Thing*, DVD, 2001.

Lubiano, Wahneema: "But Compared to What? Reading Realism, Representation, and Essentialism in *School Daze*, *Do the Right Thing*, and the Spike Lee Discourse", *Black American Literature Forum* 25:2, 1991, 253-282.

Mercer, Kobena: "Reading Racial Fetishism. The Photographs of Robert Mapplethorpe". – In K. M.: *Welcome to the Jungle. New*

Positions in Black Cultural Studies, New York, 1994, pp. 171-220.
Scott, Darieck: "Jungle Fever? Black Gay Identity Politics, White Dick, and the Utopian Bedroom." *GLQ. A Journal for Gay and Lesbian Studies* 1, 1994, 299-321.

Contributors' Addresses

Dr. Yousef Awad, Assistant Professor, English Language & Literature Department, Faculty of Foreign Languages, University of Jordan, Amman 11942, Jordan.

Prof. Dr. Christiane Bimberg, Technische Universität Dortmund, Institut für Anglistik und Amerikanistik, Emil-Figge-Straße 50, D-44227 Dortmund, Germany.

Heike Buschmann, MA, Universität Paderborn, Institut für Anglistik und Amerikanistik, Warburger Straße 100, D-33098 Paderborn, Germany.

Jun.-Prof. Dr. Simon Dickel, Ruhr-Universität Bochum, Englisches Seminar, Universitätsstraße 150, D-44780 Bochum, Germany.

Professor Patricia Duncker, English and American Studies, Centre for New Writing, University of Manchester, Oxford Road, Manchester M13 9PL, United Kingdom.

Dr. Sonja Frenzel, Universität zu Köln, Graduiertenschule zur Förderung der Fachdidaktiken, Zentrum für Lehrer/innenbildung (ZfL), Albertus-Magnus-Platz, D-50923 Köln, Germany.

Wolfgang Funk, Leibniz-Universität Hannover, Englisches Seminar, Königsworther Platz 1, D-30167 Hannover, Germany.

Mark Hall, MA ABIPP AHEA, Faculty of Art Design and Technology, School of Art and Design, University of Derby, Markeaton Sreet, Derby DE22 3AW, United Kingdom.

Dr. Elahe Haschemi Yekani, Humboldt-Universität zu Berlin, Institut für Anglistik und Amerikanistik, Unter den Linden 6, D-10099 Berlin, Germany.

Dr. Sandra Heinen, Goethe-Universität Frankfurt am Main, Institut für England- und Amerikastudien, Grüneburgplatz 1, D-60629 Frankfur am Main, Germany.

Dr. Florian Kläger, Westfälische Wilhelms-Universität Münster, Englisches Seminar, Johannisstraße 12-20, D-48143 Münster, Germany.

Prof. Dr. Gabriele Linke, Universität Rostock, Institut für Anglistik/Amerikanistik, August-Bebel-Str. 28, D-18051 Rostock, Germany.

Dr. Timo Lothmann, Rheinisch-Westfälische Technische Hochschule Aachen, Institut für Anglistik, Amerikanistik und Romanistik, Abteilung Anglistische Sprachwissenschaft, Kármánstraße 17-19, D-52062 Aachen, Germany.

Prof. Dr. Ingrid von Rosenberg, Kolberger Platz 2, D-14199 Berlin, Germany.

Prof. Dr. Elke Schuch, Fachhochschule Köln, Institut für Translation und Mehrsprachige Kommunikation, Mainzer Straße 5, D-50678 Köln, Germany.

Antje Schumacher, MA., Rheinisch-Westfälische Technische Hochschule Aachen, Institut für Anglistik, Amerikanistik und Romanistik, Abteilung Anglistische Sprachwissenschaft, Kármánstraße 17-19, D-52062 Aachen, Germany.

Prof. Dr. Merle Tönnies, Universität Paderborn, Institut für Anglistik und Amerikanistik, Warburger Straße 100, D-33098 Paderborn, Germany.